Friedrich Schiller

PLAYS

Intrigue and Love
and
Don Carlos

The German Library : Volume 15

Volkmar Sander, General Editor

Friedrich Schiller

PLAYS

Intrigue and Love
and
Don Carlos

Edited by Walter Hinderer
Foreword by Gordon A. Craig

CONTINUUM · NEW YORK

2003

The Continuum International Publishing Group Inc
15 East 26th Street, New York, NY 10010

Printed in the United States of America

Library of Congress Cataloging in Publication Data

Schiller, Friedrich, 1759–1805.
Plays.

(The German library; v. 15)
Translation of: Kabale und Liebe and Don Carlos.
Contents: Intrigues and love—Don Carlos.
I. Schiller, Friedrich, 1759–1805. Don Carlos.
1983. II. Hinderer, Walter, 1934–   III. Title. IV. Series.
PT2473.K3H5   1983   832'.6   83-7741
ISBN 0-8264-0274-7   ISBN 0-8264-0275-5 (pbk.)

Acknowledgments will be found on page 347, which
constitutes an extension of the copyright page.

Contents

Foreword

During the First World War, Thomas Mann, in a book called *Reflections of an Unpolitical Man,* wrote that German humanism was opposed to politics from the ground up. "In the German concept of *Bildung,*" he wrote, "the political element is basically missing. After fifty years of the Empire, the words of the young Nietzsche are still valid for cultivated Germans: 'He who has the *furor philosophicus* within him will have no time for the *furor politicus.*'"

This is a curious passage on two counts. It does not seem to have occurred to Mann that the war that was raging while he wrote was, in part, the consequence of the lack of interest in, and understanding of, politics that was shared by so many of his countrymen. And he forgot, or chose to ignore the fact, that one of Germany's greatest writers did not find a preoccupation with philosophy or, indeed, with *Bildung* incompatible with the most intense interest in politics. That writer was Friedrich Schiller.

It is true that, unlike some of his contemporaries, Schiller was not induced by the tumultuous political events of his time—the coming of the French Revolution and its ultimately shattering effects in his own country—to become an activist. If his first plays reflected the revolutionary aspirations of his age, he was not tempted, like Georg Forster for example, to try by his own efforts to realize them. When the Bastille fell, he was intent upon his duties as professor of history and philosophy at the University of Jena; during the Terror, he was composing his *Letters on the Aesthetic Education of Mankind;* and when the French legions began their systematic conquest of his country he devoted himself to literary production. Even so, his interest in contemporary politics never flagged; no member of his generation reflected more deeply upon the tendencies of his time, on the great struggle of men and nations for what he once called "mankind's mighty objects, power and freedom," and no one had such chillingly accurate perceptions of the seductiveness of the former and the deep ambiguity of man's devotion to the latter.

Schiller's thinking about the relationship between power and freedom is most explicit in his plays, and this is not accidental. The poet regarded the theater as a moral institution, "the common channel," he once said, "through which the glow of wisdom flows from the intelligent superior part of society and spreads itself in gentle streams through the whole state." He believed that the dramatist should be the preceptor of his people, and this is what he set out to become himself, by means of plays that would not only excite and entertain audiences but also instruct them and possibly help lay the foundations for a better and freer society.

This is nowhere more apparent than in the two plays included in this volume. Written within three years of each other in the decade before the outbreak of the French Revolution, both are, on one level, plays about parental authority and filial rebellion. But it would be a very obtuse reader who failed to perceive the political passion that informs them. *Intrigue and Love,* one of the first social dramas in German literature, is a powerful attack upon the evils of absolutism in the petty German states of the eighteenth century, whose rulers disposed of the lives of their subjects as if they were their own property. *Don Carlos* is a more balanced and sophisticated treatment of the same theme in the world of the Great Powers; based upon a story by the Abbé de Saint-Réal about the tragic fate of the son of Philipp II of Spain, it was undertaken, Schiller wrote in a letter, to correct "the lack of German plays that deal with great persons of state."

In both dramas, freedom from arbitrary authority, the right of the individual to live his life as he chooses, is a major theme, and the passages that deal with it have an eloquence that explains why the triumphant revolutionaries in France in 1789 made Schiller an honorary citizen of the Republic. But it cannot be said that they provide any evidence that their author believed that there was much hope of such freedom being realized in his own time. The political

world that he describes in these plays has such endurance and
resilience that even a cataclysm like the fall of the power-brokers
Wurm and Walther in *Intrigue and Love* cannot be expected to
make it change its ways. The structures of authority are too strong
to be toppled easily (even momentary deviations from their norms
by the ruler himself are quickly corrected, as the intervention of
the Grand Inquisitor in *Don Carlos* proves), and they are able to
defeat the rebelliousness of ordinary subjects either by brutal
suppression or by the corruptive powers in their possession..

In *Intrigue and Love,* the only person who is truly free is Luise,
who is realistic enough to see that her lover's defiance of court
society will be ineffective and courageous enough to accept death
as the means of self-liberation. All of the others have, consciously
or unconsciously, made concessions to the system that have com-
promised their independence. One suspects, after the scene with
the purse of gold, that Miller's self-reliance is less perfect than he
claims; Ferdinand's ties with the court are too close to make either
his love for Luise, which is sustained more by childish defiance and
jealousy than by any other emotions, or his plans for flight credi-
ble; and Lady Milford's illusion of freedom is the result as much
of her own vanity and self-indulgence as it is of her lover's deceit.
In *Don Carlos,* even the Marquis of Posa, who speaks of freedom
with such fervor, has been corrupted by the political world in which
he lives. In the pursuit of his political objectives, he has no scruple
about betraying his friends, and in his advice to the King there is
what seems to modern ears to be a suggestion of proneness to
authoritarian behavior, for he is clearly just as willing to be ruth-
less in his choice of means to achieve his ends as the Grand Inquisitor is in his determination to defeat them.

Schiller was too discriminating a political observer to see power
only in its negative aspects. He was fully aware that it was the
indispensable factor in the political process, a force for good as
well as for evil; and in *Don Carlos* he has presented an incisive
analysis of the problem of the responsibility of power. The tragedy
of the King is that he feels that he cannot permit in himself the
weaknesses of ordinary human beings and that his private feelings
must be subordinate to his duties as ruler. There is no doubt that
he has allowed this conviction to turn him into a monster, whose
relations with his wife and son have hardened into rigid formality,

any violation of which, however trivial, arouses in him groundless suspicions and fears for the welfare of the State. It is a tribute to Schiller's great force as an artist that he can make us see the human face behind the ceremonial mask and sense the burden of responsibility that weighs Philipp down. The anguish of the man who must sustain the system alone, since most of his associates are bound to him only by fear or ambition, is palpable in the great soliloquy in which the King betrays his own vulnerability.

> I need the truth—to dig its silent source
> Out from the gloomy rubble of what's false
> Is not the lot of kings. But give me just
> That one unusual man . . .
> . . . who can help me find it— . . .

Heinrich Heine once wrote of *Don Carlos* that in it "love of the future . . . shines forth like a forest of flowers." If that is true, it is also true that Schiller's hope that his fellow Germans might progress toward a juster and more equitable form of society was accompanied by the conviction that this would be possible only if they learned to understand the realities and ambiguities of the political process. Because he contributed so much to that understanding by his dramas of intrigue, ambition, and the manipulation of power, Benno von Wiese is perhaps justified in calling him "the only example of a great political writer among the Germans."

GORDON A. CRAIG

Introduction

I

When speaking of German Classicism, it is usually Goethe and Schiller we mean, along with the versatile *homme de lettres* Wieland and the influential theoretician Herder, who found a firm place in the Weimar of Duke Karl August. Although Goethe has since become the more widely-known poet, nineteenth-century Europe—particularly in the East—with its nationalistic and emancipatory ideals clearly belonged to Friedrich Schiller. On 4 January 1824, Goethe wrote to Johann Peter Eckermann that Schiller, who today is considered to have been a champion of the common man during his time, was actually considerably more aristocratic than he; yet Schiller took up the cause of republicanism versus tyranny early. In *Fiesco,* Schiller denounces the nobility as "abortions of ambition and weakness" (IV, 14), and the title character states in his decisive monologue: "Fiesco, the republican! the Duke Fiesco? . . . On this steep precipice the boundaries of virtue terminate: here heaven and hell are separated" (II, 19).

In Schiller's early play, *Robbers,* political, public, and social values are represented alongside private and humane ones; fame counterposes the "love of a father" and the "arms of Amelia" (I, 2). In *Fiesco* (IV, 14), Leonore compares the "Elysium" that is love with the "clanking jailhouse chains" of the thirst for power; and in the Wallenstein trilogy, Max projects the idyllic life of the virtuous hero but the commanding officer himself sees only one alternative: "I must use violence or suffer" (*Wallenstein's Death,* II, 2). In his plays, Schiller ("Monsieur Gille"), who was later to become an honorary citizen of the French Revolutionary Regime, juxtaposed republic and duchy, bourgeoisie and monarchy, freedom and tyranny, love and egoism, humanity and political mind, sensitivity and intrigue, as examples of good and bad modes of behavior. While such idealistic tyrants as Karl Moor, Ferdinand, and Marquis Posa pervert the *ius naturale* because of an overwhelming enthusiasm, Schiller's negative heroes, calculating despots such as Franz Moor, Gianettino Doria, Fiesco, and Wallenstein subscribe to the doctrine that "right is with the strongest—the limits of our power constitute our laws" (*Robbers,* I, 1).

Whereas the absolute despots and "abortions of ambition and weakness" (Franz Moor, Fiesco, President von Walther, King Philipp) are condemned at the dramatic Last Judgment, the faults of the positive heroes, whose errors stem from overenthusiasm and idealism, may be corrected at any time. Both Karl Moor and Marquis Posa sacrifice themselves in order to appease "affronted laws" and "perverted order" (*Robbers,* V, 2). A negative action in the public arena is put right by a spontaneous, humane act; thus Schiller the dramatist demonstrates that a political and public action will only be good if it originates in the right humane attitude. In the context of Schiller's philosophical writings, this means that the attainment of the progressive state is dependent on the fulfillment of the corresponding individual and humane prerequisites. "Alone the character of the citizens creates and upholds the state," wrote Schiller in a letter of 13 July 1793 to a noble patron, the Duke of Augustenburg, "and makes political and bourgeois freedom possible." This, too, is the reason that Schiller, as he explains in his essay *On Pathos* does "not wish to appeal to the citizen of the state in the man, but to the man in the citizen of the state." The political reform which Schiller—not least of all because of the developments in the French Revolution—increasingly supported could only be brought about by a thorough reform of man, a process which he described in great detail in his program for aesthetic education. A renaissance in political awareness was the goal of Schiller's writings, of his philosophy. According to his own testimony, he would gladly "say farewell to the Muse forever, should the extraordinary really come to pass: political legislation based on reason, man respected and treated as an end in himself, homage paid to law and true freedom the foundation of the state."

II

Friedrich Schiller, the most famous playwright of the Goethe era and a well-known historian, philosopher, and poet, a symbol of will-power, and a committed and tireless promoter of human rights and of intellectual and political freedom, was born on 10 November 1759 in the small Swabian town of Marbach. He was drafted into Duke Karl Eugen's Military Academy in Stuttgart, where, in 1778, he received a physician's degree. Schiller remained a regiment's doctor for only a short period, though, as after the success of his first play, *Robbers,* which will be included in Volume 14 of the German Library, he fled the Duchy of this despotic ruler who had ordered him to desist from further dramatic endeavors.

Schiller traveled about Germany, was associated in 1783–84 with the theater in Mannheim and then settled in Leipzig and Dresden for two years as the guest of Christian Gottfried Körner, who later became one of his closest friends. In 1787, Schiller arrived in the Weimar of Goethe, Herder, and Wieland; besides plays and poetry, he had become deeply interested in history and when he moved in 1788 to Jena, it was to become a professor of history. In 1790 he married Charlotte von Lengefeld and finished his major historical studies on the Netherlands and the Thirty Years' War. In 1791, he began to read Kant, resulting in a series of profound and influential aesthetic and philosophical essays. After a trip back to his Swabian homestate, a close cooperation began between Schiller and Goethe. They discussed in depth Schiller's play about Wallenstein, which was finished in 1799. Schiller also composed numerous ballads (in competition with Goethe), and wrote several more plays, such as *Maria Stuart* (1800), *The Maid of Orleans* (1801), *The Bride of Messina* (1803), and *William Tell* (1804). Schiller was working on his last (unfinished) play, *Demetrius,* at the time of his death on 9 May 1805.

Volume 15, the first volume of Schiller's works in the German Library, will be followed by two volumes containing the dramatic masterpiece *Wallenstein* and Schiller's last completed work, *William Tell* (Volume 16); the third Schiller volume, Volume 17, will include, besides *Maria Stuart,* the main aesthetic writings.

III

Thomas Mann praised Schiller's unmistakable theatrical style as "the most brilliant, rhetorically the most fascinating theatrical style that has ever been created in Germany and maybe in the whole world." This sweeping statement may, in consideration of Sophocles and Shakespeare, be rather exaggerated, but there is no question that Schiller, despite his predecessors Lessing and Lenz, created a moving, effective language for German theater which had not previously existed. Whereas the fascination of Goethe's dramas stems from the atmosphere, from the poetical depiction of the conscious and unconscious psychological processes, Schiller emphasizes "dramatic situations," effect, and emotion. In Schiller, that which is private becomes public, the character is revealed in the action. As Schiller himself expresses it in his *Prologue* to the Wallenstein trilogy, his themes are "the great objects of mankind/Tyranny and freedom." For Schiller, the idea of humanity takes precedence over the manmade institutions, state and society, and this idea is the yardstick by which he measures both the actions of a single individual and the achievements of an entire society. This attitude is evident in the plays contained in this volume: *Intrigue and Love*, which Schiller wrote in Bauerbach between December 1782 and February 1783 (revisions took until the end of 1783; the play was first staged at Frankfurt on 13 April 1784 and two days later in Mannheim); and *Don Carlos*, which Schiller began in the early months of 1783. Parts of the latter appeared between 1785 and 1787 in the magazine *Rheinische Thalia*, and the book edition came out in June of 1787. In 1801, an edited, briefer version appeared. 1788 saw the publication of Schiller's *Letters on Don Carlos*. The play itself was first presented in 1787 in Hamburg, then in Leipzig, Dresden, and Riga.

The combination of the public and the private that is characteristic of Schiller is evident in the action of both *Intrigue and Love* and *Don Carlos*. In the former, Ferdinand von Walther, the overly enthusiastic noble lover, refuses to accept class limitations; he fears only the "limits" of Luise's love. He cooly confronts his father, the calculating, plotting politician, with his own "notions of greatness and good fortune" and declares, not without pride: "my ideal of good fortune withdraws more contentedly within myself. All my desires lie buried within my heart" (I, 7). Upon learning of his father's plan to marry him to the Duke's mistress, Ferdinand speaks of "penetrating his cabals" and holding fast to the "giant handiwork of his love." He brushes the Lady Milford off rather brusquely, though he does not fail to be a bit impressed by her, confesses to her his love for the commoner, Luise, and threatens uncompromisingly: "We shall see whether *fashion* or *humanity* will lose the day" (II, 3).

To Ferdinand, his love for Luise has become a question of to be or not to be, taking precedence over all other responsibilities. He fails to notice that his absolute idealism renders him the same sort of egotistical tyrant that he despises in his father. "True greatness of mind," wrote Schiller in his eleventh *Letter on Don Carlos*, "leads no less to the violation of the freedom of others than does selfishness and the lust for power." Similar to Ferdinand in this way are Marquis Posa, who temporarily subordinates his political ideals to his friendship with Carlos, and Carlos himself, who appears to devote himself only to his love for his step-mother, the Queen, neglecting his political responsibility to Flanders.

That which neither Ferdinand, with his arrogance, nor the accusation of the servant (II, 2), through whom Schiller condemns the practice of the German princes of trading soldiers in return for riches, can achieve, is achieved by Luise in her conversation with the—deep-down noble—Lady Milford: that is, the sudden appearance of virtue and greatness, in short, of humanity, in the Lady's character. Luise, the sacrificial victim of Ferdinand's despotism and jealousy, finally elicits an altruistic gesture from the egotistical idealist, Ferdinand, at the end of the play. In the mute drama of Luise Miller, the contradictory elements of her time, politics and emotion, class society and love, responsibility and freedom, religion and phantasy, are dramatically represented.

In *Don Carlos*, Schiller proclaimed the emancipatory ideals of the eighteenth century and "the spread of a more pure, gentle humanity," a goal he described in greater depth in his eighth *Letter on Don Carlos*. King Philipp, the cold, calculating tyrant, is undoubtedly ennobled by the idealistic plea of the politically progressive Marquis Posa (sixth *Letter on Don Carlos*). Just as the Marquis intends to use his friendship with Carlos and the latter's love for the Queen for his own political goals, he also wants to win Philipp for his ideas of freedom and humanity and to reconcile bourgeois happiness with nobility (III, 10), whereas Philipp longs only for a friend "with heart both pure/And open, with a spirit bright and eyes/Unbiased" (III, 5). Nevertheless, part of the climax of the drama occurs when the King, who in II, 2 still refuses to accept "tears" as "everlasting confirmation of humanity" and criticizes his sensitive son as a pitiful dreamer, finally cries (IV, 24). He who "perverted the laws of humanity" and minted "actions like his three-penny pieces" (spoken of the Duke in *Intrigue and Love*, II, 3) confesses that, through this youth, Marquis Posa, "a new/And better morning dawned" for him (*Don Carlos*, V, 9). He seems to have his revenge for the fact that his supposed friend Posa intended to sacrifice him to his idol, humanity, and at the end, he hands his son over to the Inquisition.

Whereas Don Carlos finally renounces his egotistical love for the Queen in order to further his friend Posa's political ideals, Philipp remains a tyrannical, inhumane ruler. When the play opens, the concern is that the Infante might endanger the art of statesmanship (II, 10) with new ideas of freedom of thought and respect for mankind; at its close, the terrible power which continues to dominate Philipp and which has its spies and traitors everywhere has been revealed. The Grand Inquisitor, a blind ancient of ninety years, accuses the calculating *homo politicus,* Philipp, of compromising with dreamers and idealists and dismisses his yearning for a friend with the cynical words: "Why a man? What are, then, men to you but numbers, nothing more. Must I/Now hear the lessons of my gray-haired pupil/About the elements of princely skill?" (V, 10). The old man even accuses the King of having wanted to shake off the "chains" of the Church, to "be free and unique," but the sacrifice of his son brings about a reconciliation between the rival powers. The terrible words of the King, as he delivers his son into the hands of the Grand Inquisitor, still have a jolting effect on the audience. The merciless Inquisition and its instruments of torture, which remain on the stage, urgently call attention to the "enthusiastic plan to bring about the most auspicious state that is attainable to human society," as Schiller describes the aims of the two friends (and, one must add, of the Queen) in his eighth *Letter on Don Carlos.*

IV

Schiller's impact in the Old and perhaps also in the New World may be partially due to his instinct for the convincing phrase, the poetic word, and to that contagious—and still valid—theatrical style of which Thomas Mann spoke. These may, too, be those elements which tempted and still tempt so many playwrights to "Schillerize." But what inspires Schiller's public is also the idealistic substance and quality of his drama. Many of his plays are so eminently stageable that errors in the motivation behind the action can be overlooked, something that is not generally true of German drama of the eighteenth and nineteenth centuries. On 1 July 1826, Goethe ruefully—and in reference to his own work—penned these lines to the above-mentioned Johann Peter Eckermann: "A play which was not written cleverly and intentionally for the stage will not work, no matter what you try to do with it, there will always be something recalcitrant and out of place about it." Like his historical and philosophical writings, Schiller's drama aims from the start at public effectiveness, at a basic change in the structure of society, that is, of the people of his time. For according to Schiller, mankind could only develop through the efforts of men. This fundamental theme may partially explain the new creative possibilities which are continually being discovered in Schiller's works, in Germany and abroad, at different times and in different art forms. The unmistakable Schillerian quality has been retained in other media, in the operas of Giuseppe Verdi, for instance, who was repeatedly inspired by Schiller's works: *Giovanna d'Arco,* 1845; *I Masnaderi,* 1847; *Luise Miller,* 1849; and *Don Carlos,* 1867. During a lecture in Mannheim on 26 June 1784, Schiller described his area of impact as follows: "The theater is more than any other public institution of the state a school of practical wisdom, a guide through political life, a fitting key to the most secret doors of the human soul." Theater such as this has never lost its effectiveness.

W.H.

INTRIGUE
AND LOVE

CHARACTERS

PRESIDENT VON WALTHER, *at the court of a German sovereign*
FERDINAND, *his son, a Major*
CHAMBERLAIN VON KALB
LADY MILFORD, *the sovereign's mistress*
WURM, *private secretary to the sovereign*
MILLER, *member of the city orchestra, or, as they are in some
  places called, a professional musician*
HIS WIFE
LUISE, *his daughter*
SOPHIE, *chambermaid to the Lady*
A VALET *of the sovereign*
VARIOUS SECONDARY CHARACTERS

ACT I

Scene 1

A room in the musician's house

Miller is just getting up from his armchair and putting aside his violincello. At a table sits Mrs. Miller, still in her nightgown and drinking her coffee.

MILLER *(pacing rapidly back and forth)*: Once and for all! This business is getting serious. My daughter and the Baron are getting to be the talk of the town. My house is getting a bad name. The President will get wind of it and . . . short and sweet: I'm forbidding the gentleman my house.

WIFE: You didn't lure him to your house. You didn't throw your daughter at him.

MILLER: So I didn't lure him to my house; so I didn't throw my daughter at him: who will take notice of that? I was the master of the house. I should have kept my daughter more strictly in line. I should have talked turkey to the Major . . . or else gone and spilled the whole thing to His Excellency the daddy. The young Baron will get off with a jawing, that's for sure, and all hell will break loose on the fiddler.

WIFE *(sipping the last of a cup)*: Stuff and nonsense! What can break loose on you? Who can do anything to you? You follow your profession and pick up pupils where you can get them.

MILLER: But tell me this: what's going to come of the whole business? Marry the girl he cannot. There's no question of his marrying her, and as for having her for his . . . God help us! No thanks!—I'm telling you: when one of these M'sieus has helped himself here, there, and everywhere, when he's made the rounds through the Devil knows what all, then my fine scamp develops a taste for digging for fresh water. Just you watch out, just you watch out: even if you had an eye in every knothole and stood guard over every drop of blood in her blushes, he'll wheedle her right out from under your nose, and give the girl one, and take himself off, and there'll be the girl with a bad name for the rest of her life and left an old maid; or else, if she relished the trade, she'd carry it on. *(hitting his brow with his fist)* God in heaven!

WIFE: God's mercy protect us!

MILLER: There's need of protection. Where else can a scatterbrain like that very well turn his attention? The girl is pretty . . . slender . . . has a nice ankle. It can be any old way in the upper story and they'll overlook that in you womenfolk, so long as the dear Lord hasn't left you lacking *par terre*.—Once my whipper-snapper gets that point through his head: whoop-de-do! the light dawns on him, the way it does for Rodney* when he gets the scent of a Frenchman and all sails have to be spread and off he goes, and . . . I don't blame him. A man's a man, that much I do know.

WIFE: If you could just read the lovely *billets doux* the gentleman is always writing to your daughter. Dear Lord! Then it's crystal-clear how it's a case of sheer beauty of soul with him.

MILLER: That's the limit! Hitting the bag when you mean to hit the donkey. Anybody with a message to the good old flesh has to do no more than send the good heart as messenger. How did I do it? Once things get so far clear that the souls are in agreement, presto! the bodies have their example set for them. The common folk ape the gentry, and in the end the silvery moon has been nothing but a pander.

WIFE: But just take a look at the magnificent books the Major has brought into the house. Your daughter is forever saying her prayers out of them.

---

* George Brydges Rodney (1718–1792), the English Admiral who had defeated the French fleet under De Grasse (who had aided the Americans at Yorktown in 1781) in Caribbean waters on April 12, 1782.

MILLER *(giving a whistle):* Ho, ho! Praying! You catch on. The rough and ready broths of Nature are too coarse for His Grace's macaroon-stomach. He has to have them fancied up first in the hellish pest-kitchen of the writers. Into the fire with that filth! With that, the girl fills up on God knows what kind of . . . super-heavenly rigamaroles that run in the blood like Spanish fly and knock galleywest the handful of Christianity that her father is still just barely managing to hold together more or less. Into the fire, I say. The girl gets all sorts of Devil's drivel into her head, and then finally, with all that maundering around in Fools' Paradise, she can't get back home any more; she forgets, she is ashamed that her father is Miller the fiddler, and in the end she'll cheat me out of a fine, honorable son-in-law who could have worked himself so warmly into my patrons' favor.— No! Damn me! *(He jumps up heatedly.)* The pasty shall go straight to the hearth, and as for the Major . . . Yes, yes! I'll show the Major where Master Carpenter made the opening.
(He starts to go out.)
WIFE: Be nice for once, Miller. How many a pretty penny we've made just on those little somethings . . .
MILLER *(comes back and stands in front of her):* My daughter's blood money? Go to the Devil, you infamous procuress! I'll go around begging with my violin and give a concert for something warm . . . I'll smash my cello and stick manure in the soundingboard before I'll eat from the money my own child has earned with her soul and her salvation. Give up your accursed coffee and snuff, and you won't have to be sending your daughter's face to market. I filled my belly and always had a good shirt to my back before a confounded la-de-da like that stuck his nose into my sittingroom.
WIFE: Now don't fly off the handle. The way you get all hot and bothered first thing! I'm only saying that the Major musn't be *offensé'd,* because he *is* the President's son.
MILLER: There's the meat right on the platter! That's why, that's just why the business has got to be settled yet today. The President can't help but thank me, if he's an upright father. You must brush up my red plush coat and I'll have myself announced to His Excellency. I'll say to His Excellency: "Your Excellency's son has an eye on my daughter; my daughter is not good enough to be Your Excellency's son's wife, but to be Your

Excellency's son's whore my daughter is too precious, and that's all there is to it.—My name is *Miller*."

Scene 2

Enter Secretary Wurm.

WIFE: Ah! Good morning, Mr. Secretary! Do we again have the pleasure of seeing you?

WURM: The pleasure is mine, the pleasure is mine, Cousin Miller. Where a nobleman's Grace may call, my bourgeois pleasure is of no account whatsoever.

WIFE: The things you say, Mr. Secretary! His Grace, Major von Walter, does give us the *playzeer* now and again. But we do not disdain anybody because of that.

MILLER *(annoyed)*: A chair for the gentleman, wife! Will you take off your things, countryman?

WURM *(lays aside his hat and cane and sits down)*: Well! Well! And how is my to-be . . . or my once-was? . . . Not that, I certainly hope. Won't we get to see her, Mamsell Luise?

WIFE: Thank you for inquiring, Mr. Secretary. But my daughter is not at all haughty, you know.

MILLER *(in irritation, nudging her with his elbow)*: Wife!

WIFE: We are only sorry she can't have the honor of seeing you, Mr. Secretary. She has just gone to Mass, my daughter.

WURM: I am so pleased, so pleased. At least I will have a pious Christian wife in her.

WIFE *(smiles in ignorant gentility)*: Yes . . . but, Mr. Secretary . . .

MILLER *(in obvious embarrassment pinches her ear)*: Wife!

WIFE: If our house can serve you in any other way . . . with all the pleasure in the world, Mr. Secretary . . .

WURM *(with an angry look)*: In any other way? No thank you! No thank you!—Hm! Hm! Hm!

WIFE: But . . . as Mr. Secretary must himself realize . . .

MILLER *(angrily giving his wife a push from behind)*: Wife!

WIFE: Good is good, and better is better, and one can't be standing in the way of an only child's happiness, you know. *(with peasant pride)* You do take my meaning, don't you, Mr. Secretary?

WURM (*shifts uneasily in his chair, scratching himself behind the ear, and twitches at his cuffs and shirt-ruffle*): Get your meaning? Not quite . . . Oh, yes . . . Just what do you mean?

WIFE: Well . . . Well . . . I was only thinking . . . I mean (*coughs*) inasmuch, you see, as the dear Lord *partout* means to make a Lady of my daughter . . .

WURM (*jumping up from his chair*): What's that you say? What?

MILLER: Keep your seat! Keep your seat, Secretary! My wife is a silly goose. Where would a Lady come from? What kind of a donkey is sticking his long ears out of this twaddle?

WIFE: Fume away all you like. I know what I know . . . and what the Major said, he said.

MILLER (*in a rage runs for his fiddle*): Will you shut your mouth? Do you want this cello across your skull? What can you know? What can he have said?—Pay no attention to that gossip, cousin!—Out to your kitchen! March!—You're not going to take me for a cousin to a jackass and think I'm trying to social-climb with the girl? You're not going to think that of me, are you, Secretary?

WURM: I have not deserved that of you either, Maestro. You have at all times shown yourself to me as a man of your word, and my claim to your daughter was as good as signed and sealed. I have a position that can support a good householder. The President is well disposed toward me, and I cannot lack for recommendations when I try to push up higher. You see that my intentions as to Mamsell Luise are serious, and if perhaps you have been taken in by a windbag of the nobility . . .

WIFE: Mr. Secretary Wurm! More respect, if you please . . .

MILLER: Shut up, I say!—Never mind her, cousin! Things stand as before. The way I put it to you last fall, I repeat today. I will not force my daughter. If you're to her liking . . . well and good, and it is up to her how she makes herself happy with you. If she shakes her head . . . still better . . . I mean: all right! You pocket the mitten and drink a bottle with the father. The girl has to live with you, I don't. Why should I, out of pure and simple stubbornness, throw a husband at her that she can't stomach? . . . just to get the evil Fiend chasing me around in my ice-grey days as if I were his quarry . . . just to get it to sozzle in every glass of wine and to eat in every plate of soup: "You're the rascal that ruined his child!"

WIFE: And putting it plainly: I absolutely will not give my consent. My daughter was meant for something high-class, and I'll take it to court if my husband lets himself be bamboozled.

MILLER: Do you want to find your arms and legs in two, buttinski?

WURM *(to Miller):* Some fatherly advice can do a lot with a daughter; and I trust you know me, Mr. Miller?

MILLER: Plague take it! The girl must know you. What an old curmudgeon like me might see in you is not exactly the morsel for the young sweet-tooth of a girl. I'll tell you right down to a hair whether you're the man for an orchestra . . . but a female soul is too sharp even for a conductor. And then, from the heart, cousin . . . I guess I'm a blunt and forthright German of a fellow . . . you'd thank me but little for my advice in the long run. I won't advise my daughter to marry anybody . . . but I advise you against my daughter, Secretary. Let me finish what I have to say. A suitor who calls on the father for help, I wouldn't trust . . . forgive me . . . with so much as a hollow hazelnut. If he amounts to anything, he'd be ashamed to present his talents to his sweetheart through that old-fashioned channel . . . If he doesn't have the courage for it, he's a milksop, and no Luises were made for him. There! Behind her father's back he has to present his business to the daughter; he has to act so the girl will sooner send father and mother to the Devil than let him go . . . or else comes and throws herself at her father's feet and begs for God's sake to have either black death or yellow death or the Only Beloved. That's what I call a fellow! That's what I call love! And anybody that won't go that far with the womenfolk, will have to . . . stick to his quill.

WURM *(grabs up his hat and cane and stalks out of the room):* Much obliged, Mr. Miller!

MILLER *(following him slowly):* For what? For what? But you don't have anything to thank me for, Mr. Secretary. *(returning)* He doesn't hear, and off he goes . . . To me, it's poison and orpiment* just looking at that quillpusher. A suspicious, repulsive character, as if some sneaking trickster had smuggled him into God's world. . . . Those sly little mouse-eyes . . . that fiery-

---

* Orpiment (from Latin: auripigment)—"arsenic trisulphid," a deadly poison.

red hair . . . that underhung chin, just as if Nature out of pure
venom at a botched piece of work had picked up my rascal
there and flung him into some corner. . . . No! Before I throw
my daughter away on a blackguard like that, she'll sooner . . .
God forgive me for it . . .

WIFE (*spits; poisonously*): The cur! . . . But it'll keep his chops
clean for him!

MILLER: But you, with your pestilential nobleman! . . . You got
my dander up before too. . . . You're never so stupid as when
you ought for God's sake to be sensible. What was that drivel
about a Lady and your daughter supposed to mean? I tell you
he's the same as ever! You just have to let something like that
get a whiff of anything to have it trumpeted all over tomorrow
at the market-place well. That's just the kind of M'sieu that'll
go snooping around in people's houses, discuss cellar and cook,
and once an indiscreet word has slipped out of your yap . . .
bang! it's known to Prince and Mistress and President, and
you've got the sizzling lightning around your neck.

Scene 3

Enter Luise Miller with a book in her hand.

LUISE (*puts the book down, goes over to Miller and presses his
hand*): Good morning, dear father.

MILLER (*warmly*): Fine, my Luise. . . . I'm glad you think so dil-
igently of your Creator. Always remain so, and His arm will
support you.

LUISE: Oh, I am a great sinner, father!—Has he been here, mother?

WIFE: Who, my child?

LUISE: Ah, I forget there are any other human beings besides him.
My head is so confused . . . He hasn't been here? Walter?

MILLER (*sadly and earnestly*): I thought my Luise left that name
behind in church?

LUISE (*after gazing at him fixedly for a time*): I understand you,
father. I feel the knife you thrust into my conscience; but it
comes too late. I have no piety left, father . . . Heaven and
Ferdinand are tugging at my bleeding soul, and I fear . . . I fear
. . . (*after a pause*) Oh, no, dear father! When we neglect

him for the painting, the artist feels himself the most subtly praised. . . . If my joy at His masterpiece makes me overlook Him Himself, father, must that not delight God?

MILLER *(throwing himself angrily into the chair):* There we have it! This is the fruit of that godless reading.

LUISE *(walking restlessly up to a window):* I wonder where he is now? . . . The elegant young ladies that see him . . . listen to him . . . I am a wretched, forgotten girl. *(Startled at the words, she throws herself at her father's feet.)* Oh no, no! Forgive me! I won't mourn for my fate. I only want to . . . think of him a little, you know . . . that doesn't cost anything. This little bit of life . . . if I could but breathe it into a soft, caressing breeze to cool his face! . . . This little flower of youth . . . if it were a violet, and he trod upon it, and it could modestly die beneath his foot! . . . I would be satisfied with that, father. If that gnat suns itself in her rays . . . can the proud majestic sun punish it for that?

MILLER *(leans, moved, against the back of the chair and covers his face):* Listen, Luise . . . I would give these few dregs of my years if you had never seen the Major.

LUISE *(startled):* What are you saying? What? . . . No, my good father means something else. You cannot know that Ferdinand is mine, created for me, created for my joy by the Father of those who love. *(She stands in thought.)* When I saw him for the first time . . . *(more rapidly)* and the blood mounted to my cheeks, all my pulses throbbed more gladly, every heartbeat spoke, every breath whispered: This is he! and my heart recognized him it had ever lacked, and it averred: This is he! . . . and how that went echoing through the entire world that rejoiced with me! Then . . . oh then the first morning dawned within my soul. A thousand young emotions sprang up from my heart like flowers from the earth when it is springtime. I no longer saw the world, and yet I remember that it had never been so beautiful. I no longer knew any God, and yet I had never loved Him so much.

MILLER *(hurries to her, clasps her to his bosom):* Luise . . . dear . . . magnificent child . . . take my hoary old head . . . take everything . . . everything . . . but the Major . . . God is my witness . . . I can never give him to you.

(Exit.)

LUISE: I do not want him now either, my father. This scanty dew-drop of time . . . a dream of Ferdinand already drinks it rapturously up. I renounce him for this life. Then, mother, . . . then, when the barriers of discrimination collapse . . . when all the hateful husks of rank burst from us . . . and human beings are only human beings . . . I shall bring nothing with me but my innocence. Father has so often said, you know, that adornment and splendid titles will be cheap when God comes, and hearts will rise in price. Then I shall be rich. Then tears will be reckoned as triumphs, and beautiful thoughts as ancestors. Then I shall be aristocratic, mother! . . . What would he have then over his sweetheart?

WIFE *(jumping up)*: Luise! The Major! He's jumping over the board fence. Where shall I hide?

LUISE *(beginning to tremble)*: Stay here, mother!

WIFE: Lord in heaven! How do I look? . . . Why, I'll be put to shame. I mustn't be seen like this before His Grace.

(Exit.)

Scene 4

Enter Ferdinand von Walter, who flies to Luise. She sinks down pale and faint on a chair. He remains standing in front of her. They gaze at one another for a time in silence. Pause.

FERDINAND: You are pale, Luise?

LUISE *(rises and falls upon his neck)*: It is nothing! Nothing! You are here. It is past.

FERDINAND *(taking her hand and bringing it to his lips)*: And my Luise still loves me? My heart is as it was yesterday; is yours still so too? I fly here only to see if you are cheerful, then to go away again and be so too. . . . You aren't.

LUISE: But I am, I am, my beloved.

FERDINAND: Tell me the truth! You aren't. I see through your soul as through the clear water of this diamond. *(He points to his ring.)* Here no flaw can appear without my noticing it . . . no thought crosses this countenance that could escape me. What is the matter? Quick! If I but know this mirror clear, no cloud comes over the world. What is troubling you?

LUISE (*looking at him mutely and meaningfully for a while, then with sadness*): Ferdinand! Ferdinand! If you but knew how beautifully the bourgeois girl appears in that language. . . .

FERDINAND: What is this? (*surprised*) Girl! Listen! How do you happen upon that word? . . . You are my Luise. Who says you should be anything more? Don't you see, faithless girl, in what coolness I surprise you? If you were all love for me, would you have had time to make a comparison? When I am with you, my reason melts away into a glance . . . into a dream of you when I am absent, and you still have shrewd wit along with your love? . . . For shame! Every moment lost over that sorrow was stolen from your youthful friend.

LUISE (*taking his hand, but shaking her head*): You want to lull me into forgetting, Ferdinand. . . . You want to tempt my eyes away from the abyss into which I must most certainly plunge. I see into the future . . . the voice of fame . . . your reproaches . . . your father . . . my nothingness. (*In fright she suddenly lets go his hand.*) Ferdinand! A dagger above you and me! . . . They will separate us!

FERDINAND: Separate us! (*He springs up.*) Whence do you draw this premonition, Luise? Separate us? . . . Who can dissolve the bond of two hearts, or rip apart the tones of a chord? . . . I am a nobleman . . . but let us see whether my patent of nobility is older than the plan of the infinite universe, or my coat of arms more valid than the script of heaven in Luise's eyes, which says: "This woman is for this man." . . . I am the President's son. All the more reason. Who else but a love can sweeten the curses that my father's oppression will bequeath to me?

LUISE: Oh, how I fear him . . . your father!

FERDINAND: I fear nothing . . . nothing . . . except the limits of your love. Let obstacles come like mountains between us, and I will take them for steps and fly across them into my Luise's arms. Storms of adverse fate shall fan my feeling higher, *perils* will but make my Luise the more charming. . . . So, no more about fear, my love. I myself . . . I will watch over you, like an enchanted dragon over subterranean gold. . . . Entrust yourself to *me!* You need no other angel. . . . I will throw myself between you and fate . . . receive every wound for you . . . for you, catch every drop from the cup of joy . . . and bring them to you in the chalice of love. *(tenderly embracing her)* On this arm my Luise shall go dancing through life; fairer than it sent you forth, heaven shall have you back again and with wonderment acknowledge that only love put the final touches upon a soul. . . .

LUISE *(pushing him away, in great emotion)*: No more! I beg you, be silent! . . . If you knew . . . let me . . . you do not know that your hopes assail my heart like Furies.

(She starts to leave.)

FERDINAND *(detaining her)*: Luise? What's this? What's this? What has come over you?

LUISE: I had *forgotten* these dreams and was happy. . . . Now! Now! From *this day* on . . . the peace of my life is gone. . . . Wild wishes . . . I realize . . . will rage within my bosom. . . . Go. . . . May God forgive you! . . . You have cast a firebrand into my young, peaceful heart, and it will never, never be extinguished.

(She rushes out. Speechless, he follows her.)

Scene 5

A room in the President's palace

Enter the President, with the cross of an order around his neck and a star to one side, and Secretary Wurm.

THE PRESIDENT: A serious attachment! My son? . . . No, Wurm, you will never make me believe that.

WURM: Your Excellency has the grace of demanding proof from me.

THE PRESIDENT: That he should pay court to bourgeois riffraff . . . speak flatteries . . . and for all I care, chatter about emotions . . . these are all things I find possible . . . find forgivable . . . but . . . and the daughter of a musician yet, you say?

WURM: Music Master Miller's daughter.

THE PRESIDENT: Pretty? . . . Of course that goes without saying.

WURM *(briskly)*: The finest specimen of a blond, who, it wouldn't be too much to say, could still cut a figure beside the first beauties of the court.

THE PRESIDENT (*laughing*): You tell me, Wurm . . . that you have an eye on the creature. . . . I see that. But you see, my dear Wurm . . . the fact that my son has feeling for the lady gives me hope that the ladies do not hate him. He can get somewhere at court. The girl is *beautiful,* you say. It pleases me in my son that he has *taste.* If he deceives the little fool with solid intentions . . . still better. . . . By that I see that he has *cleverness* enough to lie for his purse's sake. He can become *President.* If he gets still further . . . splendid! That signifies to me that he has *luck.* . . . If the farce ends with a healthy grandchild . . . incomparable! Then I'll drink one bottle more of malaga to the good prospects of my family tree and pay the prostitution fine for his wench.

WURM: All I wish, Your Excellency, is that you may not find it necessary to drink that bottle for your *consolation.*

THE PRESIDENT (*seriously*): Wurm, recall that once I believe, I stubbornly believe; and I rage when I am angry. . . . I'll take it as a joke that you wanted to set me on him. That you would have liked to get a rival off your neck, I heartily believe. That the *father* was to serve as your cat's paw when you were at pains to cut my son out with the *girl,* that, again, I find comprehensible. . . . And that you have such a fine head-start toward becoming a rascal, even delights me. . . . Only, my dear Wurm, you must not try to make game of me too. . . . Only, understand me, you must not push the trick to the point of impinging on my principles.

WURM: Forgive me, Your Excellency! Even if in actuality . . . as you suspect . . . jealousy was at play here, at least it was so with the eyes alone and not with the tongue.

THE PRESIDENT: And I should think it might be dispensed with altogether. Stupid devil, what difference does it make to you if you get the coin fresh from the mint or from the banker? Console yourself with the local gentry; . . . knowingly or otherwise . . . there is rarely a marriage made among us where at least half a dozen of the guests . . . or of the attendants . . . cannot geometrically estimate the bridegroom's paradise.

WURM (*bowing*): Here, I like being a bourgeois, my Lord.

THE PRESIDENT: What's more, you can shortly have the pleasure of paying your rival back in the finest way for his sport. Right now the proposition lies in the privy chamber, that, upon the arrival of the new duchess, Lady Milford will, for form's sake, receive her congé and, to make the illusion complete, will enter upon a marriage. You know, Wurm, how much my consequence depends upon the Lady's influence . . . how the mainspring of my power is in general meshed with the passions of the sovereign. The Duke is looking for a match for Milford. Someone else can turn up . . . conclude the bargain, wrest the sovereign's confidence over to himself along with the lady, and make himself indispensable to him. . . . Now, in order to keep the sovereign in my family's net, my Ferdinand shall marry Milford. . . . Is that clear to you?

WURM: So my eyes smart. . . . At least, the *President* has demonstrated here that the *father* is only a *beginner* in comparison to him. If the Major shows you the *dutiful son* the way you have shown him the *tender father*, your demand may come back protested.

THE PRESIDENT: Fortunately I have never been worried about the execution of a decision when I could step in with a SO SHALL IT BE! . . . But look now, Wurm, this has brought us back again to the previous point. I am going to announce his marriage to my son yet this afternoon. The face he shows me will either justify your suspicion or controvert it altogether.

WURM: My Lord, I humbly beg your forgiveness. The dark look that he will absolutely dependably show you can be reckoned quite as properly to the account of the bride you are bestowing upon him as to the one you are taking away from him. I entreat of you a still sharper test. Choose the most unexceptionable match in the country for him, and if he says Yes, you can have Secretary Wurm drag a ball and chain for three years.

THE PRESIDENT *(biting his lips):* Devil!

WURM: It just can't be otherwise. The mother . . . who is stupidity itself . . . blabbed too much to me in her simplicity.

THE PRESIDENT *(pacing back and forth, choking back his anger):* All right! This morning yet.

WURM: Only, Your Excellency should not forget that the Major . . . is the son of my master.

THE PRESIDENT: *You* will be protected, Wurm.

WURM: And that the service of sparing you an unwelcome daughter-in-law. . . .

THE PRESIDENT: Is worth the return service of helping you to a wife? . . . That too, Wurm!

WURM (*bowing with satisfaction*): Eternally yours, my Lord!
(*He starts to go.*)

THE PRESIDENT: What I told you in confidence earlier, Wurm . . . (*threateningly*) If you blab . . .

WURM (*laughing*): Then Your Excellency will disclose my forged documents.
(*Exit.*)

THE PRESIDENT: I can count on you, all right! I hold you by your knavery like a stag-beetle on a string.
(*Enter a valet.*)

THE VALET: Chamberlain von Kalb . . .

THE PRESIDENT: Comes as if called. . . . He is welcome.
(*Exit the valet.*)

Scene 6

Enter Chamberlain von Kalb in a rich but tasteless court costume, with chamberlain's keys, two watches, and a sword, chapeau bas, and with his hair done à la hérisson.* With a great shriek he flies toward the President, spreading an aroma of musk over the whole audience in the pit. The President.

CHAMBERLAIN (*embracing him*): Ah, good morning, dear fellow! How did you rest? How did you sleep? . . . Do forgive me for having this pleasure so late. . . . urgent business . . . the menu . . . invitations . . . the arrangement of couples for tonight's sleighride . . . ah! . . . and then I had to be present at the levée too, you know, and announce the weather to His Highness.

THE PRESIDENT: Yes, Chamberlain, you simply could not get away.

CHAMBERLAIN: On top of that, a rascal of a tailor stood me up.

---

*Chapeau bas—"three-cornered hat;" *à la hérisson*—"hedgehog style," i.e. with his powdered wig a mass of pointed curls.

THE PRESIDENT: But everything is fine now?

CHAMBERLAIN: That isn't all. . . . One *malheur* follows upon another today. Wait till you hear!

THE PRESIDENT *(absent-mindedly):* Is that possible?

CHAMBERLAIN: Wait till you hear! I had barely got out of the coach when the stallions shy, stamp, lash out, so that . . . think of it! . . . the filth of the street splashes all over my breeches. What to do? For Goodness' sake, put yourself in my place, Baron! There I stood. It was late. It's a day's trip . . . and in that costume before His Highness . . . merciful God! What occurs to me? I feign a fainting spell. They carry me headlong into the coach. I go home at top speed . . . change my clothes . . . go back . . . and: guess what? I am still the first one in the antechamber. . . . What do you think of that?

THE PRESIDENT: A magnificent impromptu of the human intelligence . . . But, all this aside, Kalb . . . you have already spoken, then, with the Duke?

CHAMBERLAIN *(importantly):* For twenty and one-half minutes.

THE PRESIDENT: Well, I declare! . . . So you doubtless have an important piece of news for me?

CHAMBERLAIN *(seriously, after some silence):* His Highness is wearing a *merde d'oye* coat today.*

THE PRESIDENT: Fancy that! . . . No, Chamberlain, but I have a better piece of news for you. The fact that Lady Milford will become the wife of Major von Walter is surely something new to you?

CHAMBERLAIN: Think of it! . . . And is it all settled?

THE PRESIDENT: *Signed,* Chamberlain. . . . And you will oblige me if you go without delay to prepare the Lady for his call and to acquaint the entire capital with my Ferdinand's decision.

CHAMBERLAIN *(delighted):* Oh, with a thousand pleasures, dear fellow! . . . What more could I wish for? . . . I fly immediately. . . . *(embracing him)* Farewell! In three quarters of an hour the whole city will know of it.

(He prances out.)

THE PRESIDENT *(laughing at the departing Chamberlain):* Let peo-

---

* Goosedung green *(merde d'oye)* was the fashionable color of the 1782 Paris season, as Mercier's *Tableau de Paris,* published that year, shows.

ple go on saying that these creatures are of no use in the world
. . . Now, I fancy, my Ferdinand will *have to* want to, or else
the whole city will be caught in a lie.

(He rings. Enter Wurm.)

Send my son in.

*(Exit Wurm. The President paces up and down,
lost in thought.)*

Scene 7

Enter Ferdinand, accompanied by Wurm, who directly leaves.

FERDINAND: You sent for me, Sir. . . .

THE PRESIDENT: Unfortunately I have to, if I want to enjoy my
son's company for once. . . . Leave us alone, Wurm.

(Exit Wurm.)

Ferdinand, I have been watching you for some time and I no
longer find that open and impulsive youthfulness which used to
delight me so. A curious gloom clouds your face . . . You avoid
me . . . you avoid your circle . . . Shame! . . . At *your* age
people will forgive ten indiscretions sooner than a single show
of moodiness. Leave that to me, dear son. Leave me to work
for your happiness and think of nothing but playing into my
schemes. . . . Come! Embrace me, Ferdinand!

FERDINAND: You are very gracious today, father.

THE PRESIDENT: Today, you rogue . . . and this same today still
with that sour look? *(seriously)* Ferdinand! . . . For *whose*
sake have I trod this dangerous path to the sovereign's heart?
For *whose* sake have I fallen out forever with my conscience
and with heaven? . . . Listen, Ferdinand . . . I am speaking
with my son . . . for *whose* sake did I make room by the re-
moval of my predecessor . . . a story which cuts the more
bloodily into my inmost being the more carefully I conceal the
knife from the world! Listen to me! Tell me, Ferdinand: for
whose sake did I do all that?

FERDINAND *(falling back with horror)*: Surely not for mine, father? Surely the bloody reflection of that outrage is not to fall
on *me*? By the almighty God, it would be better not to have
been born than to serve as the excuse for that misdeed.

THE PRESIDENT: What was that? What? But I will put it down to your novel-mentality . . . Ferdinand . . . I will not fly into a passion, impudent boy. . . . Is *this* the way you reward me for my sleepless nights? *This* way for my restless care? *This* way for the eternal scorpion of my conscience? . . . On me falls the burden of responsibility . . . on me the curse and the judge's thunder. . . . You receive your good fortune at second remove . . . the crime does not adhere to the inheritance.

FERDINAND (*raising his right hand toward heaven*): I hereby solemnly renounce an inheritance which only reminds me of an abominable father.

THE PRESIDENT: Listen to me, young man. Do not provoke me! . . . If it all went according to your notions, you would go creeping in the dust your whole life long.

FERDINAND: Oh, that is still better, father, than if I went creeping around the throne.

THE PRESIDENT (*choking back his anger*): Hm! . . . You must be compelled to recognize your good fortune. Where ten others by utmost exertion cannot make the climb, you are effortlessly lifted up in your sleep. At age twelve you were Ensign. At twenty, Major. I managed that with the sovereign. You will take off your uniform and enter the minister's post. The sovereign spoke of the Privy Council . . . ambassadorships . . . extraordinary favors. A splendid prospect is open before you . . . the smooth path straight to the throne . . . to the throne itself, provided power is worth as much as its outward symbols. . . . That doesn't inspire you?

FERDINAND: Because my notions of greatness and good fortune are not quite yours. . . . *Your* good fortune seldom manifests itself except in destruction. Envy, fear, execration are the sorry mirrors in which the highness of a ruler smiles at itself . . . tears, curses, despair, the ghastly meal at which these vaunted favorites of fortune revel and from which they rise drunken, and in that state stagger into eternity before the throne of God. . . . My ideal of good fortune withdraws more contentedly within myself. All my desires lie buried within my *heart*.

THE PRESIDENT: Masterful! Perfect! Magnificent! After thirty years, back over the first lecture! . . . A pity my fifty-year-old head is too tough for learning! . . . But . . . not to allow this rare talent to get rusty, I will set someone at your side with whom you can practice this gaudy folly to your heart's content. You will make up your mind . . . make up your mind yet today . . . to take a wife.

FERDINAND *(falling back in consternation):* Father!

THE PRESIDENT: Without standing on ceremony . . . I have sent Lady Milford a card in *your* name. You will without delay resign yourself to going to her and telling her that you are her fiancé.

FERDINAND: *Milford,* father?

THE PRESIDENT: If you know her . . .

FERDINAND *(overwhelmed):* What pillory in the duchy doesn't! . . . But surely I am being ridiculous, dear father, in taking your whim seriously? Would you want to be *father* to the *scoundrel son* who married a licensed harlot?

THE PRESIDENT: Better yet! I would court her myself if she would have a fifty-year-old . . . Wouldn't you want to be *son* to the *scoundrel father?*

FERDINAND: No! As God lives!

THE PRESIDENT: A piece of insolence, upon my honor! which I shall forgive for its rarity . . .

FERDINAND: I beg you, father, leave me no longer in a conjecture where it becomes intolerable to call myself your son.

THE PRESIDENT: Boy, are you mad? What man of reason would not covet the distinction of playing alternate with the ruler of his country?

FERDINAND: You become a riddle to me, father. *Distinction* you call it . . . *distinction,* to share with a ruler even where he crawls lower than *human beings?*

(*The President bursts out laughing.*)

You can laugh . . . and I will pass over that, father. With what face shall I appear before the meanest laborer who at least receives, in his wife, a whole body by way of dowry? With what face shall I appear before the world? Before the sovereign? Before the harlot herself, who would wash out the stains of her honor in my shame?

THE PRESIDENT: Where in the world do you get your mouth, boy?

FERDINAND: I implore you by heaven and earth, father! You cannot become as happy by this flinging away of your only son, as you make him unhappy. I will gladly give you my life, if that can get you up higher. I have my life from you; I will not hesitate for a moment to sacrifice it for your greatness. . . . My *honor*, father! . . . if you take *that* from me, then it was a frivolous knave's trick to give me life, and I am forced to curse my *father* as well as the *pander*.

THE PRESIDENT (*amicably, as he claps him on the shoulder*): Fine, my dear son! I see now that you are a *splendid* fellow and worthy of the best wife in the duchy. . . . You shall have her. . . . By noon today you shall become engaged to the Countess von Ostheim.

FERDINAND (*startled anew*): Is this hour appointed to shatter me totally?

THE PRESIDENT (*casting a watchful glance at him*): Where, presumably, your honor has no objection to offer?

FERDINAND: No, father. Friederike von Ostheim could make any other man the happiest man in the world. (*to himself, in utmost confusion*) What his *malice* left still whole in my heart, his kindness rends to pieces.

THE PRESIDENT (*still not taking his eye off him for a moment*): I am waiting for your gratitude, Ferdinand. . . .

FERDINAND (*rushing to him and ardently kissing his hand*): Father! Your favor kindles all my emotion into flame . . . Father! My warmest thanks for your heartfelt intention . . . Your choice is beyond reproach . . . but . . . I cannot . . . I am not in a position to . . . Have pity on me! . . . I cannot love the Countess.

THE PRESIDENT (*falling back a step*): Aha! Now I have the young gentleman. So he walked into his trap, the sly hypocrite . . . So it was not honor that the Lady robbed you of? . . . It was not the *person*, but *marriage* that you abhorred?

(*Ferdinand stands at first as if turned to stone,
then he starts up and is about to run away.*)

Where are you going? Stop! Is this the respect you owe me?
(*The Major comes back.*)

You have been announced to the Lady. The sovereign has my word. City and court are correctly informed. . . . If you make a liar out of me, boy . . . in front of the sovereign . . . the Lady . . . the city . . . make a liar out of me in front of the court

. . . Listen, boy . . . or *if I get to the bottom of certain tales!*
Stop! Aha! What all of a sudden blows out the fire in your
cheeks?

FERDINAND (*white as snow and trembling*): How? What? It is certainly nothing, father!

THE PRESIDENT (*fixing a fearful look upon him*): And *if* it is something . . . and if I get on the track of where this insubordina-
tion is coming from. . . . Ha! boy! The mere suspicion of it
makes me rage. Go this minute! The mounting of the guard is
beginning. You will be at the Lady's as soon as the password
has been given . . . When I move out, a dukedom trembles.
Let's see whether a headstrong youth of a son will master me.
(*He goes out and comes back once more.*)
I tell you, boy, you will be there, or flee my wrath!
(*Exit.*)

FERDINAND (*waking out of dull stupefaction*): Is he gone? Was
that a father's voice?—Yes, I will go to her . . . I will go to her
. . . and tell her things, and hold a mirror up to her . . .
worthless creature! And if you want my hand even *then* . . . in
the face of the assembled nobility, military, and people . . .
Gird yourself with all your England's pride! . . . I will repudiate you . . . I, a German youth!
(*He hurries out.*)

ACT II

Scene 1

*A room in the palace of Lady Milford. At the right stands a sofa,
at the left a grand piano.*

*The Lady, in a free but charming négligée and with her coiffure
still not made up, is sitting at the piano, improvising. Sophie, her
maid, is coming away from the window.*

SOPHIE: The officers are breaking up. Guard-mount is over . . .
but I still see no Walter.

LADY (*very uneasily, as she rises and does a turn through the*

room): I don't know what has come over me today, Sophie.
. . . I have never been this way before. . . . So you didn't see
him at all? . . . Never mind . . . he will not be in any hurry.
. . . It lies on my heart like a crime. . . . Go, Sophie . . . have
them bring me out the wildest racer in the stable. I must get out
into the open air . . . see people and blue sky and ride myself
lighter about the heart.

SOPHIE: If you are feeling indisposed, my Lady . . . summon as-
sembly here. Have the Duke dine here, or have the ombre table
at your sofa. Do you suppose I would have the sovereign and
the whole court at my beck and call and put up with a pesty
mood that was bothering me?

LADY *(throwing herself down on the sofa):* Oh please, spare me!
I'll give you a diamond for every hour that I can get them off
my neck. Am I to paper my rooms with these people? . . . They
are wretched, sorry persons who are horrified if a warm and
heartfelt word escapes me, who stand with mouths and noses
wide open as if they saw a ghost . . . slaves of a single mari-
onette-string, which I control more easily than my crochet-work.
. . . What am I to do with people whose souls work just like
their watches? Can I find pleasure in asking them anything when
I know in advance what they will answer? Or in exchanging
words with them when they do not have the heart to be of a
different opinion than I? . . . Away with them! It is vexing to
ride a steed that won't even take the bit into his teeth.
(She steps up to the window.)

SOPHIE: But you will surely make an exception of the sovereign,
Lady? The handsomest man . . . the most ardent lover . . . the
cleverest head in his whole country!

LADY *(coming back):* Because it is *his* country . . . and only a
princedom, Sophie, can serve as an adequate excuse for my taste.
. . . You say people envy me. Poor thing! They should pity me,
rather. Of all those who drink at the breasts of Majesty, the
favorite comes off worst, because she alone sees the great and
wealthy man in beggar's posture. . . . It is true, he can, with
the talisman of his greatness, summon up every desire of my
heart, like a fairy palace, out of the ground. . . . He can set the
essence of two Indias upon a table . . . evoke paradises out of
wildernesses . . . make the springs of his country leap in proud

arches toward the sky, or let his subjects' marrow go up in the puff of a piece of fireworks . . . But can he also command his *heart* to beat *greatly and ardently* against a *great and ardent heart?* Can he wring his starving brain to a single beautiful emotion? . . . My heart is famished amid all this fullness of the senses, and what good to me are a thousand better feelings when all I can do is check upsurges of passion?

SOPHIE *(looking at her in amazement):* But how long is it that I have been in your service, my Lady?

LADY: Because not until today do you come to know me? . . . It is true, dear Sophie . . . I sold my honor to the sovereign; but my heart I have kept free . . . a heart, good friend, which is still perhaps worthy of a man . . . over which the poisoned wind of the court has passed only like a breath upon a mirror. . . . Believe me, my dear, I would long since have asserted it against this sorry sovereign if I could but prevail upon my ambition to yield my rank to a lady of the court.

SOPHIE: And this heart submitted so willingly to ambition?

LADY *(quickly):* As if it had not already been revenged! . . . were not avenging itself even now! . . . Sophie *(significantly, as she lets her hand fall upon Sophie's shoulder)* we women can choose only between *ruling* and *serving,* but the highest bliss of *power* is still but a wretched makeshift if we are denied the *greater* bliss of being slaves to a man we love.

SOPHIE: A truth, my Lady, that I expected to hear *last of all* from you!

LADY: And why, my Sophie? Isn't it obvious by this childish wielding of the *scepter* that we are fit only for *leading-strings?* Have you not seen by my moody fickleness . . . by these wild pleasures of mine, that they were meant only to drown out still wilder desires in my bosom?

SOPHIE *(falling back in astonishment):* Lady!

LADY *(more animatedly):* Satisfy these! Give me the man I am now thinking of . . . whom I worship . . . whom I must *possess,* Sophie, or die. *(melting)* Let me hear it from his mouth, that tears of love gleam more beautifully in our eyes than jewels in our hair, *(ardently)* and I'll throw this sovereign's heart and his princedom at his feet, I'll flee with this man, flee to the remotest wilderness in the world . . .

SOPHIE *(looking at her with alarm):* Heavens! What are you doing? What has come over you, Lady?

LADY *(in confusion):* You turn pale? . . . Have I perhaps said too much? . . . Oh, then let me bind your tongue with my confidence . . . Hear still more . . . hear everything . . .

SOPHIE *(looking anxiously around):* I fear, my Lady . . . I fear . . . I no longer need to hear it.

LADY: The union with the Major . . . you and the world are under the illusion that it is a *court intrigue* . . . Sophie . . . do not blush . . . do not be ashamed of me . . . it is the work . . . *of my love.*

SOPHIE: Oh Lord! What I intuited!

LADY: They let themselves be talked into things, Sophie . . . the weak sovereign . . . the cunning courtier Walter . . . the preposterous Chamberlain . . . Each one of them will swear that this marriage is the most infallible means of rescuing me for the Duke and knitting the bond between us all the more securely. . . . Yes! of undoing it forever! of breaking that shameful chain forever! . . . Liars belied! Outwitted by a weak woman! . . . You yourselves are now bringing me my beloved. That was precisely what I wanted . . . Once I have him . . . I have him . . . Oh then *forever* Good Night, hateful grandeur . . .

Scene 2

Enter an old valet of the sovereign's carrying a jewel casket.

THE VALET: His Serene Highness the Duke recommends himself to my Lady's favor and sends you these jewels for your wedding. They have just arrived from Venice.

LADY *(having opened the casket, falls back with fright):* Man! What did your Duke pay for these stones?

VALET *(with a black look):* They did not cost him a farthing.

LADY: What? Are you mad? *Nothing?* . . . and *(as she takes a step away from him)* you give me a look as if you would thrust a dagger through me . . . These inestimably precious stones cost him *nothing?*

VALET: Yesterday seven thousand sons of the land left for America . . . They pay for everything.

LADY (*suddenly puts the jewelry down again and paces rapidly through the room; to the valet, after a pause*): Man, what is the matter with you? I do believe you are weeping?

VALET (*wiping his eyes, in a fearful tone, trembling in every limb*): Jewels like *those* . . . I too have a couple of sons among them.

LADY (*turning away with a shudder and grasping his hand*): But none taken by force?

VALET (*laughing horribly*): Oh Lord . . . No . . . every one of them volunteers! A few saucy lads or so stepped up front and asked the Colonel how dear the sovereign was selling a yoke of human beings . . . But our most gracious ruler had all regiments march out on the parade ground and had the loudmouths shot down. We heard the rifles crack, saw their brains splatter the pavement, and the whole army shouted: "Hurrah! Off to America!" . . .

LADY (*falling with horror upon the sofa*): My God! My God! . . . And I heard nothing? And I noticed nothing?

VALET: Yes, my Lady . . . Why did you have to ride off to a bear-hunt with our master just as they were making all the noise for starting off? . . . You should not have missed the magnificence, as the shrilling trumpets announced to us that it was time, and wailing orphans pursued a living father in one place while in another place a frantic mother ran to spit her suckling infant on bayonets, and as bridegrooms were torn from brides with sabre blows, and we greybeards stood there in despair and finally tossed our crutches after the lads into the new world . . . Oh, and all the while the deafening roll of the drums, so the All-knower would not hear us praying . . .

LADY (*rising, vehemently moved*): Away with these stones . . . They dart hell's lightnings into my heart. (*more gently to the valet*) Calm yourself, poor old man. They will come back. They will see their fatherland again.

VALET (*warmly and effusively*): Heaven knows they will! . . . At the city gate they turned around once more and shouted: "God be with you, wives and children! . . . Long live the father of our country . . . On Judgment Day we will be back!" . . .

LADY (*pacing back and forth with energetic steps*): Horrible! Dreadful! . . . They made *me* think I had dried them all, the tears of this country. . . . Terribly, terribly my eyes are opened

. . . Go . . . Tell the Duke . . . that I will thank him in person!

> *(The valet starts to leave; she drops her*
> *gold-purse into his hat.)*

And take that for having told me the truth . . .

VALET *(throwing it contemptuously back on the table)*: Put it with the rest!

> *(Exit.)*

LADY *(looking after him in amazement)*: Sophie, run after him, ask him his name! He shall have his sons back again.

> *(Sophie goes out. The Lady paces pensively up*
> *and down. A pause. To Sophie, as the latter returns.)*

Wasn't there a rumor recently that fire had laid waste a city near the frontier and reduced some four hundred families to beggary?

> *(She rings.)*

SOPHIE: How did you come to hear of that? As a matter of fact, it is so, and the majority of those unfortunates are now serving their creditors as slaves, or else are being destroyed in the shafts of the ducal silver mines.

> *(Enter a servant.)*

SERVANT: What is my Lady's command?

LADY *(giving him the jewels)*: See that this is brought to the Department of the Interior without delay! . . . It is to be converted into money at once, I so command, and the profits from it are to be distributed among the four hundred whom the fire ruined.

SOPHIE: My Lady, reflect that you are risking supreme disfavor.

LADY *(with greatness)*: Am I to wear his country's curse in my hair? *(She motions to the servant; the latter withdraws.)* Or do you want me to collapse under the terrible harness of tears like those? . . . Go, Sophie . . . it is better to have false jewels in my hair than the awareness of this deed in my heart.

SOPHIE: But jewels like those! Couldn't you have taken your poorer ones? No, really, my Lady, you are not to be forgiven for it.

LADY: Foolish girl! For this, more diamonds and pearls will fall for me in one moment than ten kings have worn in their diadems, and more beautiful ones . . .

> *(The servant comes back.)*

SERVANT: Major von Walter . . .

SOPHIE *(running to the Lady)*: Oh Lord! You turn pale . . .

LADY: The first man to strike terror in me . . . Sophie! . . . Say I am indisposed, Eduard . . . Wait! . . . Is he in good humor? Does he laugh? What does he say? Oh Sophie! I look ugly, don't I?

SOPHIE: I beg you, Lady . . .

SERVANT: Is it your command to refuse him admittance?

LADY *(stammering)*: I shall be happy to see him.
(The servant goes out.)
Speak, Sophie . . . What shall I say to him? How shall I receive him? . . . I will be tongue-tied . . . He will make fun of my weakness . . . he will . . . Oh, what is my intuition? . . . You are leaving me, Sophie? . . . Stay! . . . No, no! Go! . . . No, stay after all!
(The Major comes through the anteroom.)

SOPHIE: Collect yourself! Here he is.

Scene 3

Enter Ferdinand von Walter.

FERDINAND *(with a curt bow)*: If I am interrupting you at something, my Lady . . .

LADY *(with visible palpitations)*: At nothing, Major, that could be more important to me.

FERDINAND: I come at my father's command . . .

LADY: I am indebted to him.

FERDINAND: And I am supposed to *announce* to you that we are being married . . . So much for my father's errand.

LADY *(turning pale and trembling)*: Not your own heart's?

FERDINAND: Ministers and panders are never accustomed to ask such questions.

LADY *(with such anxiety that words fail her)*: And you *yourself* have nothing further to add?

FERDINAND *(with a glance at the girl)*: A great deal more, my Lady.

LADY *(with a sign to Sophie, who withdraws)*: May I offer you this sofa?

FERDINAND: I shall be brief, my Lady.

LADY: Yes . . . ?

FERDINAND: I am a man of honor.

LADY: Whom I esteem.

FERDINAND: A gentleman.

LADY: No better in the duchy.

FERDINAND: And an officer.

LADY *(flatteringly):* You touch here upon merits which others also have in common with you. Why do you pass over greater ones in which you are *unique?*

FERDINAND *(icily):* I do not need them here.

LADY *(with ever mounting anxiety):* But how am I to take this preamble?

FERDINAND *(slowly and with emphasis):* As the protest of honor, should you have any intention of gaining my hand by force.

LADY *(vehemently):* What is this, Major?

FERDINAND *(calmly):* The language of my heart . . . of my coat of arms . . . and of this sword.

LADY: The sovereign gave you that sword.

FERDINAND: The state gave it to me by the hand of the sovereign . . . God gave me my heart . . . my coat of arms, half a millennium.

LADY: The name of the Duke . . .

FERDINAND *(hotly):* Can the Duke pervert the laws of humanity, or mint actions like his three-penny pieces? . . . He is himself not elevated above honor, but he is able to stop its mouth with gold. He can cast ermine over his shame. I must insist, no more on this point, my Lady. . . . It is no longer a matter of rejected prospects and ancestors . . . or of this sword-tassel . . . or of the world's opinion. I am prepared to trample all those under foot as soon as you will have convinced me that the *reward* is not still *worse* than the *sacrifice.*

LADY *(hurt and walking away from him):* Major! *This* I have not deserved.

FERDINAND *(seizing her hand):* Forgive me. We are speaking here without witnesses. The circumstance that brings you and me together . . . today and never again . . . entitles me, compels me, not to withhold my most secret feeling from you. . . . I cannot get it into my head, my Lady, that a lady of so much beauty and intelligence . . . qualities that a man would prize . . . should be capable of throwing herself away on a sovereign who has learned to admire in her only her *sex,* unless the lady was *ashamed* to appear before a man with her *heart.*

LADY *(looking at him wide-eyed):* Finish what you have to say.

FERDINAND: You style yourself a British woman. Permit me . . . I cannot believe that you are a British woman. The freeborn daughter of the freest nation under heaven . . . a nation too proud to burn incense to *foreign virtue* . . . can never become the hireling of *foreign vice.* It is not possible that *you* are a British woman . . . or else the heart of this British woman must be as much *smaller* as Britain's veins pulse more greatly and more boldly.

LADY: Have you finished?

FERDINAND: One might reply that it is feminine vanity . . . passion . . . temperament . . . penchant for pleasure. Virtue has often survived honor before this. Indeed, many a one who with shame entered these lists has reconciled the world with herself afterwards by noble actions and ennobled the ugly handiwork by a fair usage. . . . But then why this monstrous impressment of the country now, which was never like this before? . . . This, in the name of the duchy. . . . I have finished.

LADY *(with good humor and with loftiness):* This is the first time, Walter, that anyone has ventured such speech to me, and you are the only person to whom I answer for it. . . . For having rejected my hand I esteem you. For blaspheming against my heart I forgive you. That you are in earnest about that, I do not believe. Anyone who presumes to speak insults of this kind to a lady who needs no more than a night to ruin him utterly, must concede that lady a *great soul,* or else . . . be insane. . . . For putting the blame for the country's ruin on my breast, may Almighty God forgive you, Who will one day set you and me and the sovereign in confrontation. . . . But you have also challenged the Englishwoman in me, and to reproaches of this sort my fatherland must have a reply.

FERDINAND *(leaning on his sword):* I am eager for one.

LADY: Hear then what I have never confided to anyone except yourself, nor ever intend to confide to any human being.—I am not the adventuress, Walter, that you take me for. I could make my boast and say: I am of princely blood . . . of the race of ill-fortuned Thomas Norfolk, who fell as a victim of the Scottish Mary. . . . My father, the king's High Chamberlain, was charged with having treasonable intelligence with France and by a sentence of the Parliaments was condemned and beheaded. . . . All our possessions passed to the Crown. We ourselves were expelled from the land. My mother died on the day of the execution. I . . . a girl of fourteen . . . fled to Germany with my nurse . . . a casket of jewels . . . and this family cross, which my dying mother with her final blessing placed upon my bosom.

FERDINAND *(becomes thoughtful and fixes warmer glances upon the Lady.)*

LADY *(continuing with ever increasing emotion):* Ill . . . without a name . . . without protection or means . . . a foreign orphan, I came to Hamburg. I had learned nothing except a bit of French . . . a little crochet-work and the piano . . . I understood all the better how to eat off gold and silver, how to sleep under damask covers, how to make ten servants fly at my beckoning, and how to accept the flatteries of the great ones of your sex. . . . Six years had already been wept away. . . . The last jeweled pin was gone . . . my nurse died . . . and then my fate brought your Duke to Hamburg. I happened to be strolling along the bank of the Elbe, gazing into the river, and had just begun to toy with the fancy of whether *that stream* or *my grief* were the *deeper.* . . . The Duke saw me, pursued me, found out my place of stay . . . lay at my feet and swore he *loved* me. *(She checks herself amid great emotion, then continues in a tearful voice.)* All images of my happy childhood now woke anew with seductive shimmer. . . . Black as the grave there yawned before me a comfortless future . . . My heart was burning for another heart . . . I sank upon his. *(rushing from him)* And now you condemn me!

FERDINAND *(deeply moved, rushing after her and holding her back):* Lady! Oh heavens! What do I hear? What have I done? . . . Horribly my sacrilege is revealed to me. You can never forgive me.

LADY *(coming back and having made an effort to compose herself):* Listen further. The sovereign, to be sure, took my defense-

less youth by surprise . . . but the blood of the Norfolks re-
belled within me: "You, a princess born, Emilia (it cried), and
now a ruler's concubine?" . . . Pride and destiny struggled in
my bosom when the sovereign brought me here and all of a
sudden the most appalling scene confronted my eyes. . . . The
debauchery of the great of this world is the insatiable hyena that
seeks victims with its ravening hunger. . . . Dreadfully had it
already raged in this country . . . separating bride and bridegroom . . . even rending asunder the divine bond of marriages
. . . here it had wiped out the tranquil happiness of a family
. . . there exposed a young, inexperienced heart to ravaging
pestilence, and dying learners hissed forth their teacher's name
amid curses and spasms. . . . I took a stand between lamb and
tiger, exacted a princely oath from him in an hour of passion,
and that abominable victimization was forced to cease.

FERDINAND (*rushing about the room in the most vehement agitation*): No more, my Lady! No further!

LADY: That dreary epoch had yielded place to a still drearier one.
Court and harem now swarmed with the dregs of Italy. Giddy
Parisiennes toyed with the dread scepter, and the people bled
beneath their caprices. . . . They all lived their day. *I* saw them
sink to the dust beside me, for I was more of a coquette than
all of them. I removed the bridle from the tyrant, who lan-
guished voluptuously in my embrace . . . your fatherland, Walter, felt a human hand for the first time and fell trustingly upon
my bosom. (*a pause during which she looks at him meltingly*)
Oh, to think that the man by whom alone I should like not to
be misjudged must now compel me to swagger and to sear my
quiet virtue in the light of admiration! . . . Walter, I have blasted
prisons open . . . torn up death sentences, and shortened many
a hideous eternity in the galleys. Into incurable wounds I have
at least poured soothing balsam . . . brought down powerful
transgressors in the dust, and rescued the *lost* cause of innocence, often with an amorous tear. . . . Ah, youth, how sweet
that was to me! How proudly my heart could refute every accusation of my princely blood! . . . And now comes the man
who *alone* ought to reward me for all of that . . . the man
whom my exhausted destiny perhaps created by way of repara-

tion for my previous life . . . the man whom I already embrace
with ardent longing in my dreams . . .

FERDINAND *(interrupting her, utterly staggered):* Too much! Too
much! This is against our agreement, my Lady. You were supposed to clear yourself of accusations, and you make a criminal
out of me. Spare . . . I entreat you . . . spare my heart, which
is torn with shame and raging remorse . . .

LADY *(holding his hand fast):* Now or never! The heroine has stood
firm long enough . . . you must yet feel the weight of these
tears. *(in the tenderest tone)* Listen, Walter . . . if an unfortunate woman . . . irresistibly, all-powerfully attracted to you . . .
presses herself to you with a heart full of glowing, inexhaustible
love . . . Walter . . . and you even now still pronounce the
frigid word "honor" . . . if this unfortunate woman . . .
weighed down by the feeling of her disgrace . . . satiated with
vice . . . heroically uplifted by the call of virtue . . . throws
herself *thus* . . . into your arms *(She embraces him entreat-
ingly and solemnly.)* . . . *saved* by *you* . . . seeks through *you*
to be given back to heaven, or *(with her face averted from him
and in a hollow, quivering voice)* in order to *flee from your
image,* obedient to the dread call of despair, goes reeling down-
ward into still more hideous depths of vice . . .

FERDINAND *(wrenching himself free from her, in the most frightful
distress):* No, by the High God! I cannot endure this . . . Lady,
I must . . . Heaven and earth lie upon me . . . I must make a
confession to you, Lady!

LADY *(fleeing back from him):* Not now! Not now, by all that is
holy . . . not at this horrible moment when my torn heart is
bleeding from a thousand dagger-thrusts . . . Life or death
though it be . . . I must not . . . I will not hear it.

FERDINAND: Oh yes, oh yes, best Lady! You must. What I am
going to tell you now will lessen my guilt and be a warm apol-
ogy for the past. . . . I was deceived in you, my Lady. I expected . . . I wanted to find you worthy of my contempt. I
came here firmly determined to insult you and to earn your
hatred. . . . It would have been well for both of us if my plan
had succeeded! *(He is silent for a time; then softly and more
shyly)* I am *in love,* my Lady . . . in love with a girl of the

middle class . . . Luise Miller . . . the daughter of a musician. *(The Lady goes pale and turns away from him; he goes on more animatedly.)* I know what I am rushing into; but even if prudence bids *passion* be silent, *duty* speaks all the more loudly. . . . *I* am the guilty party. *I first* rent the golden peace of her innocence . . . lulled her heart with presumptuous hopes and treacherously exposed it to wild passion. . . . You will remind me of rank . . . of birth . . . of my father's principles . . . but I am in love. . . . My hope rises higher, the more Nature has fallen out with convention . . . My decision and the common prejudice! . . . We shall see whether *fashion* or *humanity* will lose the day.

> *(The Lady has meanwhile withdrawn to the
> furthest end of the room and is holding her hands
> over her face. He follows her there.)*

You wanted to tell me something, my Lady?

LADY *(in the tone of the most vehement grief):* Nothing, Lord von Walther! Nothing, save that you are destroying *yourself* and *me* and *a third person besides.*

FERDINAND: A third person besides?

LADY: We can *not* be happy with each other. Yet we must fall as victims to your father's undue haste. Never shall I have the heart of a man who gave me his hand only under duress.

FERDINAND: Duress, Lady? Gave under duress? And yet still gave? Can *you* compel a hand without a heart? *You* rob a girl of the man who is that girl's entire world? *You* tear a man from the girl who is that man's entire world? You, my Lady . . . a moment ago the *admirable British woman?* You can do that?

LADY: Because I must. *(with eagerness and vigor)* My passion, Walter, yields before my tenderness for you. My *honor* can no longer do so. . . . Our union is the talk of the whole country. All eyes, all arrows of mockery are intent upon me. The affront is indelible if a subject of the sovereign's rejects me. Remonstrate with your father. Defend yourself as best you can . . . I shall leave no stone unturned.

> *(She swiftly goes out. The Major stands in
> speechless rigidity. A pause. Then he rushes
> out through the double doors.)*

Scene 4

A room in the musician's house—Miller, Mrs. Miller, Luise.

MILLER *(entering the room precipitately):* It's just the way I said before!

LUISE *(running to him in distress):* What, Father? What?

MILLER *(rushing back and forth like mad):* Bring me my Sunday coat . . . quick . . . I must head him off . . . and a white dress shirt! . . . It's just the way I thought right from the start!

LUISE: For heaven's sake! What?

MRS. MILLER: What is the matter? What is it?

MILLER *(tossing his wig into the room):* Get that to the wig-dresser right away! . . . What's the matter? *(rushing up to a mirror)* And my beard is an inch long again . . . What's the matter? . . . What's going to happen, you crow's carrion? . . . The devil is loose, and may thunderation strike you!

WIFE: You see! Right away put everything on me.

MILLER: You? Yes, hell's fire! And who else? This morning with your diabolical nobleman! . . . Didn't I say so right at the time? . . . Wurm blabbed.

WIFE: Oh, what of it? How can you know that?

MILLER: How can I know that? . . . There! . . . Some fellow of the minister's is hanging around the main entrance and asking after the fiddler.

LUISE: It is the death of me.

MILLER: And you too, with your forget-me-not eyes! *(laughing maliciously)* It's a fact, if the devil really wants to get you, he has a pretty daughter born to you. . . . I've got that straight now!

WIFE: How do you know it has anything to do with Luise? You may have been recommended to the Duke. He may want you in his orchestra.

MILLER *(grabbing his cane):* Sulphur-rain of Sodom on you! . . . Orchestra! . . . Yes, where you, you procuress, will yowl treble and my blue backside will put in the bass. *(throwing himself into a chair)* God in heaven!

LUISE *(sitting down again, deathly pale):* Mother! Father! Why am I all at once so frightened?

MILLER *(jumping up again from his chair):* But that ink-splotcher will come within gunshot of me! . . . I'll set him on the run! . . . In this world or in the next . . . if I don't thrash his body and soul to a pulp and write all the Ten Commandments on his hide, and all seven supplications of the Lord's Prayer and all the books of Moses and the prophets besides, till the black-and-blues can still be seen at the resurrection of the dead . . .

WIFE: That's it! Curse and rant! As if that will help get rid of the devil. Help, holy Lord God! Where to turn now? How are we to manage this? What shall we do now? Well, speak up, father Miller! *(She runs about the room, wailing.)*

MILLER: I shall go straight to the minister. I'll open my yap first. . . . I'll make a statement myself.—You knew before I did. You should have given me a hint. The girl would still have listened to reason. There still would have been time . . . but no! . . . there had to be some dickering, there had to be some fishing. And you went and added fuel to the fire! . . . Now look out for your pimping fee. Eat your own mess! I'll take my daughter by the arm and walk across the border with her.

Scene 5

Ferdinand von Walter rushes breathlessly into the room. The others.

FERDINAND: Has my father been here?

LUISE *(starting up in terror):* His father? Almighty God!

WIFE *(clasping her hands together):* The President! It is all up with us!

MILLER *(laughing malignly):* Praise God! Praise God! Now we're in for it!

(all together)

FERDINAND *(hastening to Luise and clasping her tight in his arms):* You are *mine,* though heaven and hell come between us!

LUISE: My death is certain. . . . Go on speaking . . . you pronounced a dread name . . . your father?

FERDINAND: Nothing. Nothing. It is overcome. See, I have you again. You have me again. Oh, let me draw breath beside this heart! It was a dreadful hour.

LUISE: What hour? You are killing me!

FERDINAND (*stepping back and looking at her meaningfully*): An hour, Luise, when between my heart and you an *alien* figure intruded . . . when my love faded pale before my consciousness . . . when Luise ceased to be *everything* to her Ferdinand . . . (*Luise covers her face and sinks down upon the chair. Ferdinand goes swiftly to her, stands before her speechless and with fixed glance, then suddenly leaves her; with great emotion.*) No! Never! Impossible, Lady! It is asking *too much!* I cannot sacrifice this innocence to you. . . . No, by the infinite God! I cannot violate my oath, which out of these eyes, set as in death, admonishes me as loudly as the heaven's thunder.—Lady, gaze here . . . gaze here, unnatural father! . . . I am to murder this angel? I am to pour hell into this heavenly bosom? (*hurrying to her with resolution*) I mean to lead her before the universal Judge's throne, and if my love is a crime, let the Eternal say so. (*He takes her by the hand and raises her from the chair.*) Take courage, my dearest! . . . You have won. As victor I return from the most perilous of battles.

LUISE: No! No! Conceal nothing from me! Pronounce it, this horrible doom. You name your *father?* You named the *Lady?* . . . Shudders of death seize me . . . they say she will marry.

FERNINAND (*falling numb at Luise's feet*): Me, unhappy woman!

LUISE (*after a pause, with quiet, quavering tone and with dreadful calm*): Well . . . why am I startled then? . . . That old man there has told me so often enough . . . I was never willing to believe him. (*A pause, then she throws herself loudly weeping into Miller's arms.*) Father, here is your daughter once more . . . Forgive me, father! . . . Your child cannot help it if this dream was so beautiful and . . . the waking is now so fearful . . .

MILLER: Luise! Luise! . . . Oh God, she is beside herself . . . My daughter, my poor child . . . A curse upon the seducer! . . . A curse upon the woman who was her pander!

WIFE (*throwing herself, wailing, upon Luise*): Do I deserve this curse, my daughter? God forgive you, Baron! . . . What has this lamb done that you should murder her?

FERDINAND (*rushing to her, full of resolution*): But I shall penetrate his cabals . . . I shall rend asunder all these iron chains of prejudice . . . freely, as a man, I shall choose, so that these insect-souls will grow dizzy looking aloft at the giant-handi-work of my love.

(He starts to leave.)

LUISE *(tottering up from her chair and following him):* Stay! Stay! Where are you going? . . . Father . . . Mother . . . in this anxious hour he is deserting us!

MILLER *(laughing frenziedly):* Deserting us! Of course! Why not? . . . Why, *she* has surrendered everything to him! *(taking hold of the Major with one hand and of Luise with the other)* Patience, Sir! The way out of my house passes only over *this* girl here. . . . Wait for your father first, if you are not a scoun-drel. . . . Tell how you stole into her heart, deceiver, or else, by God! *(hurling his daughter at him, wildly and vio-lently)* you shall first crush underfoot this whimpering worm, whom love for you has *thus* dishonored!

FERDINAND *(coming back and pacing up and down in deep thought):* To be sure, the President's power is great . . . pater-nal authority is a big word . . . crime itself can hide in its folds . . . he can carry things far with it . . . very far! . . . But to the ultimate only *love* can go . . . Here, Luise! Your hand in mine! *(He seizes it violently.)* As surely as God will not de-sert me in my final breath! . . . The moment that parts these two hands will also rip asunder the thread between *me* and *cre-ation.*

LUISE: I am afraid! Look away! Your lips are trembling. Your eyes roll dreadfully . . .

FERDINAND: No, Luise. Do not tremble! It is not madness that speaks through me. It is the precious gift of heaven, *decision* at this crucial moment when the oppressed bosom can fetch breath only by something unheard of . . . I love you, Luise . . . you shall be preserved for me, Luise. . . . Now to my father!

(He swiftly hurries out and runs . . . into the President.)

Scene 6

Enter the President with a retinue of attendants. The others.

PRESIDENT *(as he enters):* There he is now.

ALL *(are terrified)*

FERDINAND *(falling back several steps):* In the house of innocence.
PRESIDENT: Where a son learns obedience to his father?
FERDINAND: Spare us the . . .
PRESIDENT *(interrupting him, to Miller):* You are the father?
MILLER: City musician Miller.
PRESIDENT *(to the wife):* You the mother?
WIFE: Yes, yes, the mother.
FERDINAND *(to Miller):* Father, take your daughter away . . . she is going to faint.
PRESIDENT: Useless precaution! I will bring her to. *(to Luise)* How long have you known the son of the President?
LUISE: About him I have never inquired. Ferdinand von Walter has been visiting me since November.
FERDINAND: Adore her.
PRESIDENT: Have you received assurances?
FERDINAND: A few minutes since, the solemnest possible before the countenance of God.
PRESIDENT *(angrily to his son):* For the confession of *your* folly you will be given a sign. *(to Luise)* I am waiting for an answer.
LUISE: He vowed love to me.
FERDINAND: And will keep that vow.
PRESIDENT: Must I order you to be silent?—Did you accept that vow?
LUISE *(tenderly):* I returned it.
FERDINAND *(in a firm voice):* The union is sealed.
PRESIDENT: I'll have that echo thrown out. *(maliciously to Luise)* But he did pay you cash every time?
LUISE *(attentively):* I do not quite understand the question.
PRESIDENT *(with biting laughter):* No? Well, I only mean . . . every trade, as they say, has its gold foundation . . . *You* too, I trust, have not given your favor away for nothing . . . Or were you, perhaps, satisfied with the mere *jointure?* Eh?
FERDINAND *(starting wildly up):* Hell! What was that?
LUISE *(to the Major with dignity and annoyance):* Lord von Walter, you are now free.
FERDINAND: Father! Virtue demands *respect* even in beggar's garb.
PRESIDENT *(laughing louder):* A humorous assumption! The father is supposed to respect his son's *whore.*

LUISE (*collapsing*): Oh heaven and earth!

FERDINAND (*with Luise and simultaneously drawing a dagger on the President, but quickly lowering it again*): Father! You once had a life to demand of me . . . It is now paid. (*putting up his dagger*) The bond-note of filial duty lies there torn to pieces . . .

MILLER (*who until now has been standing timidly off to one side, stepping forward in emotion, alternately gnashing his teeth with rage and with teeth chattering from apprehension*): Your Excellency . . . a child is a father's work . . . saving Your Grace . . . and anyone calling the child a jade is boxing the father's ears, slap after slap. . . . That's more or less the tariff with us . . . saving Your Grace.

WIFE: Lord and Saviour help us! . . . Now the old man is cutting loose . . . on our heads the thunderbolt will fall.

PRESIDENT (*who has only half heard*): Is the pimp bestirring himself too? . . . We'll have something to say to each other shortly, pimp.

MILLER: Saving Your Grace, my name is Miller, if you want to hear an adagio . . . with strumpets I cannot serve you. As long as the court has its own stock of them, the supply is not up to us middle class people. Saving Your Grace.

WIFE: In heaven's name, husband! You will destroy wife and child.

FERDINAND: You are playing a role here, my father, where you could at least have spared yourself witnesses.

MILLER (*coming closer, more stoutheartedly*): In plain German, saving Your Grace, Your Excellency rules the country. *This* is my living room. My most devoted compliment, if some day I bring a petition, but an uncivil guest I throw out the door . . . saving Your Grace.

PRESIDENT (*white with fury*): What is that? (*He advances upon him.*)

MILLER (*cautiously drawing back*): That was only my opinion, so to speak, Sir . . . saving Your Grace.

PRESIDENT (*aflame*): Ha, rascal! In jail you can express your presumptuous opinion . . . Away! Fetch beadles! (*Several of his retinue go out; the President rushes full of fury about the room.*) Father to jail! . . . to the pillory with mother and trollop daughter! . . . Justice shall lend its arm to my fury! For this insult I shall have horrible satisfaction. . . . Trash like this should shatter my plans and pit father and son against one another with impunity? . . . Ha, you cursed lot! I will sate my hatred on your destruction, the whole brood of you; father, mother, and daughter, I will immolate to my burning vengeance.

FERDINAND *(stepping calmly and resolutely among them):* Oh no, you don't! Have no fear! *I* am here. *(to the President with submissiveness)* No undue haste, my father! If you love yourself, no show of force! . . . There is a region of my heart where the word *father* has never yet been heard. . . . Do not invade *that.*

PRESIDENT: Worthless boy! Be silent! Do not rouse my ire still more!

MILLER *(coming to himself out of a dull stupefaction):* Look after your child, wife. I am going to the Duke. The court tailor . . . God has sent me this inspiration . . . the court tailor is studying the flute with me. He will not fail me with the Duke.

(He starts to go.)

PRESIDENT: To the Duke, you say? . . . Have you forgotten that I am the threshold over which you must jump or break your neck? . . . To the Duke, you blockhead? . . . Try it, when you are lying in living death a tower's depth below ground in prison, where night flirts with hell and sound and light turn around and go back again. Then rattle your chains and whimper: More punishment than I deserve.

Scene 7

Enter the beadles. The others.

FERDINAND *(rushing to Luise, who falls half dead into his arms):* Luise! Help! Save her! Terror has overwhelmed her.

MILLER *(seizes his Spanish cane, puts his hat on, and braces himself for attack.)*

WIFE *(throws herself on her knees before the President)*

PRESIDENT *(to the beadles, showing his decoration):* Lay hands on them, in the name of the Duke! . . . Away from that trollop, boy! . . . Fainting or not . . . once she has her iron necklace on, they'll wake her up with the stones they'll throw.

WIFE: Mercy, Your Excellency! Mercy! Mercy!

MILLER *(jerking his wife to her feet):* Kneel before God, old howl-whore, and not before . . . rascals, as long as I have to go to jail anyway!

PRESIDENT *(biting his lips):* You may be miscalculating, knave. There are still gallows standing empty. *(to the beadles)* Do I have to tell you again?

(The beadles move upon Luise.)

FERDINAND *(jumping up from beside her and placing himself in front of her, fiercely):* Who dares? *(He draws his sword together with its sheath and defends himself with the hilt.)* Let anybody dare to touch her who hasn't also rented his skull to the courts. *(to the President)* Spare yourself! Don't drive me any further, my father!

PRESIDENT *(to the beadles, threateningly):* If you hold your bread dear, cowards . . .

(The beadles seize Luise anew.)

FERDINAND: Death and all devils! Back, I say!—Once again! Have mercy on yourself! Do not drive me to the ultimate, father!

PRESIDENT *(enraged, to the beadles):* Is this your zeal of office, villains?

(The beadles lay hold more spiritedly.)

FERDINAND: If it must be, then *(as he draws his sword and wounds several of them)* Justice forgive me!

PRESIDENT *(full of anger):* Let me see whether I too will feel that sword.

(He seizes Luise himself, yanks her to her feet, and gives her over to one of the beadles.)

FERDINAND *(laughing in exasperation):* Father, father, you are making a biting caricature of the godhead, who was so poor a judge of people as to make *bad ministers out of perfect hangman's helpers.*

PRESIDENT *(to the others):* Away with her!

FERDINAND: Father, she shall stand in the pillory, but *with* the Major, the President's son. . . . Do you still insist on it?

PRESIDENT: The sight will be all the more comical.—Away!

FERDINAND: Father, I will defend the girl with my honor as an officer.—Do you still insist on it?

PRESIDENT: The swordbelt at *your* side is used to being pilloried.—Away! Away! You men know my will.

FERDINAND *(pushing one beadle aside, seizing Luise with one arm, and with the other drawing his sword on her):* Father! Before you dishonor my spouse, I will run her through with my sword.—Do you still insist on it?

PRESIDENT: Do it, if your blade has a point on it.

FERDINAND *(letting go of Luise and glancing fearfully toward heaven):* Thou, Almighty, art witness! No *human* means have I left untried. . . . I must proceed to the *devilish* one.—Conduct her to the pillory, and meanwhile *(shouting in the President's ear)* in the capital I will be telling a story *of how one gets to be President.*

(Exit.)

PRESIDENT *(as if thunderstruck):* What's that? . . . Ferdinand! . . . —Let her go!

(He rushes after the Major.)

ACT III

Scene 1

A room in the President's palace

Enter the President and Secretary Wurm.

PRESIDENT: The trick was ill-fated.

WURM: As I feared, my Lord. Force always *embitters* fanatics, but never *converts* them.

PRESIDENT: I had set my highest hopes on that stroke. Here is how I had it figured out: once the girl is *disgraced,* he will have to resign as an officer.

WURM: Very fine. But it should really have come to *disgrace.*

PRESIDENT: And yet . . . now that I think it over with a cool head . . . I shouldn't have let myself be cornered. It was a threat he would doubtless never have made good.

WURM: Surely you don't really think that. No folly is too fantastic for exasperated passion. You tell me the Major has always shaken his head at your regime. I believe it. The principles he brought back from the universities I just could not see, from the start. What good would fanciful dreams about greatness of soul and personal nobility be anyway at a court where the greatest wisdom is that of being great and small in proper tempo and in a skillful way? He is too young and too fiery to find the slow and devious gait of intrigue to his taste, and nothing will set his ambition going but what is great and adventurous.

PRESIDENT *(with annoyance):* But how will that sagacious observation help our enterprise?

WURM: It will direct Your Excellency's attention to the wound, and perhaps also to the dressing. A character like that . . . permit me . . . should either never have been made a *confidant* or else never have been made an *enemy*. He abhors the means by which you rose. Perhaps, up to now, it was only the *son* who checked the *traitor's* tongue. Give him the chance of really repudiating the former, make him think, by dint of repeated attacks upon his passion, that you are not the tender *father*, and the dutiful feelings of the patriot will surge to the fore in him. Indeed, just the odd fancy of making so notable a sacrifice to justice could, of itself, hold charm enough for him to bring his very father tumbling down.

PRESIDENT: Wurm . . . Wurm . . . You're taking me up to the edge of a ghastly abyss there.

WURM: I want to draw you back away from it, my Lord. May I speak candidly?

PRESIDENT *(sitting down):* Like one damned soul to its fellow in damnation.

WURM: Forgive me then . . . You have, it seems to me, your supple diplomacy to thank for the whole of the *President;* why did you not also entrust the *father* to it? I recall with what openness you talked your predecessor into a game of piquet that time and floated half the night away with friendly Burgundy at his house, and yet that was the very night that was to set off the big bomb and blow the good man sky-high.—Why did you show your son the enemy? He never should have found out that I knew about his love-situation. You could have undermined the romance from the girl's side and kept your son's heart. You could have played the clever general who does not take on the enemy at the center of his troops, but creates division in the ranks.

PRESIDENT: How could that be done?

WURM: In the simplest way . . . and the cards are not yet completely misdealt. Suppress for a time the fact that you are the father. Do not compete against a passion which any opposition will only make more powerful. . . . Leave it to *me* to hatch out by your fire the worm that will devour it.

PRESIDENT: I am eager to do so.

WURM: I would need to have a poor understanding of the barometer of the soul, or the Major is frightful in jealousy, as in love. Render the girl suspicious to him . . . plausibly or otherwise. A *grain* of yeast suffices to drive the whole mass into a destructive ferment.

PRESIDENT: But where to get that grain?

WURM: There we have the point. . . . First of all, Sir, make clear to me how much you have at stake with the Major's further refusal . . . to what degree it is important to you to end this romance with the girl of the middle class and to bring about the union with Lady Milford.

PRESIDENT: Can you still ask, Wurm? . . . My entire influence is in danger if the match with the Lady falls through, and, if I force the Major, my neck.

WURM (*cheerily*): Now be so kind as to listen.—Around the Major we shall spin a net of cunning. Against the girl we shall bring your total power to play. *We shall dictate to her a billet doux to a third party and neatly slip it into the Major's hands.*

PRESIDENT: A crazy notion! As if she would so quickly accommodate herself to writing her own death warrant?

WURM: She will *have to,* if you are willing to give me a free hand. I know that good heart backwards and forwards. She has no more than two mortal sides through which we can storm her conscience . . . her father and the Major. The latter will be absolutely out of the game; we can all the more freely manage with the musician.

PRESIDENT: As for example?

WURM: After what Your Excellency told me about the scene in his house, nothing will be easier than threatening the father with proceedings involving capital punishment. The person of the favorite and keeper of the seal is more or less the shadow of Majesty . . . offenses against the one are infractions against the latter. At least I intend to drive the poor devil into a tight corner with this trumped-up bogeyman.

PRESIDENT: But . . . the business shouldn't really turn serious.

WURM: Not at all . . . only far enough as is needed to force the family into a tight spot. So we shall, with all discretion, arrest the musician—to make the distress the more acute, the mother could be taken along too—we shall talk about a capital indictment, about the gallows, about perpetual imprisonment, and we shall make the *daughter's letter* the sole condition for his release.

PRESIDENT: Good! Good! I understand.

WURM: She loves her father . . . even to idolatry, I might say. The danger to his life . . . or to his liberty at least . . . the reproaches of her conscience for having been the cause of it . . . the impossibility of possessing the Major . . . finally the bewilderment of her head, which I shall undertake *myself* . . . it cannot fail . . . she will *have to* walk into the trap.

PRESIDENT: But my son? Will he not get wind of it right off? Will he not become more furious?

WURM: Let that be *my* worry, my Lord. . . . Father and mother will not be released until the whole family has sworn a corporal oath to keep the entire matter secret and to confirm the deception.

PRESIDENT: An oath? What good will an oath do, blockhead?

WURM: Nothing among *us,* my Lord. With *these* people, everything.—And now just see how neatly we both achieve our ends in this way. The girl loses the Major's love and her reputation for virtue. Father and mother pitch their strings a trifle lower, and once they are thoroughly toned down by blows of fate of this sort, they will wind up by acknowledging it as mercy when I give the daughter back her reputation by the offer of my hand.

PRESIDENT *(laughing and shaking his head):* Yes, I admit myself outdone, you scoundrel. The web is satanically fine. The scholar surpasses his master.—Now the question is: to *whom* shall the love note be addressed? With *whom* shall we associate her in suspicion?

WURM: Necessarily with someone who stands to gain everything by your son's decision, or else to lose everything.

PRESIDENT *(after some reflection):* I can't think of anyone but the Chamberlain.

WURM *(shrugging his shoulders):* He wouldn't be exactly to *my* taste, if my name were Luise Miller.

PRESIDENT: And why not? Odd! A dazzling wardrobe . . . an atmosphere of *eau de mille fleurs* and musk . . . at every silly word a handful of ducats . . . and all that should not be able to corrupt the delicacy of a wench of the middle classes? O good friend, jealousy is not that scrupulous. I'll send for the marshal.

(He rings.)

WURM: In the meantime, while Your Excellency is taking care of this matter and of the arrest of the musician, I will go and draw up the aforementioned love letter.

PRESIDENT *(walking over to the writing stand):* Which you will bring up to me for perusal as soon as it is done.

(Exit Wurm. The President sits down to write.
Enter a valet. He rises and gives him a paper.)

This order for arrest must go to the courts without delay . . . another of you will request the Chamberlain to come to me.

VALET: The lord has just driven up.

PRESIDENT: Better still . . . but the arrangements must be made with caution, you are to say, so that no commotion results.

VALET: Very well, Your Excellency.

PRESIDENT: You understand? In all secrecy.

VALET: Very well, Your Excellency.

(Exit.)

Scene 2

Enter the Chamberlain. The President.

CHAMBERLAIN *(precipitately):* Just *en passant,* my dear fellow. . . . How are you? How are you doing? . . . This evening there is the gala *Opéra Dido* . . . the most superb fireworks . . . an entire city burns down . . . surely you will come and see it burn too? Eh?

PRESIDENT: I have fireworks enough in my own household to carry all my splendor sky-high. . . . You come opportunely, my dear Chamberlain, to advise me in a matter, and help me actively, a matter that will be the making of both of us, or else our utter ruin. Sit down.

CHAMBERLAIN: Don't alarm me, sweet man.

PRESIDENT: As I say . . . the making of both of us, or else our total ruin. You know my project with the Major and the Lady. You comprehend also how indispensable it was to establish both our fortunes. Everything may fall through, Kalb. My Ferdinand won't do it.

CHAMBERLAIN: Won't do it . . . won't do it . . . Why, I've already told it all around town. The marriage is on everyone's lips.

PRESIDENT: You may be left standing as a windbag in front of the whole town. He loves someone else.

CHAMBERLAIN: You're joking. Is that any obstacle anyway?

PRESIDENT: With this bullhead, the most insuperable one.

CHAMBERLAIN: Can he be so insane as to thrust his *fortune* away? Eh?

PRESIDENT: Ask him that and see what he says!

CHAMBERLAIN: But, *mon Dieu!* what can he say?

PRESIDENT: That he intends to reveal to the whole town the crime by which we rose . . . that he intends to denounce our forged letters and vouchers . . . that he intends to send us both to the executioner's ax . . . that is what he can say.

CHAMBERLAIN: Are you out of your mind?

PRESIDENT: That is what he did say. That is what he was already of a mind to go about. . . . I hardly talked him out of it by my uttermost abasement. What have you to say to this?

CHAMBERLAIN *(with a sheepish look):* My mind has stopped dead.

PRESIDENT: We could let that pass. But at the same time my spies bring me word that Lord High Cup Bearer von Bock is on the point of suing for the Lady.

CHAMBERLAIN: You drive me wild. *Who*, did you say? Von Bock, you say? . . . Are you also aware that we are mortal enemies? Are you also aware of why we are so?

PRESIDENT: The first I hear of it.

CHAMBERLAIN: Dear fellow! You shall hear and you will be frantic. . . . If you still remember the court ball . . . it's going on twenty-one years ago now . . . you know, the one where they were dancing the first *anglaise* and the hot wax from a chandelier dripped on Count von Meerschaum's domino . . . Oh heavens, you surely still must remember it!

PRESIDENT: Who could forget a thing like that?

CHAMBERLAIN: You see! In the heat of the dance Princess Amalia had lost a garter. . . . Everybody, as is understandable, is in a state of alarm . . . von Bock and I . . . we were still gentlemen-in-waiting . . . we are creeping all over the redoubt-room floor looking for the garter . . . finally I spot it . . . von Bock sees it . . . von Bock goes for it, tears it out of my hands . . . I ask you! . . . takes it to the princess and triumphantly snatches her bow of thanks away from me—What do you think of that!

PRESIDENT: Impertinent!

CHAMBERLAIN: Snatches her bow of thanks away from me . . . I feel I'm about to faint. Never did anyone experience such a *malice*. . . . Finally I get my courage up, approach Her Serene Highness, and say: "Gracious Lady! Von Bock was fortunate enough to hand your Serene Highness the garter, but he who first sighted the garter rewards himself in silence and does not speak."

PRESIDENT: Bravo, Chamberlain! Bravissimo!

CHAMBERLAIN: And does not speak . . . But I shall hold it against von Bock till Judgment Day . . . the low, sneaking sycophant! . . . And as if that weren't enough . . . as we both fall down at the same time onto the garter, von Bock knocks all the powder out of my right hair-puff, and I am ruined for the whole party.

PRESIDENT: That is the man who will marry Milford and become the first personage at court.

CHAMBERLAIN: You thrust a knife into my heart. Will? Will? Why will he? Where is the necessity?

PRESIDENT: Because my Ferdinand won't do it, and nobody else has turned up.

CHAMBERLAIN: But don't you know of a single means of bringing the Major around? . . . No matter how bizarre, how desperate! . . . What in the whole world can be so repugnant as not to be welcome to us now in order to cut out the hated von Bock?

PRESIDENT: I know of only *one thing*, and that is up to you.

CHAMBERLAIN: Up to *me*? And that is?

PRESIDENT: To set the Major at odds with his beloved.

CHAMBERLAIN: Set at odds? How do you mean? . . . And how do I do it?

PRESIDENT: The game is won as soon as we make the girl suspect in his eyes.

CHAMBERLAIN: That she *steals,* you mean?

PRESIDENT: No, no! Would he believe that? . . . that she is carrying on with somebody else.

CHAMBERLAIN: And this somebody else?

PRESIDENT: Must be *you,* Baron.

CHAMBERLAIN: Be I? I? . . . Is she of the nobility?

PRESIDENT: What's the good of that? What a notion! . . . A musician's daughter.

CHAMBERLAIN: Of the middle classes, then? That won't do. Eh?

PRESIDENT: What won't do? Stuff and nonsense! Who under the sun will take it into his head to ask a pair of plump cheeks for their family tree?

CHAMBERLAIN: But consider, a married man! And my reputation at court!

PRESIDENT: That is something else again. Forgive me. I had not realized that the *man of blameless morals* meant more to you than *the one of influence.* Shall we drop this conversation?

CHAMBERLAIN: Be sensible, Baron! It was not understood *that way.*

PRESIDENT *(icily):* No . . . no. You are quite right. I'm tired of it too. I'll drop the whole business. I wish von Bock good luck with the prime ministership. There is still a world elsewhere. I shall request my dismissal from the Duke.

CHAMBERLAIN: And *I?* . . . It's all very well for you to talk, you! You're a university man! But *I?*—*Mon Dieu!* What am I if His Highness dismisses me?

PRESIDENT: A *bon mot* of day before yesterday. Last year's fashion.

CHAMBERLAIN: I beseech you, dear, precious man! . . . Stifle that thought! I will make the best of anything.

PRESIDENT: Are you *willing* to lend your name to a *rendezvous* that this Miller girl will propose to you in writing?

CHAMBERLAIN: As God is my witness! I will lend it.

PRESIDENT: And to drop the letter somewhere where it will not fail to catch the Major's eye?

CHAMBERLAIN: For example, at parade I will knock it out with my handkerchief, as if by accident.

PRESIDENT: And to assert your role as her lover, to the Major?

CHAMBERLAIN: *Mort de ma vie!* I'll show him! I'll take away the saucy fellow's appetite for *my* amours.

PRESIDENT: That's the way I like to hear it. The letter must be written yet today. You must come around for it before evening and go over your role with me.

CHAMBERLAIN: Just as soon as I have paid sixteen calls that are of the utmost *importance*. So forgive me if I take my leave of you without delay.

(*He leaves.*)

PRESIDENT (*ringing*): I shall be counting on your subtlety, Chamberlain.

CHAMBERLAIN (*calling back*): Ah, *mon Dieu!* Why, you know me.

Scene 3

The President and Wurm.

WURM: The fiddler and his wife have been arrested successfully and without any fuss. Would Your Excellency like to read over the letter now?

PRESIDENT (*after reading it*): Splendid! Splendid, Secretary! The Chamberlain has also risen to the bait. . . . Poison like this couldn't help but turn health itself into festering leprosy. . . . Now straight to the father with the proposals, and then warmly to the daughter.

(*They go out in opposite directions.*)

Scene 4

A room in Miller's dwelling—Luise and Ferdinand.

LUISE: I beg you, cease. I do not believe any more in happy days. All my hopes have sunken.

FERDINAND: And mine have risen. My father is aroused. My father will train all his guns on us. He will force me to play the inhuman son. I no longer answer for my filial duty. Fury and despair will extort from me the black secret of his murderous deed. The son will deliver the father into the executioner's hands. . . . The danger is at its *utmost*—and the utmost danger had to exist if my love was to venture its giant leap. . . . Listen, Luise! . . . A thought as great and as bold as my passion forces its way up before my soul. . . . *You*, Luise, and *I* and *love!* . . . Does not all heaven lie within that circle? Or do you still need a fourth thing?

LUISE: Stop. No more. I grow pale at what you are about to say.

FERDINAND: If we have no further claim to make upon the world, then why go begging for its approval? Why hazard where nothing is won and everything can be lost? . . . Will this eye not sparkle just as ravishingly, whether it is mirrored in the Rhine or in the Elbe, or in the Baltic Sea? My fatherland is where Luise loves me; your footprints in wild, sandy deserts are more interesting to me than the cathedral in my native land. . . . Will we miss the splendor of cities? Wherever we may be, Luise, a sun rises and a sun sets . . . spectacles beside which the most exuberant flight of the arts grows pale. If we no longer serve God in any temple, night will arise with inspiring awesomeness, the changing moon will preach us penance, and a reverent churchful of stars will pray with us. Shall we exhaust ourselves in conversations of love? . . . A smile of my Luise's is matter for centuries, and the dream of life is over before I have fathomed this tear.

LUISE: And can you have no other obligation besides your love?

FERDINAND *(embracing her)*: Your peace is my holiest one.

LUISE *(very seriously)*: Then be still and leave me. . . . I have a father who has no fortune beyond his only daughter . . . who will be sixty years old tomorrow . . . who is certain of the President's wrath. . . .

FERDINAND *(swiftly interrupting)*: Who will accompany us. Therefore no further reproach, love. I shall go, convert my valuables into money, and raise sums on my father's credit. It is permissible to rob a thief, and are his treasures not the fatherland's blood-money? . . . At the stroke of one o'clock past midnight a carriage will drive up here. You will throw yourselves into it. We shall flee.

LUISE: With your father's curse pursuing us? . . . a curse, reckless man, that not even murderers pronounce without its being heard, which Heaven's vengeance sustains even for the thief on the wheel, which would hunt us like a ghost, mercilessly, from sea to sea?—No, my beloved! If only sacrilege can preserve you for me, I still have the strength to lose you.

FERDINAND (*stands still and darkly murmurs*): Really?

LUISE: To *lose* you!—O the thought is beyond limits horrible . . . monstrous enough to pierce the immortal spirit and to fade the glowing cheek of joy . . . Ferdinand! To lose you!—Yet one does lose only what one has come to possess, and your heart belongs to your social class. . . . My claim was sacrilege, and with a shudder I renounce it.

FERDINAND (*his face distorted and gnawing his bottom lip*): You renounce it?

LUISE: No! Look at me, dear Walter! Do not gnash your teeth so bitterly. Come! Let me give life to your dying courage now by my example. Let *me* be the heroine of this moment . . . giving back a runaway son to his father . . . renouncing an alliance that would rend asunder the seams of the bourgeois world and bring the universal and everlasting order down in ruins. . . . *I* am the criminal . . . my heart has been given to wanton, foolish desires . . . my unhappiness is my *punishment;* but leave me now the sweet, flattering illusion that it was my *sacrifice.* . . . Will you begrudge me that pleasure?

> (*Ferdinand, in his distraction and fury, has seized
> a violin and tried to play on it.—Now he rips
> the strings apart, smashes the instrument on the
> floor, and bursts forth in loud laughter.*)

Walter! God in heaven! What was that for? . . . Control yourself! . . . This hour calls for control. . . . It is a *parting* one. You have a heart, dear Walter. I *know* it. . . . Warm as life itself is your love, and boundless as infinity.—Bestow it upon a *noblewoman* and a worthier one . . . she will not envy the happiest of her sex—. (*suppressing her tears*) *Me* you shall see no more . . . let the vain, deceived girl weep out her grief within solitary walls; no one will trouble about her tears.—Empty and dead is my future . . . and yet I shall ever and again smell the withered bouquet of the past. (*as she gives him her trembling hand with averted face*) Farewell, Lord von Walter.

FERDINAND (*starting up from his stupefaction*): I shall flee, Luise. Will you really not follow me?

LUISE (*who has sat down at the back of the room and covered her face with both hands*): My duty bids me remain and endure.

FERDINAND: Serpent, you lie! Something else is holding you here!

LUISE (*in the tone of the deepest inward grief*): Remain of that conjecture—it will perhaps make you less miserable.

FERDINAND: Cold duty against fiery love! . . . And I am supposed to be hoodwinked by this fairy tale? . . . A lover is holding you, and woe to you and to him if my suspicion is confirmed!
(*He goes swiftly out.*)

Scene 5

Luise alone. She remains motionless and mute for a time yet in the chair. Finally she gets up, comes forward, and looks about in fear.

LUISE: What is keeping my parents? . . . My father promised to be back in a few minutes, and five whole dreadful hours have already gone by . . . If an accident . . . What is coming over me? . . . Why does my breath come so anxiously?
(*Now Wurm enters the room and remains standing in the background without being noticed by her.*)
It is nothing real . . . it is nothing but the shuddering illusion of the heated blood. . . . Once our souls have drunk enough horror, the eye will behold ghosts in every corner.

Scene 6

Luise and Secretary Wurm.

WURM (*coming closer*): Good evening, Miss.

LUISE: My God! Who is speaking? (*She turns around, notices the Secretary, and falls back in terror.*) Horrible! Horrible! The most disastrous fulfillment already hastens after my dread premonition. (*to the Secretary with a look full of contempt*) Are you perhaps looking for the President? He is no longer here.

WURM: I am looking for you, Miss.

LUISE: Then I can't help feeling astonished that you didn't go to the marketplace.

WURM: Why precisely *there*?

LUISE: To fetch your fiancée down from the pillory.

WURM: Mamsell Miller, your suspicion is false . . .

LUISE *(suppressing a reply):* Of what service can I be to you?

WURM: I have been sent by your father.

LUISE *(in consternation):* Be my father?—Where is my father?

WURM: Where he isn't happy to be.

LUISE: For God's sake! Quick! An evil premonition comes over me. . . . Where is my father?

WURM: In prison, if you really want to know.

LUISE *(with a glance toward heaven):* That yet! That too yet!—In prison? And why in prison?

WURM: At the Duke's command.

LUISE: The Duke's?

WURM: Who took the affront to majesty in the person of his representative . . .

LUISE: What? What? O everlasting Almighty!

WURM: . . . in such a way that he has decided to avenge it with exemplary punishment.

LUISE: That is all I lacked! That! . . . Indeed, indeed my heart held something else dear besides the Major . . . That could not be passed over. . . . Affront to majesty . . . Heavenly Providence! Save, O save my failing faith! . . . And Ferdinand?

WURM: Chooses Lady Milford or else curse and disinheritance.

LUISE: Monstrous liberty!—And yet . . . yet he is more fortunate. He has no father to lose. To be sure, not to *have* one is damnation enough! . . . My father charged with affront to majesty . . . my beloved made to choose between the Lady or curse and disinheritance . . . Truly, it is amazing! A perfect villainy is still a form of perfection . . . perfection? No, there is still something lacking—Where is my mother?

WURM: In the work-house.

LUISE *(with a painful smile):* Now it is complete! . . . complete, and now I suppose I am *free* . . . cut off from all obligations . . . and tears . . . and joys . . . cut off from Providence. I don't really need that any more. . . . *(A dreadful silence.)* Do you perhaps have still further tidings? Go ahead and speak. Now I can hear anything.

WURM: You know what *has taken place.*

LUISE: Hence not what is still to *come?* *(Another pause, during which she scans the Secretary from head to foot.)* Poor creature! You ply a dismal trade at which you cannot possibly find blessing. To *make* people unhappy is horrible enough, but it is *monstrous* to *announce* it to them . . . to sing them the owlish dirge, to stand by while the bleeding heart quivers on the iron shaft of *necessity* and Christians doubt God. . . . Heaven preserve me! Even if every drop of anguish that you see shed were balanced by a ton of gold . . . I would not want to be 'you.— What can still happen?

WURM: I don't know.

LUISE: You don't *want* to know. . . . This message which shuns the light fears the noise of words, but the specter shows in the tomblike silence of your face. . . . What is still left? . . . You said before that the Duke intended to avenge it *with exemplary punishment?* What do you call exemplary?

WURM: Ask no further questions.

LUISE: Hear me, creature! You took lessons from the executioner. How else would you understand how to twist the iron with slow deliberateness upon the cracking joints and to tantalize the palpitating heart with the caress of pity? What fate awaits my father? . . . There is death in what you laughingly say; how does it look, that which you are keeping to yourself? Declare it. Let me have it all at once, the whole annihilating charge. What awaits my father?

WURM: A capital prosecution.

LUISE: But what is that? . . . I am an ignorant, innocent thing, with small understanding of your fearful Latin words. What is meant by capital prosecution?

WURM: Going on trial for his life.

LUISE (*steadfastly*): Then I thank you! (*She goes quickly into a side room.*)

WURM (*standing confounded*): Now where is she off to? Would the little fool be . . . ? The Devil! Surely she won't . . . I'll hurry after her . . . I must answer for her life. (*He is just about to follow her.*)

LUISE (*returning, with a cloak flung round her*): Forgive me, Secretary. I'll lock the room.

WURM: And where are you off to in such a hurry?

LUISE: To the Duke. (*She starts to leave.*)

WURM: What? *Where?* (*He holds her back in fright.*)

LUISE: To the Duke. Didn't you hear me? To that very Duke who intends to put my father on trial for his life . . . No! not *intends* to . . . *has* to put him on trial for his life because a few scoundrels wish it, who lends nothing to the whole trial for affront to majesty except a majesty and his princely signature.

WURM *(laughing uproariously)*: To the Duke!

LUISE: I know what you are laughing at . . . but I don't expect to find any mercy there anyway . . . God preserve me! only disgust . . . disgust at my outcry. I have been told the great ones of this world have not yet been taught what *misery* is . . . and don't want to be taught. I will tell him what misery is . . . I will portray for him with all the contortions of death what misery is . . . I will scream for him what misery is in tones that pulverize the bone and marrow . . . and if his hair stands on end then at the description, I will finish by shouting into his ears that in the hour of death the death-rattle begins to be heard in the lungs of earthly gods too and that the Last Judgment will rattle majesties and beggars in the same sieve.

(She starts to leave.)

WURM *(maliciously amicable)*: Go ahead, oh, go right ahead. You really can't do anything more clever. I advise you, go ahead, and I give you my word that the Duke will humor you.

LUISE *(stopping suddenly)*: What are you saying? . . . You advise me yourself to do so? *(She quickly comes back.)* Hm! What do I want to do then? It must be something loathsome since this creature advises it. . . . How do you know the sovereign will humor me?

WURM: Because he won't need to do it *for nothing*.

LUISE: Not for nothing? What price can he set on a human action?

WURM: The fair suppliant is price enough.

LUISE *(standing numb, then with faltering voice)*: All-righteous God!

WURM: And you will, I hope, not find a *father* overpriced at that favorable rate?

LUISE *(pacing up and down, in dismay)*: Yes! Yes! It is true! You are entrenched, you great ones . . . entrenched against the truth behind your own vices as if behind swords of the cherubim. . . . May the Almighty help you, father! Your daughter can die for you, but not sin for you.

WURM: That may well be news to him, the poor forsaken man—
"My Luise," he said to me, "has cast me down. My Luise will
also raise me up." . . . I hasten, Mamsell, to bring him your
answer!

(He pretends to be about to leave.)

LUISE *(hurrying after him, holding him back):* Stay! Stay! Patience! . . . How spry this Satan is when it is a matter of making people frantic! *I* cast him down. *I* must raise him up. Tell
me! Advise me! What can I do? What *must* I do?

WURM: There is only *one* way.

LUISE: And this only way?

WURM: Your father too desires . . .

LUISE: My father too? . . . What kind of a way is it?

WURM: It is easy for you.

LUISE: I know nothing more difficult than infamy.

WURM: If you will set the Major free again.

LUISE: From his love? Are you making fun of me? . . . Leaving
that to my voluntary choice which I was compelled to?

WURM: It is not meant that way, dear young lady. The Major
must withdraw first and voluntarily.

LUISE: He will not.

WURM: So it appears. Would one then be having recourse to you,
if you were not the only one who could help?

LUISE: Can I force him to hate me?

WURM: We shall try. Sit down.

LUISE *(startled):* Creature! What are you plotting?

WURM: Sit down. Write! Here are pen, paper, and ink.

LUISE *(sitting down in extreme perturbation):* What shall I write?
To whom shall I write?

WURM: To your father's executioner.

LUISE: Ha! You do know how to stretch souls on the rack.   *(She
takes the pen.)*

WURM *(dictating):* "My Lord"—

(Luise writes with trembling hand.)

"Three unbearable days have already passed—
already passed . . . and we have not seen each other."

LUISE *(startled, putting the pen down):* To whom is this letter?

WURM: To your father's executioner.

LUISE: O my God!

WURM: "Blame it on the Major . . . on the Major . . . who watches me all day long like an Argus."

LUISE *(jumping up):* Villainy the like of which was never heard of! To whom is this letter?

WURM: To your father's executioner.

LUISE *(wringing her hands, pacing up and down):* No! No! No! This is tyrannical, O Heaven! Punish humans humanly if they offend Thee, but why crush me between two horrors? why dangle me back and forth between death and infamy? Why set this bloodsucking devil on my neck?—Do what you will. I shall never write that.

WURM *(reaching for his hat):* As you wish, Mademoiselle. It is entirely at your pleasure.

LUISE: *Pleasure,* you say? At my pleasure?—Go, barbarian! Hang an unhappy man out over the abyss of hell, ask him for something, and blaspheme God by asking him if it is his *pleasure.* . . . Oh you know all too well that our hearts are bound by our natural impulses as fast as by chains. . . . From now on it is all the same! Go on dictating! I have no more thoughts. I yield to outwitting hell. *(She sits down for a second time.)*

WURM: "Who watches me all day long like an Argus" . . . You have that?

LUISE: Go on! Go on!

WURM: "Yesterday we had the President in the house. It was comical to see how the good Major defended my honor."

LUISE: Oh, fine, fine! Oh, splendid! . . . Keep right on!

WURM: "I had recourse to a fainting spell . . . to a fainting spell . . . to keep from laughing out loud."

LUISE: O Heaven!

WURM: "But soon my mask is going to become unbearable . . . unbearable . . . If I could only get away . . ."

LUISE *(stops, gets up, paces back and forth with her head down as if she were looking for something on the floor; then she sits down again and goes on writing.):* "Could only get away."

WURM: "Tomorrow he is on duty. . . . Keep an eye out for when he leaves me, and come to the appointed place . . ." Do you have "appointed?"

LUISE: I have it all!

WURM: "To the appointed place to your fond . . . Luise."

LUISE: Now all we need is the address.

WURM: "To Chamberlain von Kalb."

LUISE: Eternal Providence! A name as strange to my ears as these infamous lines are to my heart!

(She gets up and gazes during a long pause with fixed glance at the writing; finally she hands it to the Secretary with exhausted and failing voice.)

Take it, Sir. It is my honorable name . . . it is Ferdinand . . . it is the entire bliss of my life that I now place in your hands . . . I am a beggar!

WURM: Oh, no! Do not despond, dear Mademoiselle. I feel cordially sorry for you. Perhaps . . . who knows? . . . I might still be able to overlook certain things . . . Truly! By God! I am sorry for you.

LUISE *(looking at him fixedly and penetratingly)*: Do not finish what you are saying, Sir. You are on the way to wishing yourself something horrible.

WURM *(about to kiss her hand)*: Suppose it were this dainty hand . . . how then, dear young lady?

LUISE *(grandly and awesomely)*: Because I would strangle you on the wedding night and would then with rapture let myself be stretched upon the wheel. *(She starts to leave, but quickly comes back.)*   Are we through now, Sir? May the dove fly away now?

WURM: Just one more trifling matter, Miss. You must come with me and take the sacrament that you will acknowledge this letter as written of your own free will.

LUISE: God! God! Thou must Thyself provide the seal to insure the works of hell?

(Wurm draws her away.)

ACT IV

Scene 1

A room in the President's palace

Ferdinand von Walter, with an open letter in his hand, comes rushing in through one door as through another comes a valet.

FERDINAND: Wasn't there any Chamberlain there?

VALET: Major, His Excellency the President is asking for you.

FERDINAND: Damnation! I'm asking you whether there wasn't any Chamberlain there?

VALET: The gentleman is sitting upstairs at the faro table.

FERDINAND: The gentleman shall, in the name of all of hell, come down here.

(The valet goes out.)

Scene 2

Ferdinand, left alone, runs through the letter, sometimes standing numb, sometimes plunging wildly about.

It is not possible! not possible! That heavenly integument conceals no such devilish heart.—And yet! yet! Even if all the angels came down and gave warrant for her innocence . . . if heaven and earth, if creation and Creator conjoined to give warrant for her innocence . . . it is still her *hand*. . . . An unheard-of, colossal betrayal such as humanity never experienced before! . . . So *that* was why flight was so persistently opposed! . . . *For this* . . . O God! now I wake up, now everything is revealed to me! For *this* the claim to my love was renounced with so much heroic courage, and even *I* was all but, all but taken in by the heavenly mask!

(He rushes more swiftly about the room, then stands thoughtfully still again.)

To fathom me so totally! . . . To respond to every bold emotion, to every slight, shy tremor, to every fiery surge . . . to

divine my soul in the subtlest nuance of a tremulous whisper
. . . to calculate me in a tear . . . to accompany me to every
precipitous peak of passion, to meet me at the brink of every
vertiginous chasm . . . God! God! and all that was nothing but
a *grimace?* . . . Grimace? . . . Oh, if falsehood is so fast of
color, how does it happen that no devil has yet lied his way into
the kingdom of heaven?

When I disclosed to her the danger to our love, with what
convincing deception that false girl went pale! With what triumphant dignity she nullified my father's insolent derision, and yet
at that very moment the woman felt guilty . . . What? Did she
not withstand truth's ordeal by fire . . . the hypocrite fell into
a faint. What language will you use now, Feeling? Even co-
quettes fall into a faint. Wherewith will *you* justify yourself,
Innocence? . . . Even whores fall into a faint.

She knows what she has done to me. She has seen my entire
soul. In the blush of our first kiss my heart came visibly into my
eyes—and she felt nothing? Felt perhaps only the triumph of her
skill?—When my blissful madness fancied it was encompassing
all of heaven in her and my wildest wishes were silent? Before
my spirit stood no thought but eternity and that girl . . . God!
and she felt nothing? Felt nothing but that her design had succeeded? Nothing but that her charms had been flattered? Death
and vengeance! Nothing but that I was betrayed?

Scene 3

The Chamberlain and Ferdinand.

CHAMBERLAIN *(mincing into the room):* You expressed the wish,
my dear fellow . . .

FERDINAND *(muttering under his breath):* To break a scoundrel's
neck. *(aloud)* Chamberlain, this letter must have fallen out of
your pocket during parade . . . and *I* *(with a malicious laugh)*
was fortunate enough to be the finder.

CHAMBERLAIN: You?

FERDINAND: By the funniest coincidence. Settle that with Providence.

CHAMBERLAIN: You can see how startled I am, Baron.

FERDINAND: Read it! Read it! *(walking away from him)* If I
make too poor a lover, perhaps I show all the better promise as
a procurer.
> *(While the other is reading, he goes over to the
> wall and takes down two pistols.)*

CHAMBERLAIN *(throwing the letter on the table and starting to go
away):* Damn!

FERDINAND *(leading him back by the arm):* Patience, dear Chamberlain. The tidings, I fancy, are pleasant. I want my finder's
reward.
> *(Here he shows him the pistols.)*

CHAMBERLAIN *(falling back in consternation):* You will be reasonable, dear fellow.

FERDINAND *(in a loud, terrible voice):* More than enough to send
a rascal like you into the other world!
> *(He forces one pistol upon him and at the same
> time pulls out his handkerchief.)*

Take it, Here, take hold of this handkerchief! . . . I have it
from the bawd.

CHAMBERLAIN: Across the handkerchief? Are you mad? What are
you thinking of?

FERDINAND: Take hold of this end, I say! Otherwise, you know,
you'll miss your aim, coward! How he trembles, the coward!
You should thank God, coward, that you're getting something
into your skull for the first time.
> *(The Chamberlain runs away.)*

Easy! We'll take care of that.
> *(He overtakes him and bolts the door.)*

CHAMBERLAIN: In the room, Baron?

FERDINAND: As if it were worth a trip outside the city wall with
you? . . . Sweetheart, it will sound all the louder, and that will
doubtless be the *first* noise you ever made in the world.—Take
aim!

CHAMBERLAIN *(wiping his brow):* And you want to risk your precious life this way, young man full of hopes?

FERDINAND: Take aim, I say. I have nothing more to do in this
world.

CHAMBERLAIN: But *I* have all the more, my most excellent fellow.

FERDINAND: *You,* fellow? What, you? . . . To be a stop-gap where *men* make themselves scarce? In one minute's space to grow seven times long and seven times short, like a butterfly on a pin? To keep a log of your master's bowel-movements and to be the butt of his wit? Just as good, I'll lead you around with me like some rare marmot or other. You shall dance like a tame monkey to the howling of the damned, fetch and carry, sit up and beg, and jollify eternal Despair with your fawning tricks.

CHAMBERLAIN: Whatever you command, Sir! as you please . . . Only take the pistols away!

FERDINAND: See him standing there, the son of sorrows! . . . Standing there in mockery of the sixth day of creation! As if a Tübingen book-dealer had pirated him from the Almighty! . . . A pity though, an everlasting pity for the ounce of brain that earns such little interest in that thankless skull. That single ounce would have helped the baboon all the way on to human status, where now it only makes a fraction of sense . . . And to share her heart with *this?* . . . Monstrous! Inexcusable! . . . A fellow more suited to wean one away from sin than to instigate it.

CHAMBERLAIN: Oh! God be eternally praised! He's turning witty.

FERDINAND: I'll let him off. The tolerance that spares the maggot shall work to his benefit as well. You meet him, shrug your shoulders, and maybe even marvel at the shrewd economy of heaven that even feeds creatures on dregs and lees, that sets a table for the raven at the gallows and for the courtier in the slime of Majesties. . . . Finally you even marvel at the mighty regulation of Providence, which in the spiritual world too keeps blindworms and tarantulas on wages for the export of poison. . . . But *(as his fury is renewed)* on my blossom, I tell you, the vermin shall not crawl or *(grabbing the Chamberlain and knocking him roughly about)* I will squash you to a pulp like this, and this, and again like this.

CHAMBERLAIN *(moaning to himself)*: O my God! If one could just get away from here! A hundred miles from here in the Bicêtre* in Paris, and just not be with this one!

FERDINAND: Knave! What if she is no longer *pure?* Knave! What if you *enjoyed* where I *adored?* *(more furiously)* Gloated where I felt myself a god! *(suddenly silent, then fear-*

---

*The Bicêtre was a hospital in Paris for the aged and the insane.

fully) You would be better off, knave, to flee to hell than have my anger catch you in heaven! . . . How far did you get with the girl? Confess!

CHAMBERLAIN: Let me go. I will reveal everything.

FERDINAND: Oh! It must be more wonderful to *make illicit love* with that girl than to *revel,* no matter how *celestially,* with others. . . . If she did choose to play the wanton, if she did choose, she could debase the value of the *soul* and palm off lust as counterfeit virtue. *(putting the pistol to the Chamberlain's heart)* How far did you get with her? Confess, or I'll shoot!

CHAMBERLAIN: There's nothing . . . absolutely nothing to it. Be patient for a minute. You've been betrayed, you know . . .

FERDINAND: And you remind me of it, you scoundrel? . . . How far did you get with her? Confess, or you're a dead man!

CHAMBERLAIN: *Mon Dieu!* My God! I *am* talking . . . just listen to me . . . Your father . . . your own father . . .

FERDINAND *(more furiously):* Pandered his own daughter* for you? And how far did you get with her? Confess, or I'll murder you!

CHAMBERLAIN: You're mad. You don't listen. I never saw her. I don't even know her. I know absolutely nothing about her.

FERDINAND *(falling back):* You never saw her? Don't even know her? Know absolutely nothing about her? . . . The Miller girl is *lost* on account of you, and you deny her thrice in one breath?—Away, vile creature! *(He hits him with the pistol and pushes him out of the room.)* For your ilk the powder hasn't been invented!

Scene 4

Ferdinand, after a long silence during which his features evolve a dreadful idea.

FERDINAND: Lost! Yes, unhappy girl! . . . *I* am. And *you* are too. Yes, by almighty God! If I am lost, so are you! . . . Judge of the world! Demand her not of me! The girl is mine! I surrendered the whole world to Thee for the girl, renouncing Thy entire

---

* The Chamberlain says "Your father" ("*Ihr Vater*"), but by a coincidence of German grammar *Ihr Vater* also means "her father," and Ferdinand fatefully misinterprets the words.

glorious creation. Leave the girl to me. . . . Judge of the world! Yonder a million souls whimper after Thee . . . that way turn the eye of Thy mercy . . . let me act in my own way, Judge of the world! *(as he folds his hands terribly)* Should the rich and well-to-do Creator begrudge one soul, which happens to be the vilest one in all His creation? . . . The girl is mine! I, once her god, am now her devil!

(casting his eyes hideously into a corner)

To be tied with her for an eternity upon one wheel of damnation . . . eye rooted in eye . . . hair standing on end against hair . . . and our hollow whimperings blended into one . . . and then to repeat my endearments, and then to sing her vows back to her . . . God! God! The marriage is a dreadful one . . . but everlasting!

(He starts to hurry out. Enter the President.)

Scene 5

The President and Ferdinand.

FERDINAND *(falling back)*: Oh!—My father!

PRESIDENT: It is very good that we encounter one another, my son. I come to announce something pleasant to you, something, dear son, that will most certainly surprise you. Shall we sit down?

FERDINAND *(gazing at him fixedly for a long time)*: My father! *(going over to him in stronger agitation and grasping his hand)* My father! *(kissing his hand and falling on his knees before him)* O my father!

PRESIDENT: What is it, my son? Get up. Your hand burns and trembles.

FERDINAND *(with wild, fervent feeling)*: Forgive my ingratitude, my father! I am an infamous creature. I misjudged your kindness. You meant it so fatherly with me—Oh! You had a prophetic soul . . . now it is too late . . . Forgive me! Forgive me! Your blessing, my father!

PRESIDENT *(counterfeiting an innocent air)*: Get up, my son! Consider, you are talking riddles to me.

FERDINAND: That Miller girl, my father! . . . Oh, you do know human beings . . . your rage was so justified then, so noble, so paternally warm . . . your warm paternal zeal erred only as to method . . . that Miller girl!

PRESIDENT: Do not torture me, my son. I curse my harshness! I have come to apologize to you.

FERDINAND: Apologize to *me!* . . . Curse to *me!* . . . Your disapproval was wisdom. Your harshness was heavenly sympathy.—That Miller girl, father . . .

PRESIDENT: Is a sweet and noble girl. . . . I withdraw my overhasty suspicion. She has won my respect.

FERDINAND (*leaping up, much shaken*): What? You too? . . . Father! You too! . . . And no doubt, my father, a creature like Innocence itself? . . . And it is so human to love that girl.

PRESIDENT: Shall we say: it is a crime not to love her.

FERDINAND: Unheard-of! Monstrous! . . . And you usually have such a way of seeing right through hearts! You even saw her with the eyes of hatred! . . . Dissimulation unparalleled! . . . That Miller girl, father . . .

PRESIDENT: Is worthy of being my daughter. I count her virtue as ancestors and her beauty as gold. My principles yield before your love—She is yours!

FERDINAND (*plunging wildly out of the room*): This was all I needed! . . . Farewell, my father.

PRESIDENT (*going after him*): Stay! Stay! Where are you rushing off to?

(*Exit.*)

Scene 6

A very magnificent room in the Lady's residence

Enter the Lady and Sophie.

LADY: Then you saw her? Will she come?

SOPHIE: This very moment. She was still in her morning dress and wanted only to change her clothes in all haste.

LADY: Don't tell me anything about her . . . silence . . . I tremble like a criminal at seeing this fortunate girl who feels so terribly in harmony with my heart. . . . And how did she act upon receiving the invitation?

SOPHIE: She seemed aghast, became pensive, looked at me with wide eyes, and was silent. I was prepared for her excuses, when, with a glance that completely surprised me, she replied, "Your Lady orders me to do what I was going to request myself tomorrow."

LADY *(very uneasily):* Leave me, Sophie. Have pity on me. I shall have to blush if she is merely a common woman, and if she is more, lose courage.

SOPHIE: But my Lady . . . that is no mood in which to receive a rival. Remember who you are. Summon your birth, your rank, your power, to your aid. A still prouder heart must uplift the proud splendor of your appearance.

LADY *(absentmindedly):* What is the little fool chattering about?

SOPHIE *(maliciously):* Or is it perhaps coincidence that the most precious jewels happen to be glittering on you today? Coincidence that the most opulent material happens to clothe you today . . . that your antechamber swarms with footmen and pages, and that the girl of the middle classes is expected in the most princely hall of your palace?

LADY *(pacing up and down full of exasperation):* Accursed! Intolerable! To think that women have such lynx-eyes for feminine weaknesses!—But how low, how low I must already have fallen, to have such a creature fathom me!

(Enter a valet.)

VALET: Mamsell Miller . . .

LADY *(to Sophie):* Away with you! Remove yourself! *(threateningly, as Sophie still hesitates)* Away! Those are my orders!

(Sophie goes out. The Lady takes a turn through the room.)
Good, I'm glad I have gotten agitated. I am as I wanted to be. *(to the valet)* The Mamsell may come in.

(The valet goes out.)
(She throws herself upon the sofa and strikes a genteelly indifferent pose.)

Scene 7

Luise Miller timidly enters and remains standing at a great distance away from the Lady. The Lady has turned her back to her

*and attentively observes her for some time in the mirror that stands
opposite.*

LUISE *(after a pause):* Madam, I await your commands.

LADY *(turning around toward Luise and barely nodding her head;
coldly and aloofly):* Aha! You are here? . . . Doubtless the
Mamsell . . . a certain . . . What is your name, now?

LUISE *(somewhat sensitively):* My father's name is Miller, and Your
Grace sent for his daughter.

LADY: Right! Right! I recall . . . the poor fiddler's daughter they
were talking about recently. *(after a pause, to herself)* Very
interesting, but still no beauty . . . *(aloud to Luise)* Step closer,
my child. *(again to herself)* Eyes that have had their share of
weeping . . . how much I like those eyes! *(again aloud)*
Closer . . . Come right up.—Good child, I do believe you're
afraid of me!

LUISE *(grandly, in a resolute voice):* No, my lady. I scorn the judgment of the mob.

LADY *(to herself):* Just see! . . . And this defiance she got from
him. *(aloud)* You have been recommended to me, Mamsell.
You are said to have learned something and to be well-bred
otherwise as well. . . . Well, I am prepared to believe it. . . .
Neither would I take the whole world to doubt the word of so
warm a sponsor.

LUISE: But I do not know anyone, my Lady, who would take the
trouble to seek a patroness for me.

LADY *(pointedly):* Trouble for the client, or the patroness?

LUISE: That is over my head, my Lady.

LADY: More cunning than this frank appearance leads one to suspect? Luise is your name? And how young, if one may inquire?

LUISE: Sixteen, past.

LADY *(quickly getting up):* Now it comes out! Sixteen years old.
The first pulsebeat of this passion! . . . The first consecrating
silvery tones on the untouched keyboard! . . . Nothing is more
enticing. . . . Sit down. I like you, dear girl. . . . And he too
loves for the first time . . . what wonder that the rays of a
single dawn should meet? *(very amicably, taking her hand)* I
insist upon it, I am going to make your fortune, dear. . . .
Nothing, nothing but the sweet, early, fleeting dream. *(tapping
Luise on the cheek)* My Sophie is getting married. You shall
have her place. . . . Sixteen years old! It cannot last.

LUISE *(respectfully kissing her hand):* I thank you for this favor, my Lady, *as if* I were in a position to accept it.

LADY *(falling back in indignation):* Just see the great lady! Young misses of *your* background usually think themselves fortunate when they find employment. . . . Where do *you* expect to turn, then, my precious? Are those fingers too dainty for work? Is it your bit of pretty face that makes you so haughty?

LUISE: My face, my Lady, is as little my own as my background.

LADY: Or perhaps you think that will never come to an end? . . . Poor creature, whoever put that in your head . . . let him be who he may . . . played a hoax on both of you. Those cheeks are not gilded in the fire. What your mirror passes off on you as solid and everlasting is only a thin veneer of tinsel which sooner or later will come off on your adorer's hands.—What will we do *then?*

LUISE: Pity the adorer, my Lady, who bought a *diamond* because it seemed to be set in *gold.*

LADY *(unwilling to pay any heed to this):* A girl of your years always has two mirrors simultaneously, the real one and her admirer. . . . The obliging complaisance of the latter makes up for the rough forthrightness of the former. One accuses of an ugly pock-mark. By no means, says the other, it is a dimple of the Graces. You nice children believe from the former only what the latter has told you; you skip from one to the other until you finally confuse the statements of both.—Why do you stare at me so?

LUISE: Forgive me, my Lady . . . I was just feeling sorry for that magnificently flashing ruby for not being able to know that its possessor inveighs so sharply against vanity.

LADY *(blushing):* No evasions, my pert Miss! . . . If it isn't the promise of your figure, what in the world could keep you from choosing a position which is the only one where you can learn manners and society, the only one where you can shed your bourgeois prejudices?

LUISE: And also shed my bourgeois innocence, my Lady?

LADY: Silly objection! The most unruly knave is too timid to impute anything derogatory to us, if we do not meet him with encouragement ourselves. Show who you are. Assume honor and dignity, and I'll warrant your youth against all temptation.

LUISE: Permit me, my Lady, to venture to doubt that. The palaces of certain ladies are often the refuges of the most wanton pleasure. Who would trust the poor musician's daughter to have the heroic courage to throw herself into the midst of the pestilence and still shun infection? Who would go so far as to dream that Lady Milford kept an eternal scorpion for her conscience, or that she spent sums of money to have the advantage of blushing every moment with shame? . . . I am candid, my Lady. . . . Would the sight of me delight you when you were setting out for a pleasure? Would you put up with it when you came back from one?—Oh, better, better, you left latitudes to separate us . . . left seas to flow between us! . . . Beware, my lady! . . . Hours of abstinence, moments of *exhaustion* might occur . . . serpents of remorse might attack your heart, and then . . . what torture of the rack for you to read in your serving girl's face the *serene repose* with which innocence is wont to reward a pure heart. *(She takes a step backwards.)* I do beg your forgiveness.

LADY *(pacing about in great inner turmoil)*: Intolerable for her to say that to me! Still more intolerable that she should be right! *(stepping up to Luise and looking fixed into her eyes)* Girl, you will not outwit me. *Opinions* do not speak this warmly. Behind these maxims lurks a fiery interest that pictures *my* service as particularly abhorrent . . . that makes your talk so heated—that I *(threateningly)* must discover.

LUISE *(calmly and nobly)*: And *if* you were to discover it now? And if the contemptuous kick of your heel were to arouse the offended worm whose Creator still gave it a sting against mistreatment?—I am not afraid of your revenge, my Lady.—The poor sinner on the ignominious execution-chair laughs at the destruction of the world. . . . My misery has risen so high that candor itself cannot increase it. *(after a pause, very earnestly)* You wish to raise me up out of the dust of my background. I do not wish to debate this suspicious favor of yours. I only wish to inquire what could have induced my Lady to think me the little fool who was ashamed of her background? What could have justified her in setting herself up as the creator of my good fortune before she so much as knew whether I would be willing to accept my good fortune from *her* hands? . . . I had rent asunder my eternal claim to this world's joys. I had forgiven my good fortune for its over-haste . . . Why do you remind me of it anew? . . . When even deity veils its radiance from its creatures' sight, lest the most exalted seraph recoil at His eclipse . . . why must human beings be so cruelly merciful? . . . How does it happen, my Lady, that your vaunted good fortune is so eager to beg *misery* for envy and admiration? . . . Does your bliss need despair that much as a foil? . . . O grant me, I pray, blindness rather, which alone can reconcile me to my barbarous lot. . . . Why, the insect in a drop of water feels as blissful as if it were in a heavenly kingdom, as happy and as joyous, until someone tells it about an ocean where navies and whales sport!— But do you really want me to be *happy*? *(after a pause, stepping suddenly up to the Lady and surprising her by asking)* Are *you* happy, my Lady?

(The latter is taken aback and quickly leaves her;
Luise follows her and puts her hand on
the Lady's heart.)

Does this heart also have the smiling appearance of your rank? And what if we were now to exchange heart for heart and destiny for destiny . . . and what if I, in childlike innocence . . . by your conscience . . . and as if you were my mother, were to ask you—would you advise me to make the exchange?

LADY *(deeply moved, throwing herself upon the sofa):* Unheard-of! Incomprehensible! No, girl! No! You didn't bring this greatness into the world with you, and for a *father* it is too youthful. Do not lie to me. I hear *another* teacher . . .

LUISE *(looking her shrewdly and sharply in the eye):* I am really astonished, my Lady, to have you hit only *now* upon this teacher, and yet you already knew about employment for me *before.*

LADY *(jumping up):* This is not to be endured! . . . Very well, then! since I cannot escape you anyway. I know him . . . I know all about it . . . know more than I want to know! *(suddenly stopping short, then with a vehemence which gradually rises almost to frenzy)* But just dare, unhappy girl . . . just dare to go on loving him now, or to be loved by him . . . What am I saying? . . . Just dare to think of him, or be one of *his* thoughts . . . I am *powerful,* unhappy girl . . . *terrible* . . . As sure as God lives, you are lost!

LUISE *(steadfastly)*: Beyond rescue, my Lady, as soon as you compel him to *love* you!

LADY: I understand you . . . but he *need* not love me! I want to triumph over this outrageous passion, repress my heart, and pulverize yours. . . . Cliffs and chasms I mean to throw between you; through the midst of your heaven I mean to pass like a Fury; my name shall frighten your kisses apart as a specter does criminals; your youthfully blooming figure shall collapse withered like a mummy in his embrace. . . . I can never be happy with him . . . but *you* shall not be either . . . realize that, wretched girl! Destroying bliss is also bliss.

LUISE: A bliss you have already been deprived of, my Lady. Do not blaspheme your own heart. You are not capable of carrying out what you so menacingly conjure down upon me. You are not capable of tormenting a creature who has done you no harm except to have felt as you have . . . but I love you for being overwrought this way, my Lady.

LADY *(who has now regained her self-control)*: Where am I? Where have I been? What have I betrayed? . . . To *whom* have I betrayed it? . . . O Luise, noble, great, godlike soul! Forgive a raving woman . . . I do not want to harm a hair of your head, my child. Wishes! Ask! I will cherish you, I will be your friend, your sister. . . . You are poor . . . see! *(taking off several jewels)* I will sell this jewelry . . . sell my wardrobe, horse, and carriage . . . everything shall be *yours,* only give him up!

LUISE *(falling back in surprise)*: Is she making fun of a desperate girl, or could she in all seriousness have had no share in the barbarous deed?—Ha, that way I could still assume the appearance of a heroine and turn my helplessness to some purpose.

> *(She stands for a while lost in thought; then she
> approaches the Lady, takes her by the hand,
> and looks straight and significantly at her.)*

Then take him, my Lady! . . . Voluntarily I resign to you the man whom they tore out of my bleeding heart with grappling-irons of hell.—Perhaps you are not aware of it yourself, my Lady, but *you* have demolished the heaven of two people in love, torn two hearts asunder that *God* had bound together; shattered a creature that was *dear* to Him as you are, that He created for joy as He did you, who has praised Him as you have, and now will never praise Him again. . . . Lady! To the ear of the Omniscient the final spasm of the trodden worm also cries . . . it will not be a matter of indifference to Him if souls in His keeping are murdered! Now he is *yours!* Now, my Lady, take him! Rush into his arms! Drag him to the altar . . . only, do not forget that in between your bridal kiss there will rush the *ghost* of a *suicide*—God will be merciful . . . there's nothing else that I can do!

(She rushes out.)

Scene 8

The Lady, standing alone and shattered and beside herself with her eyes fixed on the door through which the Miller girl has hurried away, waking finally from her state of numbness.

LADY: How was that? What has happened to me? What did the unhappy girl say? . . . Still, O Heaven! still my ear is rent by those dreadful words that condemn me: *Take him!* . . . *Whom,* unhappy girl? The gift of your death-rattle . . . the dreadful legacy of your despair! God! Have I sunk *this* low . . . so suddenly hurtled from all the thrones of my pride, that I ravenously await what a beggar-girl's generosity throws me from her last death-struggle? . . . *Take him!* And this she says in a tone of voice, this she accompanies with a look—Ha! Emilia! Was it for *this* that you overstepped the bounds of your sex? Was it for *this* that you had to vie for the glorious name of the great British *woman,* to have the ostentatious edifice of your *honor* collapse beside the higher virtue of a forsaken bourgeois wench? . . . No, proud unfortunate! No! . . . *Put to shame* Emilia Milford may be . . . but *disgraced* never! I *too* have strength to renounce.

(walking back and forth with majestic steps)

Crawl away now, weak, suffering woman! . . . Farewell, sweet, golden visions of love . . . let magnanimity alone now be my guide!—This loving couple is lost, or else Milford must wipe out her claim and be effaced from the sovereign's heart! *(after a pause, enthusiastically)* It is done! . . . The awful obstacle is removed . . . burst are all bonds between me and the Duke, this wild love is wrenched out of my heart!—Into thy arms I throw myself, Virtue! . . . Take her to thee, thy repentant daughter Emilia! . . . Ah! how good I feel! How relieved, how exalted I feel all of a sudden! . . . Grand, like a setting sun, shall I sink today from the pinnacle of my loftiness; let my splendor die with my love, and let nothing but my *heart* accompany me into this proud exile. *(walking resolutely over to the writing desk)* Now it must be done right away . . . now on the spot, before the dear youth's charms renew the bloody struggle of my heart.

(She sits down and begins to write.)

Scene 9

Enter a valet. Lady. Sophie, then the Chamberlain, finally servants.

VALET: Chamberlain von Kalb is in the anteroom with a commission from the Duke.

LADY *(in the heat of writing)*: He will stagger to his feet, the princely marionette! Indeed, the idea is funny enough too to turn the noddle of a Serene Highness like that topsy-turvy! . . . His sycophants will reel . . . the whole country will be in ferment.

(Enter Sophie.)

VALET AND SOPHIE: The Chamberlain, my Lady . . .

LADY *(turning around)*: Who? What? . . . All the better! Creatures of this sort are born for carrying loads. I will be glad to see him.

(The valet goes out.)

SOPHIE *(timidly coming closer)*: If I weren't afraid, my Lady, that it would be presumptuous . . .

(The Lady goes on writing feverishly.)

The Miller girl was beside herself as she went rushing out of the anteroom . . . you're feverish . . . you're talking to yourself.

(The Lady goes on writing.)

I am alarmed . . . What must have happened?

*(Enter the Chamberlain. He makes a thousand
bows to the Lady's back, and when she does*

not notice him, he comes closer, stands behind
her chair, tries to pull out the border of her
dress, and presses a kiss upon it.)

CHAMBERLAIN *(in an awed whisper):* Serenissimus . . .

LADY *(sprinkling sand and running through what she has written):*
He will blame me for black ingratitude. . . . I was an aban-
doned girl, he took me out of misery. . . . Out of misery? . . .
Loathsome exchange! . . . Tear up your bill, seducer! My everlasting blush pays it with interest.

CHAMBERLAIN *(after walking all around the Lady in vain):* My
Lady seems to be somewhat *distrait* . . . perhaps I'll have to be
so bold as to take it upon myself. *(very loud)* Serenissimus
sends me to ask my Lady whether this evening there shall be
Vauxhall* or German comedy.

LADY *(laughing as she gets up):* One or the other, my angel . . .
meanwhile, take this note to your Duke with his dessert. *(to
Sophie)* You, Sophie, will give the order to have the horses
hitched, and you will summon all my wardrobe-ladies to this
hall.

SOPHIE *(going out, full of consternation):* O heavens! What I fore-
boded! How will this all turn out?

CHAMBERLAIN: You are *échauffée*, dear Lady?

LADY: All the fewer lies will be told on that account . . . hurrah,
Chamberlain! There is going to be a vacancy. Good weather for
panders! *(as the Chamberlain casts a dubious glance at the
note)* Read it, read it! It is my will that the contents shall not
remain confidential.

CHAMBERLAIN *(reading, while the Lady's servants gather in the
background):*

"My Lord,
An agreement which you have so frivolously broken
can no longer be binding upon *me*. The well-being of
your country was the condition of my love. Three years
the deception has gone on. The blindfold falls from my
eyes; I abhor demonstrations of favor that drip with

---

*Open-air dancing and entertainment, so called from the famous Vauxhall Gar-
dens which were operated in London from 1661 until 1859.

the tears of subjects. . . . Bestow the love which *I* can no longer reciprocate, upon your sorrowing country, and from a *British princess* learn pity for your *German people.* An hour from now I shall be across the border.

Joan Norfolk." *

ALL THE SERVANTS *(murmuring among themselves in consternation):* Across the border?

CHAMBERLAIN *(laying the note in fright down on the table):* Heaven forbid, best and gracious Lady! The bringer's neck would have to itch as badly as the writer's.

LADY: That is your worry, man of gold . . . unfortunately I know that you and your kind strangle when parroting what others have done!—*My* advice would be to have the note baked in a venison pie, and then Serenissimus would find it on his plate . . .

CHAMBERLAIN: *Ciel!* The audacity!—But do consider, do reflect, how deeply you are putting yourself in *disgrâce,* Lady!

LADY *(turning to the assembled servant staff and speaking the following with the most fervent emotion):* You stand in consternation, good people, fearfully waiting to see how the riddle will turn out? . . . Come closer, my dear ones! . . . You have served me honestly and warmly, you have more often looked into my eyes than into my purse, your obedience has been your passion, and your pride . . . my favor!—To think that your loyalty must also be the memorial of my humiliation! A sorry fate, that my blackest days were your happy ones! *(with tears in her eyes)* I dismiss you, my children.—Lady Milford is no more, and Joan of Norfolk is too poor to discharge her debt. . . . Let my treasurer empty my privy purse among you . . . this palace remains the Duke's. . . . The poorest of you will leave here richer than his mistress. *(She extends her hands, which all of them in turn kiss with fervor.)* I *understand* you, my good people—Farewell! Forever farewell! *(regaining control of her choked feelings)* I hear the carriage driving up. *(She tears herself away, starts to leave, but the Chamberlain bars her way.)* Man of pity, are you still standing there?

*Lady Milford

CHAMBERLAIN *(who all this time has been standing and looking in mental bankruptcy at the note)*: And this note I am to deliver into the most august hands of His Princely Serenity?

LADY: Man of pity! into his most august hands, and you are to report into his most august ears that, since I cannot go barefooted to Loretto, I will work for wages to cleanse myself from the infamy of having been his mistress.

> *(She hurries out. The others all disperse in great emotion.)*

ACT V

Twilight in a room of the musician's home

Scene 1

Luise is sitting silent and motionless in the darkest corner of the room, with her head bowed upon her arm. After a long and profound pause, Miller enters, carrying a lantern in his hand. He shines the light nervously around the room without noticing Luise, then lays his hat on the table and sets the lantern down.

MILLER: She's not here either. Not here either. . . . I've been through all the streets, I've been to all our friends', I've inquired at all the city gates . . . no one has seen my child anywhere. *(after a silence)* Patience, poor, unhappy father! Wait till morning comes. Maybe then your only child will come floating in to shore.—God! God! What if my heart clung too idolatrously to this daughter of mine? . . . *This* punishment is severe, Heavenly Father, severe! I do not mean to murmur, Heavenly Father, but this punishment is severe. *(He throws himself gloomily into a chair.)*

LUISE *(speaking from the corner)*: You do quite rightly, poor old man! Learn how to lose in time.

MILLER *(jumping up)*: Are you there, my child? Are you? . . . But then why so lonely and without any light?

LUISE: That is just why I am not lonely. When it gets really black all around me, I have my best visitors.

MILLER: God preserve you! Only the worm of conscience roves with the owl. Sins and evil spirits shun the light.

LUISE: *Eternity* also, father, which speaks to the soul without intermediaries.

MILLER: Child! Child! What kind of talk is that?

LUISE (*rising and coming forward*): I have fought a hard fight. You know that, father. God gave me strength. The battle has been decided. Father! People are wont to call our sex tender and frail. Do not believe that any more. Before a spider we shrink, but the black monster *Corruption* we clasp in our arms in sport. Just by way of information, father: your Luise is merry.

MILLER: Listen, daughter! I'd rather you were howling. You would please me better that way.

LUISE: How I shall outwit him, father! How I shall cheat the tyrant! . . . Love is more cunning than malice, and bolder . . . he did not know that, the man with the dismal star. . . . Oh! they are crafty as long as they have to do only with the head, but as soon as they become involved with the heart, scoundrels turn stupid—he thought he would seal his betrayal with an oath? Oaths, father, may be binding upon the living; in death even the iron bond of the sacraments dissolves. Ferdinand will know his Luise. . . . Will you take care of this note for me, father? Will you be so kind?

MILLER: To whom, my daughter?

LUISE: Curious question! Infinity and my heart between them have not room enough for a single thought of *him* . . . When would I have been writing to anyone else?

MILLER (*uneasily*): Listen, Luise! I shall open the letter.

LUISE: As you will, father . . . but you won't make anything out of it. The letters lie there like cold corpses and come alive only to the eyes of love.

MILLER (*reading*): "You are betrayed, Ferdinand . . . A knavish trick without parallel has rent asunder the bond of our hearts, but a terrible vow held my tongue bound, and your father has stationed his spies everywhere. But if you have the courage, Beloved . . . I know of *another* place where no vow is binding any more and to which no spy of his ever goes."

(*Miller stops and looks earnestly into her face.*)

LUISE: Why do you look at me like that? But read it all the way through, father.

MILLER: "But you must have sufficient courage to walk a dark road where there are no lights save your Luise and God. You must come all *love,* leaving all your hopes at home and all your tumultuous desires; nothing will be of any use to you but your heart. If you are willing . . . then set out when the clock sounds its twelfth stroke on the Carmelite tower. If you are afraid . . . then cancel the word *strong* in front of your sex, for a girl has put you to shame."

(*Miller lays the note down, stares straight ahead of him for a long time with a pained, unwavering glance; finally he turns to her and says in a gentle, broken voice*)
And this other place, my daughter?

LUISE: You do not know, you really do not know, father? . . . Strange! The place is marked so as to be found. Ferdinand will find it.

MILLER: Hum! Speak more plainly.

LUISE: I don't just know any pleasant name for it . . . you must not be startled, father, if I call it by an ugly one. This place . . . oh, why has love not invented names! It would have given this place the most beautiful one of all. The other place, dear father . . . but you must let me finish what I have to say . . . the other place is the *grave.*

MILLER (*tottering to a chair*): O my God!

LUISE (*going to him and holding him up*): Not so, my father! These are but terrors that lurk about the word.—Take that away, and there is a bridal bed there, and over it the morning throws its golden coverlet and the springtimes strew their colored garlands. None but a howling sinner could have called death a skeleton; it is a lovely, charming youth, in the flower of life, the way they paint the god of love, only not so mischievous, a quiet, ministering spirit who lends his arm to the exhausted pilgrim soul to help her across the ditch of time, opens up the fairy castle of everlasting splendor, nods in a friendly fashion, and disappears.

MILLER: What are you planning, my daughter? . . . Will you lay hand upon yourself of your own volition?

LUISE: Do not call it that, my father. To leave a company where I am not very welcome . . . to leap ahead to a place which I can no longer do without . . . is that sin?

MILLER: Suicide is the most abominable of sins, my child . . . the only one which cannot be repented, because death and misdeed occur together.

LUISE *(standing numb):* Horrible! . . . But surely it won't happen that fast. I will jump into the river, father, and *as I am sinking* I will beg Almighty God for mercy.

MILLER: That means that you intend to repent the theft as soon as you know the stolen goods are safe. . . . Daughter! Daughter! Beware lest you mock God when you need Him most. Oh, things are far, far gone with you . . . You have given up prayer and merciful God has withdrawn His hand from you.

LUISE: Is it a crime, then, to love, father?

MILLER: If you love God, you will never carry love to the point of crime.—You have bowed me low, my only one! low, low, perhaps down to the grave. . . . But I do not want to make your heart *still* heavier. . . . Daughter! I said something before. I thought I was alone. You overheard me; and why should I keep it a secret any longer? You were my idol. Listen, Luise, if you still have room for a father's feelings . . . you were my all. Now you are no longer disposing of your own possessions. I too have all to lose. You see my hair is beginning to turn grey. The time is gradually coming on for me when the capital will stand us fathers in good stead that we laid up in our children's hearts. . . . Will you cheat me out of that, Luise? Will you make off with your father's goods and chattels?

LUISE *(kissing his hand in the strongest emotion):* No, my father. I leave the world as your great debtor and shall pay you interest through all eternity.

MILLER: Beware of miscalculating there, my child! *(very earnestly and solemnly)* Will we be meeting there again? . . . See how pale you turn! . . . My Luise understands of her self that I will very likely not be able to overtake her in that world, because I do not hasten there so *soon* as she.

> *(Luise falls into his arms, seized with dread—he clasps her with fervor to his bosom and continues in an entreating voice.)*

O daughter! Daughter! Fallen, perhaps already lost daughter! Weigh your father's earnest words! I cannot watch over you. I can take the knife away from you, but you can kill yourself with

a knitting needle. I can protect you from poison, but you can choke yourself with a string of beads.—Luise . . . Luise . . . all I can still do is *warn* you . . . will you take the risk of having your treacherous illusion fade away on the dreadful bridge between time and eternity? Will you venture up before the throne of the Omniscient with the lie: *At Thy summons,* Creator, I am here! . . . when your guilty eyes look for their mortal puppet? . . . and when this brittle god of your brain, then a worm as you are, writhes at the feet of your Judge, belies your impious confidence at that wavering moment, and refers your disappointed hopes to everlasting Mercy, which the wretched man can scarcely beg for himself . . . what then? *(more emphatically, louder)* What then, unhappy girl?
(He clasps her tighter, looks fixedly and penetratingly at her for a time, then quickly walks away from her.)
I now know of nothing else . . . *(raising his right hand)* I am responsible, judging God, for this soul no longer. Do as you will. Present your slim youth with such a sacrifice that your devils will exult and your good angels will retreat. . . . Go on! Load all your sins upon you, load also this last and most horrible one upon you, and if the load is still too light, then let my curse make up the weight. . . . Here is a knife . . . pierce your heart, and *(as he starts to rush away loudly weeping)* your father's heart!

LUISE *(jumping up and running after him):* Stop! Stop! O my father! . . . To think that tenderness compels more barbarously than tyrant's fury! . . . What shall I do? I cannot! What must I do?

MILLER: If your Major's kisses burn hotter than your father's tears . . . then die!

LUISE *(after an excruciating struggle, with some firmness):* Father! Here is my hand! I will . . . God! God! What am I doing? What do I want to do? Father, I swear . . . Alas for me, alas! A criminal whichever way I turn! . . . Father, so be it! . . . Ferdinand . . . God is looking down! . . . Thus I destroy his last memorial.
(She tears up the letter.)

MILLER *(falling drunk with joy upon her neck):* That is my daughter! Look up! You are one lover lighter, and in exchange you have made a happy father. *(embracing her amid laughter and weeping)* Child! Child! of whom I was never worthy in my life! God knows how a wicked man like me ever came by this angel! . . . My Luise, my heavenly kingdom! . . . O God! I understand little, you know, about love, but that it must be torture to stop . . . that much I do understand.

LUISE: But away from this neighborhood, my father . . . away from this city, where my playmates make fun of me and my good name is gone forever. . . . Away, away, far away from the place where so many traces of my lost happiness speak to me . . . Away, if possible . . .

MILLER: Anywhere you wish, my daughter. Our Lord God's bread grows everywhere, and He will provide ears for my fiddle too. Yes! Let everything go . . . I will set the story of your sorrow to the lute, I'll sing a song about the daughter who broke her heart to honor her father—we'll beg from door to door with the ballad, and the alms will taste delicious from the hands of those in tears . . .

Scene 2

Enter Ferdinand. The others.

LUISE *(catching sight of him first and throwing herself upon Miller's neck with a loud cry):* God! There he is! I am lost.

MILLER: Where? Who?

LUISE *(with averted face, pointing to the Major and clinging more tightly to her father):* He! He himself! . . . Just look around, father . . . He has come to murder me.

MILLER *(catching sight of him and falling back):* What? You here, Baron?

FERDINAND *(slowly coming closer, stopping opposite Luise and fixing a piercing glance upon her; after a pause):* Conscience surprised unawares, I thank you! Your confession is terrible, but it is swift and certain and saves me the torment of the rack. . . . Good evening, Miller.

MILLER: But for God's sake! What do you want, Baron? What brings you here? What does this invasion mean?

FERDINAND: I have known the time when the day was dissected

into its seconds, when yearning for me tugged at the weights of the lingering wall-clock and waited with impatience for the pulsebeat at which I should appear . . . How does it happen that I now take you unawares?

MILLER: Go away, go away, Baron! . . . If there is still a spark of humanity left in your heart, if you don't want to slay her whom you claim to love, flee, do not stay a minute longer. Blessing departed my house as soon as *you* set foot on it . . . *you* have summoned misery beneath my roof, where only joy used to be at home. Are you *still* not satisfied? Do you still want to *probe* the wound that your unhappy acquaintance has dealt to my only child?

FERDINAND: Singular father, why, I've come to tell your daughter something delightful.

MILLER: New hopes, maybe, for new despair? . . . Go, messenger of misfortune! Your face belies your wares.

FERDINAND: At last it is in sight, the goal of my hopes! Lady Milford, the most formidable obstacle to our love, has this very moment fled from the country. My father approves my choice. Fate is ceasing to persecute us. Our lucky stars are rising. . . . I am here now to make good my pledged word and to take my bride to the altar.

MILLER: Do you hear him, my daughter? Do you hear him making his jests over your disappointed hopes? O truly, Baron! it becomes the seducer well to tickle his wit on his crime.

FERDINAND: You think I am jesting. By my honor, I am not! My statement is *true*, like my Luise's love, and sacredly will I hold to it, as *she* does to her oath . . . I know of nothing more sacred. . . . You still doubt me? Still no joyous flush on the cheeks of my spouse? Odd! Falsehood must be current coin here, if truth meets with so little belief. You mistrust my words? Then believe the written evidence.

> (He throws Luise's letter to the Chamberlain
> at her.)
> (Luise unfolds it and, deathly pale, falls fainting.)

MILLER (*without noticing this, to the Major*): What does this mean, Baron? I do not understand you.

FERDINAND (*leading him over to Luise*): She has understood me all the better!

MILLER (*falling down beside her*): O God! my daughter!

FERDINAND: Pale as death! . . . Now she really pleases me, your daughter! Never was she so beautiful before, the artless, upright daughter . . . with this corpselike face of hers.—The breath of the Last Judgment, which strips the varnish of every˙ lie, has blown away the paint with which this mistress of a thousand wiles has deceived even the angels of light. . . . It is her fairest face! It is her *first real* face! Let me kiss it.

(He starts to go over to her.)

MILLER: Back! Away! Do not lay hands on a father's heart, boy! From your blandishments I could not shield her, but from your mistreatment I can.

FERDINAND: What do you want, greybeard? With you I have nothing to do. Don't interfere in a game that is so obviously lost . . . or are you maybe shrewder than I gave you credit for? Did you lend the wisdom of your sixty years to your daughter's love-intrigues and shame that venerable head with a pander's trade? . . . Oh, if that is *not* so, unfortunate old man, lie down and die . . . There is still time. You can still die amid the sweet illusion: I was a fortunate father!—An instant more, and you will pitch the poisonous adder down to its hellish homeland, curse both gift and giver, and pass to the tomb blaspheming God. *(to Luise)* Speak, wretched girl! Did you write this letter?

MILLER *(warning Luise):* For God's sake, daughter! Do not forget! Do not forget!

LUISE: Oh, this letter, my father . . .

FERDINAND: That it fell into the wrong hands? . . . Praised be chance, I say; it has wrought greater things than hair-splitting Reason has, and on that Day will stand up better than the cleverness of all wise men . . . Chance, did I say . . . Oh, Providence is at hand when sparrows fall, why not when a devil is to be unmasked? . . . I want an answer! . . . Did you write this letter?

MILLER *(aside to her, in entreaty):* Steadfast! Steadfast, my daughter! Just that one *Yes,* and everything is overcome.

FERDINAND: Comical! Comical! The father taken in too! Everybody taken in! Just see her standing there, the shameless thing, and even her tongue now refuses obedience for her final lie! Swear by God! by the dread, true God! Did you write this letter?

LUISE (*after an excruciating struggle during which she has communicated with her father by glances, firmly and decisively*): I wrote it.

FERDINAND (*standing terrified*): Luise—no! As sure as my soul lives! you're lying. . . . Even innocence will confess while on the rack of crimes it never committed . . . I asked too violently . . . didn't I, Luise? . . . You confessed only because I asked too violently?

LUISE: I confessed what is true!

FERDINAND: No, I say! No! No! You did not write it. It is not your hand at all . . . And even if it were, why should handwritings be harder to imitate than hearts are to destroy? . . . Tell me the truth, Luise . . . Or rather, no, no, do not do so, you might say yes, and I would be lost.—A lie, Luise, a lie! . . . Oh, if you only knew one now, and threw it at me with that frank angelic mien, if you would only persuade my ear, only my eye, if you but deceived this heart, no matter how abominably . . . Oh Luise! All truth could then walk right out of creation in *that* breath and the good cause could from now on bend its stiff neck in a court bow! (*in a timid, tremulous voice*) Did you write this letter?

LUISE: By God! By the dread, true God! Yes!

FERDINAND (*after a pause, in the expression of deepest pain*): Woman! Woman! . . . The face with which you stand before me *now!* . . . With that face distribute paradises, and you won't find a buyer even in the kingdom of damnation. . . . Did you know what you meant to me, Luise? Impossible! No! You did not know that you meant *everything* to me! Everything! . . . It is a poor, contemptible word, but eternity has difficulty encompassing it; universes complete their orbits within it . . . Everything! And to toy with it so criminally . . . Oh, it is terrible . . .

LUISE: You have my confession, Lord von Walther. I have condemned myself. Now go! Leave a house where you were so unfortunate.

FERDINAND: Good! Good! I am calm now . . . calm too, they say, is the ghastly stretch of country across which the pestilence has passed . . . so am I. (*after some reflection*) One more request, Luise . . . the last! My head is burning so feverishly. I need something cooling. . . . Will you make me a glass of lemonade?

(*Luise goes out.*)

Scene 3

Miller and Ferdinand both pace up and down, without saying a word, at opposite ends of the room for the length of several pauses.

MILLER (*stopping finally and gazing with a sad look at the Major*): Dear Baron, can it perhaps lessen your grief if I confess to you that I am heartily sorry for you?

FERDINAND: Never mind that, Miller. (*several more paces*) Miller, I hardly remember any more how I came to your house . . . what was the occasion for it?

MILLER: What, Major? Why, you wanted to take flute lessons from me. You no longer remember that?

FERDINAND (*quickly*): I saw your daughter. (*several more paces*) You didn't keep your word, my friend. We agreed on *peace* for my solitary hours. You betrayed me and sold me scorpions. (*noticing Miller's agitation*) No! Don't be startled, old man. (*in emotion, on his shoulder*) You are not to blame.

MILLER (*wiping his eyes*): That, all-knowing God knows!

FERDINAND (*again pacing back and forth, lost in gloomy brooding*): Strangely, oh, beyond comprehension strangely, God plays with us. By slender, imperceptible cords often hang fearful weights.—If man but knew that in *this* apple he would taste death . . . hum! . . . if he but knew that? (*pacing more vehemently up and down, then grasping Miller's hand in strong emotion*) Man! I am paying too dear for those few flute lessons—and you are not even making anything . . . you too are losing . . . losing perhaps everything. (*choked up, walking away from him*) Wretched flute playing, I should never have had the notion.

MILLER (*trying to conceal his feeling*): The lemonade is taking far too long. I think I'll see about it, if you will not take it amiss . . .

FERDINAND: There is no hurry, dear Miller (*muttering to him-*

self) especially for the father. . . . Just stay here . . . what was it I wanted to ask? . . . Oh, yes! . . . Is Luise your only daughter? You have no other children?

MILLER *(warmly):* I have no others, Baron . . . nor do I wish for any others. The girl is just right the way she is, to put my whole paternal heart in her pocket . . . I've spent my whole cash-supply of love on this daughter.

FERDINAND *(vehemently shaken):* Ha!—Maybe you had better go and see about the drink, good Miller.

(Miller goes out.)

Scene 4

Ferdinand alone.

FERDINAND: His only child! . . . Do you feel that, murderer? His only one! Murderer! Do you hear: his only one? . . . And the man has nothing in God's wide world but his instrument and this only child . . . you want to rob him of her? . . . rob? . . . rob a beggar of his last savings? Throw the lame man's crutch, broken, at his feet? What? Do I have the heart for that too?— And what if he comes hurrying home and cannot wait to count down the entire sum of his joys from this daughter's face, and steps in and she is lying there, the blossom . . . withered . . . dead . . . wantonly trodden under foot . . . his last, his only, his surpassing hope . . . Ha! and he stands there in front of her, and stands there while all Nature holds its living breath and his numbed glance fruitlessly traverses depopulated infinity, looks for God and can no longer find God and comes back emptier than before—God! God! God! But *my* father also has this one son . . . his only son, though not his only wealth. *(after a pause)* But then, what is he losing? This girl, to whom the most sacred feelings of love were merely playthings, will she be able to make her father happy? . . . She will not! She will not! And I deserve thanks besides if I crush the adder before she stings her father too.

Scene 5

Miller who returns and Ferdinand.

MILLER: You shall be served directly, Baron. The poor thing is sitting out there trying to weep herself to death. She will give you tears to drink along with the lemonade.

FERDINAND: Well would it be if it were only tears!—Since we were talking before about the music lessons, Miller . . . *(taking out a purse)* I am still your debtor.

MILLER: What? What? Go along with you! What do you take me for? That's in good hands, you know. Please don't insult me, and just let it not be, if God so wills, the last time that we are together.

FERDINAND: Who can tell? Do take it. It's for all contingencies.

MILLER *(laughing):* Oh, all right, Baron! In *that case,* I think I might risk it with you.

FERDINAND: It would be risking—Have you never heard of youths dying . . . maidens and youths, the children of hope, the castles-in-air of disappointed fathers . . . what worry and old age don't do, a thunderbolt can often accomplish . . . your Luise is not immortal either.

MILLER: I have her from God.

FERDINAND: Listen . . . I tell you she is not immortal. This daughter is the apple of your eye. You have set heart and soul on this daughter. Be careful, Miller. Only a desperate player stakes everything on one throw. They call a merchant foolhardy who loads his entire fortune in one ship.—Listen and ponder the warning.—But why don't you take your money?

MILLER: What, Sir? The whole almighty purse? What is Your Grace thinking of?

FERDINAND: Of my indebtedness . . . There! *(He throws the purse on the table so the gold pieces fall out.)* I can't keep this trash this way for an eternity.

MILLER *(dumbfounded):* What in the great God's name? That didn't ring like silver money! *(He steps up to the table and cries out in horror.)* What in the name of all the heavens, Baron? Baron? Where are you? What are you doing, Baron? I would call that absentminded *(with clasped hands)*

Why, here lies . . . or else I'm bewitched, or . . . damn me!
Here I *clutch* right into solid, yellow, honest-to-goodness gold—
No, Satan! You won't get me with this!

FERDINAND: Was it old or new wine you drank, Miller?

MILLER (*uncouthly*): Thun-der-ation! Just look at it! . . . Gold!

FERDINAND: What about it?

MILLER: Deuce take it! . . . I say . . . I ask you for the sake of
the Lord Christ . . . Gold!

FERDINAND: As a matter of fact, that is something remarkable.

MILLER (*going up to him after a silence, with feeling*): My Lord,
I am a plain, forthright man . . . if you are maybe trying to
lure me into some knavish trick . . . for with that much money
God knows nothing good is to be earned.

FERINAND (*moved*): You may be quite reassured, dear Miller. You
earned this money long ago, and God protect me from defray-
ing my expenditure with your good conscience.

MILLER (*leaping into the air like a jumping jack*): Mine then! Mine!
With the good Lord's knowledge and will, mine! (*running to
the door, shouting*) Wife! Daughter! Hurrah! Come here!
(*coming back*) But Lord in Heaven, how do I happen to come
by all this awful wealth all of a sudden? How do I deserve it?
Requite it? Eh?

FERDINAND: Not with your music lessons, Miller . . . with this
money I repay you (*seized with terror he stops short*) I repay
you (*after a pause, with sadness*) for the happy three-month
dream of your daughter.

MILLER (*taking his hand and pressing it hard*): My Lord, if you
were a simple little man of the middle class . . . (*rapidly*) and my girl didn't love you . . . I'd stab the girl! (*back
by the money, again, then downcast*) But now I have everything and you nothing, and now I'll have to blow the whole
blessed lot of it again, eh?

FERDINAND: Don't let that bother you, friend . . . I am going
away, and in the country where I plan to settle, this currency
will not pass.

MILLER (*with his eyes fixed meanwhile unwaveringly on the gold,
full of rapture*): So it stays mine? Stays?—Only, I'm sorry that
you are going away. . . . Just wait, what an appearance I'll put
in now! Will I ever cut a swath now! (*He puts on his hat and*

dashes about the room.)   And I'll give my music lessons on the Exchange, and smoke Three Kings No. 5, and if I ever sit in the cheap seats again, may the Devil take me.

(He starts to go out.)

FERDINAND: Stay here! Be still! And put your money away! *(with emphasis)*   Just for this evening be quiet, and from now on, as a favor to me, don't give any more music lessons.

MILLER *(still more heatedly, clutching him by the vest, full of fervent joy):* And, Sir! my daughter! *(letting loose of him again)*   Money doesn't make the man . . . not money . . . I have eaten potatoes or a wild partridge; full is full, and this coat here is good forever if God's dear sunlight doesn't shine through the sleeves. . . . For me, this is rubbish . . . but the girl shall profit by the good luck; whatever I can guess from her eyes that she wants, she shall have . . .

FERDINAND *(swiftly interrupting):* Quiet, quiet . . .

MILLER *(still more fervently):* And she'll learn French from the ground up, and minuet dancing, and singing, till they read about it in the papers; and she shall wear a headdress like a Councillor's daughter, and a *cul de Paris,** as they call it, and about the fiddler's daughter they shall talk for four miles around . . .

FERDINAND *(grasping his hand in the most terrible emotion):* No more! No more! In God's name, be still! Just for *today* yet, be still! Let that be the only thanks I ask from you.

Scene 6

Enter Luise with the lemonade.

LUISE *(her eyes red from weeping, her voice trembling, as she brings the Major the glass on a plate):* Please tell me if it isn't strong enough.

FERDINAND *(taking the glass, setting it down, and turning quickly to Miller):* Oh, I would almost have forgotten about it! . . . May I ask something of you, dear Miller? Will you do me a small favor?

---

* A bustle. In the original German text, Miller garbles the French phrase into "Kidebarri."

MILLER: A thousand for one! What is your command. . . .

FERDINAND: They will be expecting me at dinner. Unfortunately I am in a very bad mood. It is quite impossible for me to appear among people. . . . Will you take a walk over to my father's and present my excuses?

LUISE *(startled and quickly putting in):* Why, I can take the walk.

MILLER: To the President's?

FERDINAND: Not to him personally. You will give the message to a valet in the anteroom. . . . For identification, here is my watch. . . . I will still be here when you get back. . . . You will wait for an answer.

LUISE *(much alarmed):* But can't I just as well take care of this?

FERDINAND *(to Miller, who is on the point of starting out):* Wait, and something else! Here is a letter to my father that came this evening enclosed with one to me . . . perhaps urgent business . . . it can be delivered on the same errand—

MILLER: Very well, Baron!

LUISE *(clinging to him in the most terrible dread):* But, my father, I could take care of all this quite well, you know.

MILLER: You are alone, and it is dark night, my daughter.
(Exit.)

FERDINAND: Light your father out, Luise.
*(While she accompanies Miller out with the lamp,
he steps up to the table and drops poison in the
glass of lemonade.)*
Yes! That she shall! She shall! The powers above nod their terrible *Yes* down to me, Heaven's vengeance subscribes, her good angel deserts her—

Scene 7

Ferdinand and Luise. She comes slowly back with the lamp, sets it down, and stands on the opposite side from the Major, her gaze cast down, and glancing over at him only from time to time, timidly, furtively, and with a sidelong look. He stands on the other side and stares straight ahead. A long silence, which must prepare this scene.

LUISE: If you will accompany me, Lord von Walter, I will try something on the fortepiano. *(She opens the Pantaleon.*)*
(Ferdinand makes no reply. A pause.)
You still owe me my *revanche* at the chessboard. Shall we have a game, Lord von Walter?
(Another pause.)
Lord von Walter, the letter-case that I once promised to embroider for you. . . I have begun it . . . wouldn't you like to examine the design?
(Another pause.)
Oh, I am very wretched!

FERDINAND *(in the same position):* That might well be.

LUISE: It is not my fault, Lord von Walter, that you are so poorly entertained.

FERDINAND *(laughing insultingly under his breath):* How can you help my stupid diffidence?

LUISE: I realized that it would not do for us to be together now. I was frightened at once, I confess, when you sent my father away. . . . Lord von Walter, I suspect this moment will be alike intolerable for us . . . If you will permit me, I will go and ask some of my friends in.

FERDINAND: Oh yes, do that. And I will go right away and ask some of mine too.

LUISE *(looking at him in dismay):* Lord von Walter?

FERDINAND *(very spitefully):* By my honor! the most sensible idea that a person could possibly have in this situation. We will make a jollification out of this irksome duet, and with the aid of certain gallantries avenge ourselves on the caprices of love.

LUISE: You are in high spirits, Lord von Walter.

FERDINAND: Most extraordinarily so, enough to make the boys in the marketplace come swarming after me! No! In all truth, Luise! your example converts me . . . you shall be my teacher. They are fools who babble about eternal love. Eternal monotony repels, change alone is the salt of pleasure. . . . Agreed, Luise? I'm for it . . . we'll skip from romance to romance, wallow from mire to mire . . . you out this way . . . I out that way—

* A term used for a piano, though originally the word for a nonkeyboard dulcimer developed by Pantaleon Hebenstreit about 1695.

perhaps my lost peace will be found again in some brothel . . . perhaps then, after the merry chase, we will chance upon one another again, two moldering skeletons, with the most pleasant surprise in the world, and then, by the common family resemblance which no child of that mother ever fails to betray, we will recognize each other, the way they do in comedies, and find that disgust and shame will create a harmony which has proven impossible to the tenderest love.

LUISE: O youth! Youth! You are unhappy already; do you further want to deserve to be so?

FERDINAND *(muttering fiercely between his teeth):* I am unhappy? Who told you that? Woman, you are too wicked to feel for yourself . . . how can you judge another's feelings? . . . Unhappy, she said? . . . Ha! That word could summon my fury up from the grave! . . . Unhappy I had to become, that she knew. Death and damnation! she knew that, and still she betrayed me. . . . look, serpent! That was the only spot of forgiveness . . . your remark breaks your neck for you. . . . Up till now, I was able to extenuate your crime on the grounds of your simplicity; in my *contempt* you had all but escaped my *revenge.* *(as he hastily seizes the glass)* So, frivolous you were not . . . stupid you were not . . . you were just a devil. *(He drinks.)* The lemonade is flat, like your soul . . . Try it!

LUISE: O Heaven! Not for nothing did I fear this scene.

FERDINAND *(peremptorily):* Try it!
> *(Luise takes the glass somewhat reluctantly
> and drinks.)*
> *(Ferdinand, suddenly turning pale, walks away as
> soon as she has brought the glass to her mouth
> and hurries to the furthest corner of the room.)*

LUISE: The lemonade is good.

FERDINAND *(without turning around, shaken with a shudder):* Much good may it do you!

LUISE *(after putting it down):* Oh, if you knew, Walter, how monstrously you offend my soul!

FERDINAND: Hum!

LUISE: There will come a time, Walter . . .

FERDINAND *(coming forward again):* Oh, with *time* we have done, I fancy.

LUISE: If the present evening should fall heavy on your heart . . .

FERDINAND *(beginning to pace more vigorously and to become more uneasy, throwing aside his sash and sword):* Good night, state service!

LUISE: My God! What is the matter with you?

FERDINAND: It's hot and close . . . I'm making myself more comfortable.

LUISE: Drink! Drink! The drink will cool you.

FERDINAND: That it will, for very sure. . . . The slut is good-hearted . . . but then, so are they all!

LUISE *(rushing to his arms in the full expression of love):* That to your Luise, Ferdinand?

FERDINAND *(pushing her away):* Away! Away! Away with that soft, languishing eye. I succumb. Come in your monstrous terribleness, serpent, jump up on me, snake! . . . parade your hideous windings before me, rear your coils to the sky . . . as horrible as ever the pit beheld you. . . . Only no more angel . . . only no more angel now! . . . it is too late . . . I must crush you underfoot like an adder, or else despair . . . have pity!

LUISE: Oh, that it ever had to go this far!

FERDINAND *(watching her sidelong):* This fair work of the Heavenly Sculptor . . . who can believe it? . . . who would believe it? *(seizing her hand and holding it up)* I will not call Thee to account, Creator . . . but why then pour Thy poison into such fair vessels?—Can vice thrive in this mild latitude? . . . Oh, it is strange!

LUISE: To listen to this and have to be silent!

FERDINAND: And that sweet, melodious voice . . . how can so much harmony come out of torn strings? *(tarrying to glut his eyes on the sight of her)* Everything so beautiful . . . so full of proportion . . . so divinely perfect!—Everywhere the work of His heavenly hour of love! By God! as if the whole world had come into being solely to put the Creator in the mood for this masterpiece!—And can God have erred only in the shaping of the *soul?* Is it possible that this revolting monster came into Nature without blame? *(as he swiftly walks away from her)* Or did He see an angel emerging from beneath His chisel and hastily make good His mistake with a heart that much more wicked?

LUISE: Oh, this impious self-will! He sooner attacks Heaven than acknowledge a rash deed.

FERDINAND *(falling upon her neck violently weeping):* Once more, Luise! . . . Once more, as on the day of our first kiss, when you stammered "Ferdinand" and the first loving address came to your burning lips . . . Oh, a crop of infinite and ineffable joys seemed at that moment to be as though in bud . . . there lay eternity before our eyes like a lovely day in May; golden millennia skipped like brides past our souls.—Then I was the happy man! . . . O Luise! Luise! Luise! Why have you done this to me?

LUISE: Weep, weep, Walter. Your sadness will be more just toward me than your indignation.

FERDINAND: You deceive yourself. These are not that kind of tears . . . not that warm, sensual dew that flows like balm into the wound of the soul and sets the immovable wheel of feeling into motion again. These are isolated . . . cold drops . . . the chilly, everlasting farewell of my love. *(terribly and solemnly, as he lets his hand descend upon her head)* Tears for your soul, Luise . . . tears for the Deity, who failed here in His infinite benevolence and who is so wantonly robbed of the most glorious of His works. Oh, I feel all creation ought to don mourning crape and be dumbfounded at the example that is taking place in its midst. It is an ordinary matter for human beings to fall and for Paradises to be lost; but when pestilence rages among angels, mourning should be proclaimed throughout all Nature.

LUISE: Do not drive me to the last extreme, Walter! I have strength of soul as much as any . . . but it must be put to a human test. Walter, one word yet, and then we part.—A monstrous fate has confused the speech of our hearts. If I might open my lips, Walter, I could tell you things . . . I could . . . but harsh destiny has bound my tongue as well as my love, and I must endure having you mistreat me like a vulgar slut.

FERDINAND: Do you feel all right, Luise?

LUISE: Why this question?

FERDINAND: Otherwise I should have to feel sorry for you if you were forced to depart with this falsehood.

LUISE: I implore you, Walter . . .

FERDINAND *(amid violent agitation):* No! No! That revenge would be too Satanic! No! God preserve me! I will not carry it on into *that* world—Luise! Did you love the Chamberlain? You will leave this room no more.

LUISE: Ask whatever you will. I shall answer no further. *(She sits down again.)*

FERDINAND *(more earnestly):* Consider your immortal soul, Luise! . . . Did you love the Chamberlain? You will leave this room no more.

LUISE: I shall answer no further.

FERDINAND *(falling on his knees before her in dreadful agitation):* Luise! Did you love the Chamberlain? Before this light burns down . . . you will stand . . . before God!

LUISE *(leaping up in horror):* Jesus! What is that?—and I feel very ill.

(She sinks back down upon the chair.)

FERDINAND: Already? . . . Oh, you women and the eternal riddle! Their delicate nerves stand firm against crimes that gnaw away the roots of humanity, and a miserable gram of arsenic overthrows them.

LUISE: Poison! Poison! O Lord God!

FERDINAND: So I fear. Your lemonade was seasoned in hell. You have drunk it to your death.

LUISE: To die! To die! All-merciful God! Poison in the lemonade, and to die! . . . Oh, have mercy on my soul, God of mercy!

FERDINAND: That is the main thing. I too implore Him for it.

LUISE: And my mother . . . my father . . . Savior of the world! my poor, lost father! Is there no rescue? My youthful life . . . and no rescue! And must I go now, so soon?

FERDINAND: No rescue, you must go now . . . But be calm. We shall make the journey together.

LUISE: Ferdinand, you too? Poison, Ferdinand! From your hand? O God, forget it of him . . . God of mercy, take away the sin from him . . .

FERDINAND: Look to *your* reckoning . . . I fear it stands ill . . .

LUISE: Ferdinand! Ferdinand! . . . Oh . . . Now I can remain silent no longer . . . Death . . . death annuls all oaths . . . Ferdinand! . . . Heaven and earth contain nothing more unfortunate than you . . . I die innocent, Ferdinand.

FERDINAND *(terrified):* What's that she's saying? . . . One surely does not usually take a lie along on *this* journey?

LUISE: I am not lying . . . not lying . . . I lied only *once* all my life long . . . Oh-h! How that shivers ice-cold through my veins—when I wrote that letter to the Chamberlain . . .

FERDINAND: Ha! that letter! . . . God be praised! Now I have all my manhood back.

LUISE *(her tongue becoming thicker, her fingers beginning to jerk convulsively):* That letter . . . prepare to hear a horrible thing . . . my hand wrote what my heart condemned . . . your father dictated it.

> *(Ferdinand stands rigid as a statue through a long, dead pause, and finally falls as if struck by a thunderbolt.)*

Oh, this lamentable misunderstanding . . . Ferdinand . . . they forced me . . . forgive . . . your Luise would have preferred death . . . but my father . . . the danger . . . they did it so cleverly.

FERDINAND *(leaping up):* Praise be to God! I still do not feel the poison.

> *(He whips out his sword.)*

LUISE *(declining from weakness to weakness):* Alas! What are you doing? It is your father . . .

FERDINAND *(manifesting the uttermost fury):* A murderer and a murderer's father! . . . *With* us he shall come, so that the Judge of the world may rage only against the guilty party. *(He tries to leave.)*

LUISE: My Redeemer forgave as He was dying . . . blessing be upon you and upon him.

> *(She dies.)*

FERDINAND *(turning suddenly around and perceiving her last dying movement, falling down before the dead girl and giving way to grief):* Stop! Stop! Do not run away from me, angel of Heaven! *(He seizes her hand and quickly drops it again.)* Cold, cold and moist! Her soul has passed. *(He leaps up again.)* God of my Luise! Mercy! Mercy to the most heinous of murderers! It was her last prayer!—How lovely and fair even as a corpse! The Destroyer was touched and passed gently across those friendly cheeks . . . this gentleness of disposition was no mask . . . it has stood firm against death. *(after a pause)* But how is this? Why do I feel nothing? Will the strength of my youth save me? Thankless effort! Such is not my intention. *(He reaches for the glass.)*

Last Scene

Ferdinand. The President, Wurm, and servants all come rushing full of horror into the room, followed presently by Miller with members of the populace and servants of the law, who assemble in the background.

PRESIDENT *(with the letter in his hand)*: Son, what is this? . . . I will never believe . . .

FERDINAND *(throwing the glass at his feet)*: Then *see,* murderer!

PRESIDENT *(reeling backward; everyone stands rigid; a fearful pause)*: My son, why have you done this to me?

FERDINAND *(without looking at him)*: Oh yes, of course! I should have listened to the statesman first, to see whether the business would suit his cards? . . . Sly and admirable, I confess, the trick was, to rend the bond of our hearts asunder by jealousy. . . . A master made the calculation, only it is a pity that angry *love* was not so responsive to the wire as your wooden puppet.

PRESIDENT *(searching wild-eyed all around the circle)*: Is there no one here who would weep for an inconsolable father?

MILLER *(shouting offstage)*: Let me in! In God's name, let me in!

FERDINAND: The girl is a saint . . . for her, another must get justice.

(He opens the door for Miller, who comes rushing in with members of the populace and servants of the law.)

MILLER *(in the most dreadful anguish)*: My child! My child! . . . Poison! . . . Poison, they are shouting, has been taken here . . . My daughter! Where are you?

FERDINAND *(leading him up between the President and Luise's corpse)*: I am innocent. Thank *this* man here.

MILLER *(falling on the floor beside her)*: O Jesus!

FERDINAND: In a few words, father . . . they are beginning to become precious to me . . . I have been knavishly robbed of my life, robbed by *you.* As to how I stand with God, I tremble . . . but a scoundrel I have never been. Let my everlasting lot fall as it may . . . may it not fall on *you* . . . But I have committed a murder, *(with his voice raised terribly)* a murder that *you* will not expect me to drag *alone* up before the Judge of the world. Frankly, I lay at your door the larger, more hideous half of it; how you manage with it is for you to see to. *(leading him over to Luise*) Here, barbarian! feast your eyes on the horrible fruit of your cleverness; upon this countenance your name is written in convulsions, and the angels of death will read it. . . . May a form like this one draw the curtain before your bed when you are sleeping and give you its ice-cold hand . . . may a form like this one stand before your soul when you are dying and drive away your last prayer . . . may a form like this one stand upon your grave when you resurrect—and at the side of God when He judges you.

(*He becomes faint. Servants support him.*)

PRESIDENT (*with a terrible gesture toward heaven*): Not from me, not from me, Judge of the world! Demand these souls from *this man!*

(*He advances upon Wurm.*)

WURM (*vehemently*): From me?

PRESIDENT: Accursed man, from you! From you, Satan! . . . You, you gave me the serpent counsel . . . on *you* the responsibility . . . I wash my hands of it.

WURM: On me? (*He begins to laugh hideously.*) Jolly! Jolly! Now I know the way devils thank. . . . On me, stupid scoundrel? Was it *my* son? Was *I* your master? . . . On me the responsibility? Ha! at this sight, which chills me to the marrow in my bones! On me it should fall? . . . Now I *am willing to be* lost, but *you* shall be lost with me. . . . Up! Up! Cry "murder!" through the streets! Wake Justice up! Servants of the law, bind me! Take me away! I will reveal secrets to make the flesh creep of those that hear them. (*He starts to go.*)

PRESIDENT (*detaining him*): You wouldn't do that, madman?

WURM (*clapping him on the shoulder*): I will, comrade! I will! . . . A madman I am, that is true . . . that is your work . . . so now I will act like a madman too. . . . Arm in arm with *you* to the scaffold! Arm in arm with *you* to hell! It will tickle me, rascal, to be damned with *you!*

(*He is led away.*)

MILLER (*who all this time has been lying in mute grief with his head in Luise's lap, getting suddenly to his feet and throwing the purse at the feet of the Major*): Poisoner! Keep your accursed gold! . . . Did you mean to buy my child from me with it?

(*He rushes out of the room*)

FERDINAND *(with failing voice)*: Go after him! He is desperate . . .
somebody save the money here for him . . . it is my terrible
acknowledgement . . . Luise . . . Luise . . . I come . . .
Farewell—Let me expire at this altar . . .

PRESIDENT *(out of a dull apathy, to his son)*: Son! Ferdinand! Will
no gaze more fall upon a shattered father?

    (The Major is eased down alongside of Luise.)

FERDINAND: To merciful God this last one belongs.

PRESIDENT *(falling on his knees before him in the most terrible
affliction)*: Creature and Creator abandon me . . . Shall no
glance more fall to me as a final comfort?

    (Ferdinand extends to him his dying hand.)

(quickly standing up) He forgave me! *(to the others)* Now:
your prisoner!

    *(He goes out. The servants of the law follow him,
as the curtain falls.)*

                    Translated by Charles E. Passage

DON CARLOS

CHARACTERS

KING PHILIPP OF SPAIN
DON CARLOS, *his son, the Crown Prince*
ELIZABETH, *Philipp's Queen*
RODERICK, MARQUIS OF POSA, *a Maltese*
FATHER DOMINGO, *a priest at Philipp's Court*
THE DUCHESS OF OLIVAREZ ⎫
THE PRINCESS OF EBOLI ⎬ *All, ladies-in-waiting to the Queen*
THE MARQUISE OF MONDECAR ⎭
THE DUKES OF ALBA, FERIA, AND ⎫
   MEDINA SIDONIA ⎬ *All, courtiers*
THE COUNT OF LERMA ⎭
VARIOUS LADIES AND GRANDEES OF THE COURT
A PAGE IN SERVICE TO THE COURT
THE PRIOR OF A CARTHUSIAN MONASTERY
THE PRINCE OF PARMA
THE COUNTESS FUENTES
THE INFANTA CLARA EUGENIA, *daughter of Philipp and Elizabeth*
DON RAIMUND OF TAXIS, *the Chief Postmaster*
LUIS MERCADO, *the Queen's physician*
VARIOUS OFFICERS OF THE KING'S BODYGUARD
THE GRAND INQUISITOR

ACT 1

The royal garden in Aranjuez

Scene 1

Carlos. Domingo.
DOMINGO: The lovely days here in Aranjuez
    Are at an end. Your Royal Majesty
    Departs no merrier. 'Tis clear that we
    Have stayed so long in vain. Can you not break
    This baffling silence, Prince, and open up
    Your heart bared to your father's heart? The price
    For this, his only son's tranquillity
    Can for our Monarch never be too dear.
            (Carlos looks down and remains silent.)
    Can then his wishes be denied by Heaven
    To this, the most beloved of all its sons?
    I looked on when within Toledo's walls
    Proud Karl received his subjects' adoration,
    When princes strove to kiss his hand and then
    As one—*as one*—fell down before his feet.
    Six kingdoms lay before him prostrate there.
    I was a witness when the young, proud blood
    Rose to his cheeks; I saw his bosom swell
    With royal resolution; then his gaze
    Did soar with rapture through the gathering

And broke in ecstasy—and, Prince, this gaze
Affirmed: It is enough.
               (Carlos turns away.)
                  This quiet, Prince,
This sad solemnity that we have seen
Has lingered eight long months upon your face,
The whole court's mystery, and the alarm
Of the whole kingdom, it has brought upon
Your royal father many troubled nights
And cost your mother many tears.
CARLOS *(turns around suddenly)*:   My mother?
  O heaven, grant that I may yet forget
  That he made her into my mother!
DOMINGO: Prince?
CARLOS *(reflects and passes his hand over his forehead)*:
  O noble sir—I have such awful luck
  With mothers. What I did as my first act
  Upon my entrance in this world—was kill
  My mother.
DOMINGO: Can it be, O noble Prince?
  Can self-reproach weigh on your conscience thus?
CARLOS: And my new mother—what has she done for me
  But rob me quickly of my father's love?
  My father scarcely loved me save for this:
  The merit due me as his only child.
  Now she gives him a daughter—Oh, who knows
  What slumbers hidden in the mist of time?
DOMINGO: You jest with me, my Prince, for all of Spain
  Adores its Queen, and should you be the one
  Alone to look at her with hate-filled eyes
  And at her aspect entertain shrewd thoughts?
  She is the fairest woman in the world,
  And Queen besides—and one time your betrothed.
  It cannot be, Prince, cannot be believed
  That Carlos hates what all the world doth love.
  Can Carlos hold such strangely different views?
  Take special care, my Prince, and guard that she
  Will never know how much her son dislikes her.
  That news would pain her.

CARLOS: Do you think that's so?
DOMINGO: Your Majesty need only to recall
  How in the tournament at Saragossa
  The King was slightly injured by a lance.
  The Queen sat there, her ladies round about,
  Upon the grandstand in the palace yard,
  And viewed the combat, when a cry rose up:
  "The King! He bleeds!"—The crowd was in confusion,
  A muffled murmur penetrated to
  The Queen's ear and she cries, "The Prince?" and is
  About to hurl herself down from the rail.
  "Oh, no! It is the King," comes the reply,
  "The King himself!"—"Then let the doctors come!"
  She answers, while she tries to catch her breath.
                    (after a silence)
  You lose yourself in thought?
CARLOS: I marvel at
  The King's droll priest, who practices such skill
  In entertaining us with witty tales.
                    (serious and threatening)
  But I have always heard the story told
  That sundry spies and bearers of bad tales
  Have carried out more evil in this world
  Than poison or a dagger ever could.
  You might have spared yourself the effort, sir.
  For your reward you must go to the King.
DOMINGO: You do quite right, my Prince, to guard against
  Dissemblers—but take care not to repulse
  Your friends in the same gesture with your foes.
  I mean well by you, Prince.
CARLOS: You'd best take care
  My father does not note it, else you'll lose
  Your cardinal's hat.
DOMINGO *(startled):* What do you mean?
CARLOS: Well now,
  Did he not promise when a cardinal's hat
  Is granted Spain to give it to you?
DOMINGO: Prince,
  You mock me.

CARLOS: God forbid that I should dare
 To mock the man who holds the awesome power
 To raise my father to a saint or likewise
 To damn him!
DOMINGO: 'Twere presumptuous of me, Prince,
 To strive to ferret out the secret cause
 So sacredly preserved behind your sorrow.
 But let me beg your Highness to recall:
 A refuge and retreat is offered to
 The anxious conscience by our Mother Church,
 And even kings do not possess the means
 To open up the seal of secrecy
 Provided by the Holy Sacrament.
 You know, Prince, what I mean, and I have said
 Enough for now.
CARLOS: That lies far from my thoughts,
 To tempt the master of that seal so sore!
DOMINGO: Prince, this mistrust! You fail to recognize
 Your faithful servant.
CARLOS: Then give up on me.
 That would be best. You are a holy man
 Who knows the world—but in my case you are—
 To put it frankly—overwhelmed already.
 Your path, O reverend sir, is most remote
 And leads you to a seat on Peter's chair.
 To know too much might be a burden for you.
 Just give that message to the King, who sent you.
DOMINGO: Who sent me?
CARLOS: Those were just my words. Too well
 I know that at this court I am betrayed—
 Too well I know that in the royal throngs
 A hundred eyes are hired to watch me close.
 I know King Philipp sells his only son
 And to the lowest of his lowly knaves;
 And each informer reaps a princely prize
 For every word that he can gather from me.
 He would not pay so well for noble deeds.
 I know—oh, silence! Nothing more of that!
 My heart is apt to overflow, and I
 Have said too much.

DOMINGO: It is the King's intent
To reach Madrid before the evening falls.
The courtiers gather now. Have I your leave
To go, Prince—
CARLOS: It's all right. I'll follow you.
(Domingo exits. After a moment of silence)
O Philipp, wretched as your son is wretched!
I see your soul bleed there, the victim of
The serpent called suspicion's poisonous bite.
Unhappy curiosity o'ertakes
The most appalling of discoveries.
You will go mad when you uncover them.

Scene 2

Carlos. Marquis of Posa.
CARLOS: Who comes? What do I see? Oh, you good spirit!
My Roderick!
MARQUIS: My Carlos!
CARLOS: Can it be?
Can this be true and real? Can this be you?
Oh, let me clasp you to my heart and feel
Your heart as it beats powerfully against me.
Oh, now is everything made good. In this
Embrace my aching soul is healed. I hang
Upon my Roderick's neck.
MARQUIS: Your aching soul?
Why does it ache? And what is now made good?
To listen to you makes me pause.
CARLOS: And what
Brings you from Brussels unbeknownst? To whom
Do I owe thanks for this surprise? To whom?
Need I then ask? O Providence sublime,
Forgive me, drunk with joy, this calumny!
Who else but You, most gracious One? You knew
That Carlos had no angel, and You sent
Me this one. Need I ask again?
MARQUIS: Forgive,
Beloved Prince, if your impetuous joy

Meets only with my consternation here.
It was not thus that I had hoped to see
Don Philipp's son. The red that seems to burn
On your pale cheeks appears unnatural and
Your lips do tremble as if you were ill.
What must I think, beloved Prince, for that
Is not the lion-hearted youth to whom
An oppressed people of heroic stock
Send me—I stand here not as Roderick,
Not as the playmate of the boy prince—
A representative of all mankind
Embraces you—the provinces of Flanders
Do weep in truth upon your shoulder now,
And solemnly they beg you for your help.
For their dear land is finished, if the Duke
Of Alba, servant of fanaticism,
Arrives at Brussels with his Spanish law.
The last best hope of this illustrious land
Rests with the exalted grandson of great Karl.
It falls in ruins, if your noble heart
Has lost the need to beat for humankind.

CARLOS: It falls in ruins.

MARQUIS: Oh, what do I hear!

CARLOS: You talk of times that vanished long ago.
  Once was when I, too, dreamed about a Carlos
  Whose cheeks would burn with passion when one spoke
  Of freedom—but that dream is long since gone.
  What you see here no longer is that Carlos,
  Who in Alcala took his leave from you,
  Who in a fit of sweet intoxication
  Dared to embark upon a plan to build
  Anew the Golden Age in Spain—a whim
  So childish, yet it was most beautiful!
  But now those dreams are gone.

MARQUIS: Dreams, Prince? Then they
  Were only dreams?

CARLOS: Oh, let me weep, yes, weep
  Hot, scalding tears and clutch you to my heart,
  My only friend; for I have no one here,

And there is no one in this whole, wide world
As far as land lies 'neath my father's sway,
As far as ships may sail beneath his flag,
There is no spot, not even one, whereon
I can relieve my grief with tears like these
But here. O Roderick, by all that you
And I in time to come hope for in Heaven,
I beg you, do not drive me from this place.

MARQUIS *(bends over him in speechless emotion)*:

CARLOS: Try to pretend I am an orphan child
Whom out of sympathy you drew aside.
I do not even know what "father" means—
I am a king's son—Oh, if it should be,
As my heart tells me, if you are the one,
From all the million others, who can know me,
If it is true that nature had contrived
To make another Roderick of Carlos,
With our soul's music played on fragile strings
Strung just alike at dawning of our lives,
If just one tear that comforts me a bit
Is dearer to you than my father's favor—

MARQUIS: Oh, it is dearer than the world.

CARLOS: So deep
Is my descent—and I am sunk so low—
I must remind you of our early years,
And in the name of childhood days I must
Entreat you to repay debts long forgotten,
Debts that were made when we wore sailor suits—
When you and I were just unruly boys,
Grown up together in such fellowship
That nothing bothered me except to see
Myself eclipsed by what you were—and so
I then resolved to love you without measure,
Because I lacked the strength to be like you.
So I began to pester you with ev'ry
Variety of tender brother-love.
Your proud heart gave me cold return for this.
How often I stood there—you never saw—
And hot and heavy teardrops hung upon

My lashes, when you would skip over me
And clasp far lesser children in your arms.
Oh, why just them? I would cry out in pain:
Am I not good to you with all my heart,
But you, you knelt down there so cold before me.
That was, you said, quite proper for a king's son.
MARQUIS: Have done with childish stories, Prince, that still
Can cause a blush to rise into my cheeks.
CARLOS: I never did deserve such treatment from you.
You could disdain, despise the love I proferred
But never drive me off. You could dismiss
The prince three times, but three times he returned
As supplicant, imploring you to love him
And eagerly to urge his love upon you.
What Carlos could not do occurred by chance.
Remember once, when we were playing games,
Your shuttlecock flew wild and hit my aunt,
Bohemia's Queen, full in the eye. She thought
That it was done on purpose and she told
The King while tears coursed down her cheeks.
All of the boys around the palace yard
Had to appear, to name the guilty one.
The King then vowed to punish fearfully
This treach'rous deed, and even if it were
Done by his son himself.—I saw you there
As you stood trembling in the distance. Then—
Then I stepped up and threw myself before
My father's feet. I was the one, I cried.
You must take your revenge on your own son.
MARQUIS: Oh, that you should remind me!
CARLOS: And he did!
In view of all the members of the court,
Who stood in sympathetic circle round me,
Revenge was taken on me like a slave.
I looked at you and did not cry. The pain
Caused me to grind my teeth against each other;
I did not cry. Although my royal blood
Flowed basely under unrelenting blows,
I looked at you and did not cry.—You came,

And weeping loudly you sank down before me.
Then you cried out, Yes, now my pride is broken.
I will repay you when you are the king.
MARQUIS *(extends his hand to the Prince):*
    And I will do it, Carlos. Childhood's pledge
    Now as a man I do renew. And I
    Will pay it when the time is come.
CARLOS: Now, now—
    Oh, do not hesitate—the time has come.
    The hour is here, in which you can repay.
    Your love is what I need. A fearful secret
    Is burning now within my breast. I will,
    I must reveal it. There on your pale face
    I'll read the sentence and it will be death.
    Now hear—and brace yourself—but do not answer—
    I love my mother.
MARQUIS: O beloved God!
CARLOS: No! No! I do not want forbearance. Speak!
    Speak out, that on the circle of this earth
    No misery exists that's close to mine.
    Speak, though I know already what you'll say.
    A son who loves his mother. World custom,
    All nature's order, and the law of Rome
    Condemn this passion. My pretension strikes
    Most frightfully against my father's rights.
    I know that—but no matter, I still love.
    This leads to madness or to execution.
    I love without all hope and sinfully—
    In mortal terror and in fear of death—
    I see that—oh, no matter, I still love.
MARQUIS: And does the Queen know how you feel?
CARLOS: How could
    It be disclosed; for she is Philipp's wife
    And Queen besides, and this is Spanish soil.
    Watched over by my father's jealousy,
    Encircled by the rules of etiquette,
    How could I, without witnesses, approach her?
    Eight months I've suffered through the pangs of hell
    Since I received the royal call to come

Back here, which forces me to gaze each day
Upon her but keep silence like the grave's.
Eight months, O Roderick, the pangs of hell
I've suffered as this fire has raged within;
A thousand times this horrible confession
Was on my lips about to venture forth;
Then shy and cowardly it crept again
Back to my heart. O Roderick—a moment
Alone with her—

MARQUIS: And what about your father?

CARLOS: Unhappy man! Why must you mention him?
Tell me about the terrors of my conscience,
About my father do not talk to me.

MARQUIS: Then you do hate your father?

CARLOS: No! Oh, no!
I do not hate my father—but such fear
And sinner's apprehension seizes me
At the mere mention of this fearful name.
How can I help it that love's tender seeds
Were crushed by servile care and training when
My heart was still so young. I was already
A six-year-old before I gazed upon
That awful man, the one who, as they told
Me, was my father. Early on a morning
When he had just subscribed four sentences
Of death it happened. After that I saw
Him only when a punishment was to
Be given me for an offense. My God!
I feel I am becoming bitter—so,
Away—away from here.

MARQUIS: Oh, no. You should—
You shall now open up your heart, Prince. Words
Can ease the heavy burden in your breast.

CARLOS: So often I have struggled with myself
In the wee hours when my watch was sleeping.
With hot tears coursing from my eyes I've thrown
Myself before the Blessed Virgin's form
And begged her for a filial heart—I would
Arise without that blessing. Roderick,

Reveal the answer to this mystery
Of Providence. Why of a thousand fathers
Just this one should be mine. And choosing from
A thousand better sons I should be his?
Two creatures more irreconcilable
Could never be disclosed in nature's sphere.
Why did it pick these two remote extremes
Of all the human race—take him and me
To bind together in this holy bond?
Oh, frightful fate! Why did it have to happen?
Why did two men, who've always shunned each other,
Come face to face in this one dread desire?
Here, Roderick, two hostile constellations
Appear that in the whole, long course of time
For just this once on a contiguous course
Make contact but to crash—and then to part
Eternally.
MARQUIS: This presages, I think,
A moment full of woe.
CARLOS: I think so too.
Like furies from the pit there follow me
Most awful dreams. My better self despairs,
And struggles with a host of monstrous plans;
Through labyrinthine subtleties my mind
In its most wretched contemplation moves
Until, when at the very edge of the
Declivity, it stops.—O Roderick,
If I denied the father in him.—Yes,
I see by your pale face you understand—
If ever I denied the father in him,
What would the King then be to me?
MARQUIS: Dare I
Presume to ask a favor of my Carlos?
Whate'er you have in mind to do, I beg
That you will not attempt it without me.
Now promise me?
CARLOS: I promise everything—
All that your love can offer me. I throw
Myself entirely in your care.

MARQUIS: They say
  Our monarch plans to go back to the city.
  The time is short. If ever you can hope
  To see the Queen in secret, it must happen
  Here in Aranjuez. The solitude
  Prevailing here—the habits, unrestrained,
  Are an advantage—
CARLOS: That was my hope, too,
  But it was all in vain!
MARQUIS: Not totally.
  I go just now to be presented to her.
  If here in Spain she has not changed from what
  She was in former times at Henry's court,
  Then I will find sincerity. If I
  Can gather hope for you then in her look,
  If I should find now that she is disposed
  To meet—her ladies can be drawn away—
CARLOS: And most of them are mine.—Especially
  The Lady Mondecar, whom I have won
  Because her son serves me as page.
MARQUIS: So much
  The better. Stand close by, Prince, so that at
  My sign you can appear immediately.
CARLOS: That will I do—I will—oh, just make haste.
MARQUIS: I will not lose one moment, O my Prince.
  Farewell then till we meet again.
            (Both exit to opposite sides.)

The royal household of the Queen in Aranjuez. A simple pastoral region; an avenue cuts across it, blocked from sight by the Queen's country house.

Scene 3

The Queen. The Duchess of Olivarez. The Princess of Eboli and the Marquise of Mondecar, who are coming down the avenue.
QUEEN: *(to the Marquise):*
  I want to have *you* with me, Mondecar.

For the Princess's look has bothered me
This whole long morning; you can plainly see
She scarcely knows how to control her joy
That she can leave this rustic place.
EBOLI: I will
  Not disavow, my Queen, that I rejoice
  Exceedingly to see Madrid again.
MONDECAR: And does Your Majesty not share this joy?
  Do you regret to leave Aranjuez?
QUEEN: To leave—at least this lovely neighborhood.
  Here I can be as if in my own world.
  This little place I've chosen for my own.
  Here nature welcomes me, a rustic maid;
  It was the bosom friend of my young years.
  Here I can make believe I am a child,
  And here the breath of France is wafted to me.
  Do not reproach me, to each one of us
  Our homeland sometimes calls.
EBOLI: But here it is
  So lonely and so dull! We seem to be
  Among the Trappist monks.
QUEEN: For me it is
  The opposite. I find Madrid so dull.
  What does our Duchess say to that?
OLIVAREZ: I am,
  Your Majesty, of the opinion that
  It was the custom to reside one month
  In this place, in the Pardo for another,
  And spend the winter in the residence,
  As long as kings have governed over Spain.
QUEEN: Yes, Duchess, you know well I have renounced
  Forever having any quarrel with you.
MONDECAR: And it will soon be lively in Madrid!
  The Plaza Mayor has been renovated
  To hold a bullfight there, and also we
  Are promised we shall see the Holy Court
  In an auto-da-fé—
QUEEN: We're promised that?
  Can that be gentle Mondecar?

MONDECAR: Why not?
They are but heretics that we see burned.
QUEEN: I hope my Eboli thinks differently.
EBOLI: But why, Your Majesty? For I must hope
You hold me for no lesser Christian than
The Marquise Mondecar.
QUEEN: But I forget
The place in which I am. To something else:
We spoke, I think, about the land. This month,
It seems to me, has passed by far too fast.
The many, many pleasures that I hoped
I would enjoy while biding in this place,
They have not come to pass as I had thought.
Is this the way it is with hope? I never
Had a wish that went awry before.
OLIVAREZ: You have not said, Princess of Eboli,
If Gomez entertains some hope with you?
Perhaps we'll welcome him as your betrothed?
QUEEN: Oh, yes, it's good that you reminded me.
                    (to the Princess)
I have been asked to intercede for him.
But how can I do that? The man whom I
Reward by giving him my Eboli
Must be deserving.
OLIVAREZ: O my Queen, he is
A very worthy man; he is a man
Whom our Most Gracious Majesty does honor
With royal favor, as is known by all.
QUEEN: That surely makes him very fortunate—
But whether he can love, we want to know,
And if he merits love.—Princess, this is
My question.
EBOLI *(stands mute and bewildered, her eyes cast down;*
at last she falls at the feet of the Queen):
                    O my Queen, have mercy on me
And do not let them, ah, I beg you,
Please do not let them, in the name of God,
Make me a sacrifice.
QUEEN: A sacrifice?

I need not one word more. Arise! It is
A cruel fate to be a sacrifice.
I place free trust in you. Arise! Has it
Been very long since you refused the Count?

EBOLI *(standing up):*
    Oh, it's been many months. Prince Carlos was
    Still at the university.

QUEEN *(stops short and looks at her with a searching glance):*
                    Do you
    Know why you feel this way about it?

EBOLI: Never!
    It cannot ever happen, Majesty.
    There are a thousand reasons.

QUEEN: More than one
    Is never needed. If you don't esteem him,
    That is enough for me. No more.
                (to the other ladies)
                    I have
    Not seen my baby princess yet today.
    Marquise, please bring her here to me.

OLIVAREZ *(looks at the clock):*   It is
    Not yet the time for that, Your Majesty.

QUEEN: Not yet the time when I may be a mother?
    That is too bad. Well, please do not forget
    To tell me of it when they bring her.
       *(A page appears and speaks quietly with the Royal
       Stewardess, who then turns to the Queen.)*

OLIVAREZ: Here
    Is the Marquis of Posa, Madam.

QUEEN: Posa?

OLIVAREZ: He comes straight from the Netherlands and France
    And wishes you to grant that he may bring
    Some letters from the queen, your mother, meant
    For you.

QUEEN: Is that allowed?

OLIVAREZ *(doubtfully):*   In my instructions
    There is no precedent for just this case,
    In which a grandee from Castile arrives,
    Possessing letters from a foreign court,

To be delivered to the Queen of Spain
While in her garden grove.
QUEEN: Well then, I will
Just take the risk upon myself and dare it!
OLIVAREZ: Will you permit, Your Majesty, that I
May in this case withdraw?
QUEEN: Conduct yourself,
My Duchess, as you wish.
          (*The Royal Stewardess exits, and the Queen signals
          to the page, who goes off immediately.*)

Scene 4

Queen. Princess of Eboli. Marquise of Mondecar. Marquis of Posa.
QUEEN: I bid you welcome.
Yes, welcome, Chevalier, to Spanish soil.
MARQUIS: Which I have never called my fatherland
With so much pride as I do now.
QUEEN (*to both ladies*):   This knight,
Marquis of Posa—who at Rheims did break
A lance in combat with my very father,
And three times caused by colors to prevail—
Foremost among his nation, he taught me
The credit to be gained if I would be
The Queen of Spain.
          (*turning to the Marquis*)
                    When that last time we walked
Together in the Louvre, Chevalier,
You never dreamed, I'm certain, at that time,
That you would be my guest here in Castile.
MARQUIS: That's true, Your Majesty, for at that time
I never could have dreamed that France would lose
To us the one and only thing for which
We envied them.
QUEEN: How dare you, haughty Spaniard!
The only thing?—And you say that to me,
A daughter of the House of Valois?

MARQUIS: May
  I now speak out, Your Majesty, for you
  Are one of us.
QUEEN: Your trip, I have been told,
  Took you through France as well.—What do you bring
  To me from my beloved mother there
  And from my brothers to a loving sister?
MARQUIS *(hands her the letter):*
  The royal mother I found sick, withdrawn
  From every other pleasure of this world,
  Except to know her royal daughter was
  Content upon the Spanish throne.
QUEEN: Must she
  Not be, when she has such remembrances
  Of her fond kinsmen? When her memories
  Are sweet of—Chevalier, I hear your travels
  Have taken you as guest to many courts
  And countries where you witnessed many customs
  And peoples—but they say that you still plan
  To settle in your fatherland itself?
  A greater prince within your own still walls
  Than Philipp on his throne—a man who's free!
  A true philosopher!—I do not think
  That you could ever like it in Madrid.
  It is so—peaceful in Madrid.
MARQUIS: And that
  Is more than any other part of Europe
  Rejoices in.
QUEEN: That is what I have heard.
  But I have put aside these matters of
  The world almost beyond remembering.
                    (to the Princess of Eboli)
  It seems to me, Princess of Eboli,
  A hyacinth is blooming over there.
  Please fetch it for me.
        *(The Princess goes to get it. The Queen, somewhat
        softer, to the Marquis)*
                          Chevalier, I must
  Delude myself or your arrival here

Has caused one person at this court to be
A great deal happier.

MARQUIS: I found a man
So very sad, a man who on this earth
Needs such a little cheer—

(The Princess comes back with the flower.)

QUEEN: The Chevalier
Has seen so many lands that certainly
He will have many curious tales that he
Can tell us.

MARQUIS: That is true. And to seek out
Adventure is, as you all know, a duty
To every knight, and his most sacred vow
Defending ladies in his care.

MONDECAR: From giants!
There are no giants now, you see.

MARQUIS: But force
Is for the weak at every time a giant.

QUEEN: The Chevalier is right. There are still giants,
But knights one sees quite seldom.

MARQUIS: Recently
As I was coming back from Naples, I
Was witness to a sad and touching story,
In which I was involved, because the tale
Concerned what happened to dear friends of mine.
If I was not afraid Your Majesty
Would be fatigued by listening—

QUEEN: And may
I make the choice? The curiosity
Of the Princess is not to be denied,
And I am very fond of stories, too.

MARQUIS: In Mirandola lived two noble lines
Which, being tired of jealousy and strife
Transmitted by the Ghibellines and Guelphs
Down through the ages, made a resolution
To join each other in eternal peace
Through the tight bonds of consanguinity.
The mighty Pietro's sister's son, Fernando,
Divine Mathilda, daughter of Colonna,

Were singled out of their respective lines
To join together in this splendid union.
Now, neither nature nor the world before
Had fashioned fairer creatures for each other,
Ne'er was a choice so happy or so praised.
As yet, Fernando's charming wife-to-be
Had idolized him only through his portrait—
Fernando trembled, meanwhile, scarcely hoping
That he could trust her portrait to reflect
In truth what he so ardently imagined!
In Padua where studies kept him bound
Fernando ardently anticipated
That happy moment that would bring to him
The right to kneel down at Mathilda's feet
And utter those first loving words of homage.
> *(The Queen becomes more attentive. After a moment of silence the Marquis continues the story, directing it, as far as possible in the presence of the Queen, at the Princess of Eboli.)*
Meanwhile the death of Pietro's wife gives him
His freedom. Old man that he is, he falls
A victim to the rumors that extol
Mathilda and reacts with youthful passion.
He comes! He sees!—He loves! This new emotion
Suppresses gentler voices in his nature.
The uncle seeks Mathilda's hand in marriage
And consecrates his robbery at the altar.
QUEEN: What does Fernando do?
MARQUIS: On wings of love,
The awful change of plans unknown to him,
And drunk with love, he speeds to Mirandola,
On his swift steed he comes by starlight to
The city gates—the noise of revelry,
Of dancing, and of drumming thunders toward him
From the illuminated palace windows.
He shyly, trembling, mounts the steps and looks
Unrecognized about the wedding hall,
Where in the midst of reeling merry makers
Pietro sat—an angel by his side,

An angel whom Fernando recognizes,
More glorious even than he'd ever dreamed.
One single glance shows him what had been his
And shows him, too, what he has lost forever.
EBOLI: Unfortunate Fernando!
QUEEN: Is the story
Completely finished, Chevalier?—It must
Be finished.
MARQUIS: No, not quite.
QUEEN: Did you not say
That this Fernando was a friend of yours?
MARQUIS: I never had a better friend.
EBOLI: Now do
Continue with the story, Chevalier.
MARQUIS: Here it becomes so sad—and the remembrance
Renews the pain. I beg to be released
From telling the conclusion—
                    (a general silence)
QUEEN *(turns to the Princess of Eboli):* Certainly
The time has come when I may hold my daughter.—
Princess, please bring her here to me.
        (The Princess exits. The Marquis beckons a page,
        who appears backstage and immediately exits. The
        Queen breaks the seal on the letter that the Marquis
        has given her and appears startled. Meanwhile the
        Marquis talks, privately and very earnestly, with the
        Marquise of Mondecar.—The Queen, having read the
        letter, turns to the Marquis with an inquiring glance.)
                                            You have
Not told us anything about Mathilda?
Perhaps she does not know Fernando grieves.
MARQUIS: No one has looked into Mathilda's heart—
We know great spirits suffer patiently.
QUEEN: I see you look around. Whom do you search for?
MARQUIS: I only contemplated just how happy
A certain person, whom I will not name,
Would be, if he were here.
QUEEN: And whose fault is it
That he is not?

MARQUIS *(replying spiritedly):* Then dare I, Majesty,
  To understand you as I choose? If he
  Were now to appear, would he find pardon here?
QUEEN *(alarmed):*
  Now, my Marquis? What do you mean by now?
MARQUIS: That he may hope—may he?
QUEEN *(with growing consternation):* You frighten me.
  He will not come—
MARQUIS:　　　　　　　He is already here.

Scene 5

The Queen. Carlos.

(Marquis of Posa and the Marquise of Mondecar withdraw to the rear.)
CARLOS *(having prostrated himself before the Queen):*
  So it is finally here, this precious moment,
  And Carlos dares to touch this cherished hand!—
QUEEN: What deed is this—this unexpected action,
  Foolhardy and forbidden! Sir, arise!
  We are found out. My household stands nearby.
CARLOS: I will not rise—forever will I kneel.
  Here in this place will I remain enchanted,
  And rooted to the spot.
QUEEN:　　　　　　　You are a madman!
  To what audacity my favor leads you!
  Do you not know, then, that it is the Queen,
  It is your mother, whom you are addressing
  With rash and daring words? Do you not know
  That I—that I myself must tell the King
  About this act—
CARLOS:　　　　　And then that I must die!
  But let them drag me hence and to the gallows!
  One moment to have lived in Paradise
  Is not too dearly paid for with my life.
QUEEN: And what about your Queen?
CARLOS:　　　　　　　　　　Oh, God, I go—

For must I not forsake you—must I not,
If you require me to? O Mother, Mother!
How frightfully you play with me! One nod,
One-half a look, a sound from your dear mouth
Commands me to endure or to expire.
What is there that you wish would come to pass?
What can there be under the heav'n above
That I will not give up immediately,
If you but wish it?

QUEEN: Flee then.

CARLOS: O my God!

QUEEN: O Carlos, the one thing that I implore
  With tears is that you flee!—before my ladies—
  Before my jailors find us, you and I,
  Together here and bring such signal tidings
  Straight to your father's ears—

CARLOS: Then I await
  My fate—and whether it be life or death.
  How then? Did I direct my lingering hopes
  Toward this one single magic interval
  That you present me without witnesses,
  Then to be disappointed by base fear?
  Oh, no, my Queen! The world may turn in space
  A thousand times upon its axis ere
  This favor of coincidence returns.

QUEEN: No, it will never, ever come again.
  Unhappy man! What do you want of me?

CARLOS: My Queen, the fact that I have struggled hard,
  Yes, harder than a mortal ever did,
  God is my witness—yet it was in vain!
  Gone are my hero's deeds, for I succumb.

QUEEN: No more of that—respect my peace of mind.

CARLOS: Once you were mine—mine in the world's eyes,
  Promised to me by two great thrones and granted
  By Heaven itself and Nature to be mine,
  And it was Philipp, Philipp took you from me—

QUEEN: He is your father.

CARLOS: And your husband.

QUEEN: Who
  Leaves you the greatest kingdom in the world.

CARLOS: And gives me you as mother—
QUEEN: God, you rave—
CARLOS: And does he even know how rich he is?
  Does he possess a heart to treasure you?
  I will not mourn, nay, I will even try
  To be oblivious to the happiness
  That might have been—if *he* is only happy.
  But he is not—There lies my agony!
  Oh, he is not—and he will never be.
  You took away my Heaven and for what?
  That it might be consumed in Philipp's arms.
QUEEN: Oh, loathsome thought!
CARLOS: But it is known to me
  Who was the author of this marriage—and
  I know how Philipp loves and how he woos.
  Tell me what role you play here in this land.
  The reigning Queen perhaps? That cannot be!
  If you were Queen, then how could Alba butcher?
  And how could Flanders bleed for its beliefs?
  Then are you Philipp's wife? Impossible!
  That I cannot believe. A wife possesses
  Her husband's heart—and who possesses his?
  Does he not feel the need to beg for pardon
  From his gray hair and from his scepter for
  Each tenderness escaping him in passion?
QUEEN: Who said my lot at Philipp's side was but
  A fate deserving pity?
CARLOS: My own heart,
  That feels so ardently how at my side
  It would deserve such envy.
QUEEN: Vain you are!
  And if *my* heart tells me the opposite?
  If Philipp's reverential tenderness
  Should move me as more ardent and sincere
  Than the rash eloquence of his proud son?
  And if an old man's circumspect attention—
CARLOS: That would be different—then—yes, then—forgive me,
  I little knew that you could love the King.
QUEEN: My wish and pleasure is to honor him.
CARLOS: Then you have never loved?

QUEEN: Peculiar question!

CARLOS: Then you have never loved?

QUEEN: —I love no more.

CARLOS: Because your heart, because your oath forbids it?

QUEEN: You must leave now, my Prince, and do not come
Again to me for such a conversation.

CARLOS: Because your oath, because your heart forbids it?

QUEEN: Because my duty—O unhappy man,
What use is sad discourse about the fate
That you and I must bow to?

CARLOS: That we must?
That *we* must bow to?

QUEEN: Now, what do you mean
By such a grave and somber tone?

CARLOS: I mean
That *must* is not what Carlos has in mind
But rather what he *wants;* to be the most
Unfortunate in this whole land is not
What Carlos has in mind, if it will cost
Him nothing but the changing of some laws
To be the happiest.

QUEEN: Do I hear right?
Do you still hope? Do you still dare to hope,
When everything, yes, everything is lost?

CARLOS: No thing is surely lost except in death.

QUEEN: For me? You still can hope for me, your mother?
*(She regards him long and penetratingly—
then with dignity and sternness.)*
Well then, why not? The newly chosen King
Can do much more—he can destroy by fire
The orders of the late departed one;
He can efface his portraits, and he can—
Who will prevent him—drag his body out
Of the Escurial, where it lies resting,
Into the light of day and widely strew
His defiled dust into the winds that blow.
And in the end, to finish with a flourish—

CARLOS: In God's own name, do not continue this.

QUEEN: And in the end to marry your own mother.

CARLOS: Accursed son!
   (He stands for a moment motionless and speechless.)
                    Yes, it is over. It
Is over now. I sense distinctly, clearly,
What should remain obscure to me forever.
For me you are forever—ever—gone—
Forever more!—The die has now been cast—
And you are lost to me forever. Hell
Lies in this feeling, but it would be Hell
If I possessed you.—Oh, alas, I cannot
Conceive of this, my nerves begin to break.
QUEEN: O dear, dear Carlos! How I pity you.
I feel it, too, this nameless agony
That rages now within your breast. As great
As your love is, will this pain be. As great
As it is, is your gain, if you subdue it.
May you achieve this end, courageous youth.
The prize is worthy of the valiant knight,
Is worthy of the youth whose virtue is
The virtue of a long and noble line.
Take heart, O Prince—the grandson of great Karl
Must now begin courageously to fight
Where other men, discouraged, would give in.
CARLOS: Too late! O God! It is too late!
QUEEN: To be
A man? O Carlos! How great is our virtue,
If our hearts break when in the practice of it!
For you have been raised up by Providence
Far higher than a million of your brothers.
It gave to you, its favorite, the things
It took from others, and those millions ask:
Did he deserve while in the womb already
To be more than we other mortals are?
Now you must vindicate thus Heaven's justice
And earn the right to rank first in this world
By sacrificing what no other can!
CARLOS: That I can do.—To fight for you, I have
The strength of giants, but to lose you, none.
QUEEN: Admit it, Carlos, this is but defiance

And bitterness and pride that do attract
You with such fierceness to your mother. Love,
Your heart, that you would sacrifice on me,
Belong in truth to every land that you
Will someday rule. Do you not see that you
May revel in this blessing that is yours?
Love is your greatest office. Until now
It strayed after your mother.—Now you must
Turn it and bring it to those many lands
That you will rule, and feel instead of guilt
The bliss saved for a god. Elizabeth
Was your first love. Now let your second be
The lands of Spain! How gladly, my dear Carlos,
Will I give way to this, the better lover!

CARLOS (*overwhelmed by emotion, throws himself at her feet*)
Oh, how magnificent you are!—Yes, I—
I will do everything you ask.—So be it!
                    (*He rises.*)
I stand here in the hand of the Almighty
And swear to you, I swear eternally
That—Heaven! No! I swear eternal silence,
But to forget, I cannot swear.

QUEEN: Can I
Demand from Carlos what I cannot swear
To do myself?

MARQUIS (*rushes from the avenue*): The King!

QUEEN: O God!

MARQUIS: Away.
Away from here, my Prince!

QUEEN: The King's suspicion—
It will be frightful, if he sees—

CARLOS: I stay!

QUEEN: And who will be the victim then?

CARLOS (*pulls the Marquis by the arm*):   Away!
Come, Roderick!
                    (*He leaves and then returns.*)
                    What can I take with me?

QUEEN: The friendship of your mother.

CARLOS: Friendship! Mother!

QUEEN: And take these tears sent from the Netherlands.

*(She gives him some letters. Carlos and the
Marquis exit. The Queen looks around for her ladies,
who are nowhere to be seen. As she is about to go
toward the background, the King enters.)*

Scene 6

*King. Queen. Duke of Alba. Count of Lerma. Domingo. A group
of ladies and grandees, who remain at a distance.*

KING *(looks around astonished and remains silent for a time):*
  What do I see? You here! Alone, Madam?
  And not one lady here as company?
  I am surprised—where have the women gone?
QUEEN: Most gracious husband—
KING: Why are you alone?
                            (to his retinue)
  I will demand a strict accounting for
  This inexcusable omission here.
  Who is the court official for the Queen?
  Who was the one to serve her at this time?
QUEEN: My husband, please do not be so distressed.
  I am myself the guilty one. Princess
  Of Eboli withdrew at my command.
KING: At your command?
QUEEN: Why, yes, to call the maid.
  Because I yearned so to caress our child.
KING: And for that reason sent your court away?
  But this excuses only your *first* lady.
  Where was the second?
MONDECAR *(who meanwhile has returned and joined the other
  ladies, steps forward):* Here, Your Majesty.
  I feel I am to blame—
KING: And for that reason
  I grant you ten years' time far from Madrid
  That you will spend reflecting on your lapse.
        *(The Marquise steps back with tears in her eyes.
        There is a general silence. All the bystanders
        look at the Queen dismayed.)*

QUEEN: Marquise, whom do you cry for?
                    (to the King)
                                        Gracious husband,
If I am in the wrong, then I believe
The royal crown and scepter of this land,
For which I never have contended, should
At least protect me from the need to blush.
Is there a law prevailing in this kingdom
That calls a monarch's daughter into court?
And is it force alone protects Spain's women?
Does anything protect them more than virtue?
And now forgive me, husband, for I am
Unused to see those who with joy have served me
With tears then take their leave. O Mondecar!
  (She removes her waistband and hands it to the Marquise.)
The King is angry with you—I am not—
Take this reminder of my favor with you
And of this hour.—Depart then from this land—
You have committed wrong in Spain alone;
In my homeland of France they'll wipe away
Your tears with joy.—Oh, why must I remember?
      (She leans on the Duchess of Olivarez and covers
      her face.)
In France things were so different.
KING *(in some agitation):*   Can it be
This slight rebuke caused by my love can grieve you?
One word can grieve you that the tenderest
Solicitude has placed upon my lips?
                  (He turns to the grandees.)
The vassals of my throne stand here as witness.
Did ever sleep descend upon my eyes
That I had not upon that very evening
Considered how the hearts of all my people
Inclined and even to the farthest regions?—
And should I be concerned more for my throne
Than anxious for the consort of my heart?—
My sword will always answer for my people,
My eyes alone must serve to keep your love.
QUEEN: Do I deserve this lack of trust?

KING: I am
  The richest man in the whole Christian world;
  Somewhere the sun shines always on *my* land—
  But all of that another once possessed,
  And after me another will possess it.
  But *this* belongs to me. What the King owns
  Is due to fate—Elizabeth is mine.
  This is the point where I am a mere mortal.
QUEEN: You are afraid then, Sire?
KING: This graybeard fear?
  Whenever I begin to be afraid,
  That moment I can cease to fear.
                    (to the grandees)
                                I count
  The foremost persons of my court but miss
  The first. Where is then my Infante?
                    (when no one answers)
                                Carlos,
  My son, begins to be alarming to me.
  He flees my royal presence since he came
  Back from the university to court.
  His blood is hot, why is his look so cold?
  Why is his conduct toward me so precise?
  Be vigilant. I urge you.
ALBA: Sire, I am.
  As long as my heart beats beneath this mail,
  Don Philipp may lie down to peaceful sleep.
  Duke Alba stands before your throne as do
  God's angels before Paradise.
LERMA: Dare I
  In all humility express opinions
  Conflicting with my wise King's own?—Too deep
  My veneration for Your Majesty
  To let me judge your only son with harshness.
  The hot blood of Don Carlos one may fear,
  But not his heart.
KING: You may talk thus, my Count,
  So as to prejudice a father's thoughts;
  The King's support, however, is the Duke—

No more of that—
>   *(He turns to his attendants.)*
>   I hasten to Madrid.
My royal duties call. The pestilence
Of heresy contaminates the folk,
And in the Lowlands insurrection grows.
Now it is time. Most awful warnings must
Be given that the erring be converted.
Tomorrow I redeem that solemn oath
That all the kings of Christendom have made.
My court of justice shall be an example,
My retinue is summoned to observe.
>   *(He leads the Queen away, the others follow.)*

Scene 7

Don Carlos, with letters in his hand, and the Marquis of Posa enter from opposite sides.

CARLOS: I am decided. Flanders must be saved.
  It is her wish—that is enough.
MARQUIS: But not
  A single moment can be lost. The Duke
  Of Alba has been chosen, so they say,
  As governor already.
CARLOS: In the morning
  Then I will ask to see my father and
  Demand that office for myself. It is
  The first thing I have ever dared to ask.
  How can he then deny it to me? He
  Has been unhappy with me in Madrid.
  This offers him a way to send me forth.
  And, Roderick, can I confess it to you?
  I hope for more—Perhaps I will succeed
  In showing, when I meet him face to face,
  That I, his son, am worthy of his favor.
  The voice of Nature has not touched him once.
  Now, Roderick, I'll see if he will heed
  Its power on my own lips and in his presence.

MARQUIS: At last I recognize my Carlos here.
At last you have become yourself.

Scene 8

The previous. Count Lerma.

LERMA: Just now
His Majesty has left Aranjuez.
I am to say—
CARLOS: It is all right, Count Lerma,
I plan to go there with the King.
MARQUIS *(looks as if he is about to leave. With great*
ceremony):   And is
There nothing more you wish to charge me with?
CARLOS: No, nothing, Chevalier. I wish you luck
On your arrival in Madrid. You will
Have many things to tell me about Flanders.
                (to the Count, who is still waiting)
I'm coming right away.
                        (Count Lerma exits.)

Scene 9

Don Carlos. The Marquis.

CARLOS: I understand
And I do thank you. This constraint is only
Endurable because of others present.
Are we not brothers? This charade of rank
Be in the future banished from our bond!
Let us pretend that we have just arrived
In costume at a ball, and you are dressed
In clothing that befits a slave while I
Am in the mood to wrap myself in crimson.
As long as it is carnival, we will
Maintain our roles with comical intent
Not to disturb the pleasure of the crowd.
But through the mask Carlos will beckon you
And you will clasp my hands as you pass by
And we will understand each other.

MARQUIS: Godlike
To me appears this dream, but will it fade?
Is Carlos then so sure that he can brave
The charms of absolute authority?
There is a greater day to come—a day
When this heroic mood—I want to warn you—
Will sink beneath an overwhelming trial.
Don Philipp dies and Carlos then inherits
The greatest empire in all Christendom.
A frightful fissure parts him from all mortals.
Today he is a god who yesterday
Was man. His frailties are gone. For him
All obligations wane. Humanity
—Today a word of great importance to him—
Will sell itself and follow its false gods.
Along with grief, his pity is erased,
Debauchery then wears his virtue thin,
For every folly gold comes from Peru,
For every vice his court draws devils to him.
He falls asleep enchanted in this heaven
That slaves create so cunningly around him.
Divinity endures as long as dreams.
Woe to the madman who in pity wakes him.
And what becomes of Roderick? A monarch
Diseased this way cannot endure the awe
And splendor of a friendship bold and true.
You could not bear defiance from your minion.
Nor I a prince's pride.
CARLOS: This is a real
And frightful portrait of a monarch you
Have truly drawn.—But lust alone laid bare
His heart to wickedness.—And my life has been pure,
A youth of three-and-twenty years—still pure.
A thousand others without any conscience
Have wasted in voluptuous embraces
Their spirit's better part, virility,
Which I have saved up for the future ruler.
And what could force you from my heart, if it
Cannot be done by women?

MARQUIS: I myself.
  How can I love you, Carlos, fervently,
  If I must fear you?
CARLOS: That will never be.
  Do you have need of me? Do you have passions
  That need the throne's support? Does gold attract you?
  You are a richer subject now than I
  Will be a king.—Do you desire much praise
  And honor? As a youth you had your fill
  Of that—in vain you tried to ward it off.
  Now which of us will be the true believer,
  And owe the other? Do you keep your silence
  And do you tremble from temptation? Are you
  Not certain of yourself as yet?
MARQUIS: All right.
  I yield. Here is my hand.
CARLOS: Now it is mine?
MARQUIS: Forever in the most audacious way.
CARLOS: As true and warm as you are to your Prince,
  Will you one day be also to your King?
MARQUIS: I swear it.
CARLOS: Even then when flattery
  Is clutching at my unprotected heart—
  And when these eyes have long forgotten how
  To shed the tears they used to shed—this ear
  Has turned away from supplication, will you
  Remain the fearless guardian of my virtue,
  Seize me by force, and summon to appear
  My soul, called by its own great name?
MARQUIS: I will.
CARLOS: And now one more request! To you a detail;
  To me, a king's son, it is something great.
  Will you share a fraternal bond and be
  My brother?
MARQUIS: Call me brother!
CARLOS: To the King!
  Now I fear nothing—arm-in-arm with you
  I call my century to meet this challenge.
             (They exit.)

ACT 2

In the royal palace at Madrid

Scene 1

King Philipp under a canopy. Duke of Alba at some distance from the King, with his hat on. Carlos.

CARLOS: The kingdom takes precedency, and I
  Will gladly let the Duke speak first. He speaks
  For Spain. The house of Spain is my house, too.
               (He steps back with a bow.)
PHILIPP: The Duke will wait. The Infante may speak out.
CARLOS *(turning to Alba):*
  Then I must ask *you* to be generous
  And give me the King's presence as a gift.
  A child—you know, of course—may have a lot
  Of things he will talk over with his father,
  Some things not fit to tell another. You
  Shall have the King's complete attention. I
  Want but the father for an hour's time.
PHILIPP: Here is my friend.
CARLOS: Have I perhaps deserved
  The right to hope the Duke will be mine, too?
PHILIPP: And have you ever wanted to deserve it?
  I do not like those sons who think their choice
  Is better than their fathers'.
CARLOS: Can Duke Alba
  Stand proudly here and listen to this scene?
  As truly as I live, I would not be
  Such an intruder who, without a blush
  And uninvited, seeks to force himself
  Between a son and father and remains
  Pierced by the knowledge of his nothingness.
  By God—I would not, if it cost a crown.
PHILIPP *(leaves his seat with an angry glance at the Prince):*

Withdraw, Duke Alba!
 (Alba goes toward the main entrance, through which
 Carlos had come; the King waves him toward another.)
      To my private room,
Until I call you.

Scene 2

King Philipp. Don Carlos.
CARLOS *(as soon as the Duke has left the room, goes to*
the King and falls at his feet with an expression
of deep emotion): Now you are my father.
Now you are mine again, and I give thanks
For such a favor.—Let me take your hand.—
This day is sweet!—The joy of such a kiss
Has not been granted to me for so long.
For all these years why have you locked me, Father,
Out of your heart? Oh, why? What have I done?
PHILIPP: Such wiles do not befit your heart, Infante.
Refrain from them, they do not please me.
CARLOS *(standing up):*   There!
I hear the followers of your court—my Father!
This is not good, by God! Not everything
A priest may say is good, not everything
That those dependent on a priest may say.
I am not bad, my Father—my hot blood
Is where I fail. My crime is but my youth.
I am not bad, not truly bad; although
My heart is often charged with wild emotion,
My heart is good.—
PHILIPP: Your heart is pure, I know it,
As you are in your prayers.
CARLOS: 'Tis now or never!
And etiquette's formalities give way
So that we stand here but a son and father.
'Tis now or never! Hope's bright rays I see,
And through my heart there wings an intimation
Of sweet fulfillment. Bands of happy angels

Do cause the heavens to bend low over me.
And there the Trinity looks down upon
This happy scene with sympathy! O Father!
Be reconciled!

(He falls at his feet.)

PHILIPP: Arise!

CARLOS: Be reconciled!

PHILIPP *(tries to free himself):*
Your clowning is too bold for me—

CARLOS: Too bold
The love of your own child?

PHILIPP: Now have we tears?
Disgraceful spectacle!—Now leave my sight.

CARLOS: 'Tis now or never!—Let us reconcile!

PHILIPP: Out of my sight! From battle come to me,
Though covered with disgrace, my arms shall be
Wide open to receive you then—but now
I do reject you!—Cowards guiltily
May wash themselves in these disgraceful springs.
Who feels no shame to show remorse will not
Avoid what makes him feel remorseful.

CARLOS: Who
Is this? What stranger has through error found
His way among mankind?—Humanity
Is everlastingly confirmed by tears,
The eye that's always dry was never born
Of woman.—Force those eyes that never have
Been wet with tears to learn to cry or else—
Or else in some dark hour they may have need
To make up for it.

PHILIPP: Do you expect with pretty words to shake
Your father's deep and grievous doubt?

CARLOS: His doubt?
My wish is to destroy this doubt—I want
To hang upon my father's heart—I want
To pull upon his heart with such great strength
That that rock-hard encasement built by doubt
Will fall away.—Who can they be, these men
Who drive me from the favor of my King?

What was the offer that a monk could make
A father for his son, or Alba give
As payment for a childless, wasted life?
If you want love, then here within this bosom
There is a spring more vigorous and fresh
Than in those dull and boggy reservoirs
That Philipp's gold must open first.

PHILIPP: Control
Your impudence! The men you dare so to
Abuse consist of my most proven servants.
Henceforth you will respect them.

CARLOS: Nevermore.
I know what I can be. What such a man
As Alba does can Carlos do and more.
What does a hireling care about a kingdom
That never will be his?—Why is it his
Concern if Philipp's gray hair turns to white?
Your Carlos would have loved you.—I would dread
To think that I might one day sit alone
And lonesome on a throne.

PHILIPP (*moved by these words, stands meditating. After a
pause*):   I *am* alone.

CARLOS (*going to him with spirit and warmth*):
You *were* alone. Don't hate me and I'll love
You like a child, I'll love you fervently,
Just do not hate me anymore.—How sweet,
How joyous it can be to find ourselves
Exalted in another lovely spirit,
Our joys put color in another's cheeks,
Our fears cause other hearts to palpitate,
Our sorrows bring the tears to other eyes!—
How beautiful it is and splendid, hand
In hand with a most dear beloved son,
To hasten back upon the paths of youth
And dream the dream of youth again with him!
How grand and sweet it is eternally
To live, immortal in the virtue of
His child and thus for centuries!—How fine
To plant what later a dear son will harvest,

To gather what will grow for him, to think
How bright the glow of thanks will grow! My father,
Your monks were wise to hold their tongues about
This earthly paradise.

PHILIPP (*not without emotion*): My son, my son,
You do condemn yourself. The happiness
You picture, you would never, ever grant me.

CARLOS: Almighty God may judge me!—You yourself,
You shut me out both from a father's heart
And sharing in the duties of the crown.
Up to this very day—oh, was that right
And fair—till now have I, Crown Prince of Spain,
Been like a stranger here in Spain, been like
A prisoner where I will one day rule.
Now was that just or kind?—How often I,
My father, growing red with shame, looked down
When envoys of some foreign potentates
Or sheets of news brought me accounts of what
Had happened lately in Aranjuez!

PHILIPP: So fiercely does the blood rush through your veins
That you would only harm things.

CARLOS: Give me, Father,
A thing that I might harm.—My blood does rush
Within my veins—now three-and-twenty years,
And nothing done for immortality!
I wake and know what I can be.—The call
Unto the throne reverberates as if
A follower were rousing me from slumber,
And all my youth's lost hours are exhortations
As strong as debts of honor. It has come,
That great and lovely moment that demands
I should at last remit the full pound's tax:
The history of the world is calling, fame
And honor thunder loudly from the past.
The time has come to open up for me
The boundaries of glorious fame.—My King,
Oh, do I dare to beg you for the favor
That led me hither?

PHILIPP: Yet another favor?
Well, make it known.

CARLOS: The uproar in Brabant
Is growing worse. The rebels' doggedness
Requires a strong, intelligent attack.
In order to subdue those mad fanatics
The Duke, armed with the King's authority,
Will lead the royal army into Flanders.
This duty holds such honor and how perfect
A chance to open up the gates of fame
And let your son come in!—Let me, my King,
Oh, let me lead the army. Loved am I
Throughout the Lowlands, and I dare to risk
My life as pledge for their fidelity.
PHILIPP: You are a dreamer and you speak like one.
This task requires a real man—
CARLOS: It needs
A human being, Father, and just that
Is what Duke Alba never ever has been.
PHILIPP: But only fear will tame the rioters.
And mercy would be madness.—You, my son,
Are soft and gentle, and the Duke is feared.
Desist from this request.
CARLOS: My King, I beg
You, send me with the army into Flanders
And trust my gentle soul. My name alone
Of Royal Prince will conquer as it speeds
Throughout the countryside before my flag
Where Alba's executioners lay waste.
Down on my knees I beg you'll grant me this,
The only thing I've ever asked you.—Father,
Entrust me with the Lowlands.—
PHILIPP *(examining the Infante with a penetrating look)*:
                    And my army
As well to your desire for royal power?
A dagger to my murderer!
CARLOS: O God!
Is this what I achieved? Is this the fruit
Of the great hour that took so long to come?
        (after some reflection, with less severity)
Oh, answer me more gently. Do not send
Me forth this way. I do not want to be

Dismissed so wrongly, and I do not want
To take away with me this heavy heart.
Oh, handle me more graciously. It is
The need most pressing to me, and it is
My last, most desperate attempt—I can
Not comprehend, cannot endure it, if you
Deny me *every every every* thing.—
Now you will let me leave you—plea refused,
Betrayed by thousands of the sweetest hopes.
I leave your sight.—Now your Duke Alba and
Your priest Domingo rule victorious
Where once your child lay weeping in the dust.
The host of courtiers, the anxious grandees,
The monkish band as pale as sin were witness
That you had granted me this solemn hearing.
Oh, do not shame me, Father, do not wound
Me mortally nor sacrifice me to
The mockery of the whole court that knows
That strangers revel in your favor when
Don Carlos' pleas will not prevail. As proof
That you will honor me, I beg you send
Me with the army to the Lowlands!

PHILIPP: Say
What you have said no more or earn my wrath!

CARLOS: I dare to face your royal wrath and ask
You one last time—entrust me with the Lowlands.
I should—I must leave Spain. My presence here
Is like existence under threat of death—
The heavens in Madrid lie heavy like
The knowledge of a murder. And my hope
Of remedy would be a change of heavens.
If you desire to save me—send me, Father,
Without delay to Flanders.

PHILIPP: Such a sickness
As you, my son, do suffer from requires
That you be under constant care of doctors.
You stay in Spain; the Duke will go to Flanders.

CARLOS (*beside himself*):
Oh, now encircle me, good spirits—

PHILIPP *(takes a step backwards):* Stop!
  What are these threatening incantations?
CARLOS *(with unsteady voice):* Father,
  Can this decision then not be reversed?
PHILIPP: It is the King's decision.
CARLOS: I am finished.
  (Exits severely agitated)

Scene 3

Philipp stands for a while sunken in gloomy contemplation; finally he takes a few steps up and down the hall. Alba approaches self-consciously.
PHILIPP: Be ready for the order any minute
  To take your leave for Brussels.
ALBA: Everything
  Is ready, O my King.
PHILIPP: Your power of
  Authority is sealed and lying in
  My private room. Now tell the Queen farewell
  And also take your leave from the Infante.
ALBA: I saw him as he left this room just now,
  With the appearance of a man gone mad.
  And now I see Your Royal Majesty
  Appears distressed and deeply moved besides—
  Your conversations' content was—?
PHILIPP *(after pacing back and forth):* It was
  Duke Alba.
  (The King stops and fastens him with his eye,
  ominously.)
  Gladly would I have it shown
  That Carlos *hates* my counselors, but I
  Discovered with dismay he only *scorns* them.
ALBA *(grows pale and is about to speak out):*
PHILIPP: Now not a word. I will allow you to
  Appease the Prince.
ALBA: My Lord!
PHILIPP: Now tell me, Duke,

Who was it, then, who was the first to warn me
That I had best beware Don Carlos' black
Attacks? I listened to *you* then and not
To *him*. Now I will make a test. Henceforth
My son stands nearer to my throne. Now go.

> *(The King goes into his private room. The Duke
> exits through another door.)*

An antechamber to the Queen's room

Scene 4

*Don Carlos enters through the middle door in conversation with
a page. The courtiers in the antechamber disperse in the adjoining
rooms as he enters.*

CARLOS: A letter for me? And what is this key?
  And both so secretively handed to me?
  Come closer.—Tell me where you got it!

PAGE *(mysteriously):*   This
  Was what the lady wanted, rather that
  You'd guess her name than have it told.

CARLOS *(starting back in surprise):*   The lady?
        (He examines the page more carefully.)
  What is this—and who are you, then?

PAGE: I am
  A page in service to Her Royal Highness—

CARLOS *(alarmed, goes up to him and puts his hand over the boy's
mouth):*
  Then you are doomed. Stop there! I know enough.
    *(He rips off the seal hastily and moves to the far
    end of the hall to read the letter. Meanwhile Duke
    Alba enters and, without being noticed by the Prince,
    goes by him into the Queen's room. Carlos begins to
    tremble and becomes pale and red in turn. When he
    has finished reading, he stands silent for a long
    time, his eyes fixed on the letter.—
    Finally he turns to the page.)*
  She gave you this herself?

PAGE: With her own hands.
CARLOS: She gave you this herself? Don't jest with me!
  I never read a word she ever wrote.
  I must believe you, if you will but swear it.
  If you were lying, just confess it frankly,
  And do not jest with me.
PAGE: Not jest with *whom?*
CARLOS (*looks at the letter again and regards the page*
    with an uncertain, inquiring expression. After he
    has walked the length of the hall):
  You do have parents, don't you? And your father
  Does serve the King and is a native Spaniard?
PAGE: He fell in battle at San Quentin. He
  Was Count Alonzo of Henárez and
  A colonel with the Duke of Savoy's troops.
CARLOS (*as he takes the boy's hand and fixes him meaningfully*
  with his eyes):
  The King gave you the letter?
PAGE (*sensitively*): Gracious Prince,
  Do I deserve so much mistrust?
CARLOS (*reads the letter*): "This key
  Will open the rear door of the pavilion
  Belonging to the Queen, the last of all,
  Adjoining on one side a private room,
  In which the sound of footsteps never echoes.
  Here love may freely, clearly be confessed,
  That up to now was limited to hints.
  Full favor now awaits the timorous.
  Rewards for the discreet long-suffering one."
        (*as if awakening from a stupor*)
  I do not dream—I am not mad—that is
  My right arm and that is my sword—and those
  Are written words. It is all true and real,
  And I am loved.—Oh yes, I am—I am,
  Oh, I am loved!
    (*Beside himself, rushing about the room with his arms*
    thrown up in the air)
PAGE: Then come with me, my Prince, I'll lead you there.
CARLOS: First let me get a hold upon myself.

Does not the shock of this new fortune make
Me tremble? Have I ever hoped such hopes?
Or have I ever dared to dream such dreams?
What man can learn so quickly to be God?—
Who was I and who am I now? That is
A different heaven and another sun
Than ever I did see before.—She loves me!

PAGE *(is about to lead the way):*
But this is not the place—do you forget—

CARLOS *(gripped by a sudden paralysis):*
The King, my father!
>   *(He lets his arms sink, looks timidly around,*
>   *and begins to collect his thoughts.)*
>   This is terrible—
Yes, you are right, my friend. I thank you, I
Was not just now myself entirely. That
I must keep silent, keep such happiness
Walled up within my breast is terrible.
>   *(taking the page by the hand and drawing him aside)*
Now listen to me—everything you've seen,
And all that you've not seen, shall be enclosed
Within your breast as if 'twere in a tomb.
Now go. I'll find my way. Just go. They must
Not find us here. Now go—

PAGE *(starts to leave):*

CARLOS: But wait! and listen!—
>   *(The page returns. Carlos puts a hand on his shoulder*
>   *and looks him earnestly and solemnly in the face.)*
You take away a terrible secret with you,
That like unto some deadly poisons will
Burst through the vessel wherein it is kept—
Be master of your countenance. Your head
Should never know the things your bosom guards.
Be like the lifeless speaking tube that takes
A sound and sends it on and does not hear.
You are a boy—and it is well you be one,
Continuing to play a happy part—
How well the clever writer understands
The way to choose a messenger of love!
Here will the King not look to find his vipers.

PAGE: And I, my Prince, I will be proud of it
  To know that I am richer by one secret
  Than is the King himself—
CARLOS: Oh young, vain fool,
  That is the reason you must tremble.—If
  It should occur that we should meet in public,
  You must approach me shyly with submission.
  Your vanity must never tempt you to
  Make known how much in favor with the Prince
  You are! There is no sin more heinous than
  To win my favor.—In the future, when
  You have some information for me, do
  Not speak it out, no, do not trust your lips;
  But what you have to say should never follow
  The universal road of thought. Instead
  Speak with your eyes or with your finger, thus;
  I'll listen to you with a glance. The air,
  The light around us, is a vassal, too,
  And even the deaf walls are in his pay—
  Someone is coming—
                (The door to the Queen's room
                opens, and the Duke of Alba enters.)
                Go! Farewell!
PAGE: My Prince,
  Be sure you choose the right room when you go.
                (Exits.)
CARLOS: It is the Duke.—Oh, no, oh, no! All right!
  I'll manage it.

Scene 5

Don Carlos. Duke of Alba.
ALBA *(obstructs his way):* Two words, O gracious Prince.
CARLOS: Oh, yes—that's fine—another time.
                (He starts to leave.)
ALBA: This spot
  Is not the most appropriate. Perhaps
  It would be more agreeable to you
  To give me audience in your own room?

CARLOS: What for? Here is as good a place as any.
  But just be quick—
ALBA: The thing that brings me here
  Is that I want to offer to Your Highness
  My humble thanks for what you did—
CARLOS: Your thanks?
  To me? What for?—The Duke of Alba's thanks?
ALBA: For scarcely had you left His Majesty
  Than I was notified that it was time
  For me to leave for Brussels.
CARLOS: Brussels! So!
ALBA: To whom, my Prince, can I attribute this,
  Excepting to the intercession of
  Your favor with His Majesty?—
CARLOS: To me?
  Oh, not to me—no, truly not to me.
  You're going—may you go with God!
ALBA: That's all?
  Well, that surprises me.—And does Your Highness
  Have nothing else to send with me to Flanders?
CARLOS: What else? What would there be?
ALBA: Just recently
  The fate and future of those lands required
  The presence of Don Carlos.
CARLOS: Why was that?
  Oh, yes—that's right—that was before—but this
  Is just as good, quite good, it is much better—
ALBA: I hear this with astonishment—
CARLOS (*not with irony*):   You are
  A general of skill.—Who does not know?
  The envious themselves will swear to that.
  And I—I am so young. That was the King's
  Opinion, too. The King is right, quite right.
  I see it now. I am content, and so
  Enough of that. Good luck attend you. I
  Am now, as you can see, completely—I
  Am somewhat overburdened—for the rest,
  Tomorrow or whenever you may choose
  Or when you come again from Brussels—

ALBA: What?

CARLOS *(after a silence as he perceives that the Duke
    is not leaving):*
The season is auspicious for you. You
Will travel through Milan and then Lorraine,
Through Burgundy and Germany—now, was
It not in Germany? Yes, there you're known!
It's April now: May—June—and by July,
Or at the latest by the first of August,
Then you will be in Brussels. Oh, there is
No doubt we'll soon hear of your victories.
You know the way to make your actions worth
The favor of our confidence.

ALBA *(meaningfully):*   Though I'm
Pierced by the knowledge of my nothingness?

CARLOS *(after a silence, with dignity and pride):*
Duke Alba, you are sensitive and with
Good cause. It was—I will admit it—not
Quite fair on my part to attack you thus,
When you were not in a position to
Retaliate.

ALBA: In no position?—

CARLOS *(offering his hand with a smile):* What
A shame I do not have the time just now
To fight this worthy battle with Duke Alba.
Another time—

ALBA: Prince, we both make mistakes
In very different ways. You, for example,
You see what you will be in twenty years.
I see you twenty years ago.

CARLOS: And so?

ALBA: And it occurs to me how many nights
With his most beauteous wife from Portugal—
Your real mother—that our monarch would
Have gladly given just to purchase for
His kingdom such an arm as mine? It is
Perhaps no secret to him that the art
Of propagation of a king is not
So hard as propagating kingdoms—how

Much quicker one can give the world a king
Than give a king the world.

CARLOS: That is quite true.
Duke Alba, still and all—

ALBA: And how much blood,
The blood of your own people, had to flow
Until two drops could make you to a king.

CARLOS: That is quite true, and in a few words you
Have well expressed what pride of merit can
Oppose to pride of fortune—But now let
Us hear your application, Duke.

ALBA: Oh, woe
Betide the tender babe of royalty
Who makes fun of his nurse. How peacefully
And undisturbed he sleeps upon a cushion
Made soft by all our victories. His crown
Will glitter full of jewels and not of wounds
By which it was obtained.—This trusty sword
Has written Spanish law for foreign peoples,
Before Our Lord, the Crucified, it flashes.
And draws the bloody furrows on our soil,
Where seed corn of our faith will then take root:
God is the judge in Heaven, I on earth—

CARLOS: It makes no difference whether God or devil,
You were his right arm—that I know—and now
No more of it, I beg you. There are certain
Remembrances I'd rather guard against—
I honor him my father chooses and
My father needs an Alba. That you're needed
Is not a reason why I envy him.
You are a great man.—Yes, that may be true;
I almost think it is. I only fear
You came a thousand years before your time.
An Alba, I would think, would be the man
Who would be present at the end of time!
Then when iniquity's defiance has
Consumed all Heaven's forbearance, when the crop
Of crime and sin will ripen and demand
A reaper such as earth has never seen,
Then you will stand upon the proper place.—

O God, my Paradise! my Flanders!—Still,
I should not think about it. Silence now.
It's said you carry a supply of signed
And sealed sentences of death. Your foresight
Is worthy of great praise. One need not fear
To meet with underhanded tricks. O Father,
How little did I understand. I thought
That you were hard on me when you refused
A mission where your Alba could prevail.—
Here your regard for me began.

ALBA: My Prince,
These words deserve—

CARLOS *(vehemently)*:   Yes? What?

ALBA: Here royalty
Protects you.

CARLOS *(grasping his sword)*: Satisfaction! I demand
It—draw your sword, Duke!

ALBA *(coldly)*:   Against whom?

CARLOS *(pressing him fiercely)*:   Now draw
Your sword or I will run you through.

ALBA *(draws)*:   If it
Must be then—

                    (They fight.)

Scene 6

The Queen. Don Carlos. Duke of Alba.

QUEEN *(who has stepped out of her room, alarmed)*:
                    Swords drawn!
        *(to the Prince, distressed and with a commanding
        voice)*

                            Carlos!

CARLOS *(at the sight of the Queen loses his composure,
    lets his arm fall, stands without motion or thought,
    then rushes up to the Duke and kisses him)*:
Forgiveness, Duke! And reconciliation!
        *(He throws himself without a word at the Queen's
        feet, then quickly arises and rushes out in confusion.)*

ALBA *(who stands there full of astonishment without taking his*
eyes off of them):
My God but that is strange!—
QUEEN *(stands a moment disturbed and uncertain, then*
slowly goes to her room, turns around at the door):
                          Come now, Duke Alba!
(The Duke follows her into the room.)

A private room of the Princess of Eboli

Scene 7

The Princess, with exquisite taste, beautifully but simply dressed,
is playing on a lute and singing. The Queen's page enters.
PRINCESS *(jumps up quickly)*:
He comes!
PAGE *(hastily)*: You are alone? I am surprised
To find him not already here, but he
Must surely come, in just a moment.
PRINCESS: Must?
Then he must *wish* to—so it is decided—
PAGE: He follows on my heels.—O, my Princess,
You are beloved—beloved, beloved as you
Have never ever been and no one ever was.
Oh, what a scene I looked upon!
PRINCESS *(pulls him to herself with impatience)*:
                              Make haste!
You talked to him? Speak up! What did he say?
How did he act? What were his very words?
He was embarrassed, was a bit perplexed?
And did he guess who sent the key to him?
Speak up—Perhaps he didn't guess? He did
Not guess at all? He guessed all wrong?—Well now?
And aren't you going to answer me at all?
Oh, shame on you: You've never been so stubborn
And so insufferably slow as now.
PAGE: If you will let me, gracious lady, speak?
I gave the letter and the key to him

Before the Queen's room, where the words escaped
Me that I was sent by a lady. Then
He gave a start and looked at me.

PRINCESS: He gave
A start? That's very good, but tell me more.

PAGE: I wanted to say more, but he turned pale
And snatched the letter from my hand and looked
So menacing and said he knew it all.
The letter he read through with consternation
And then began to tremble.

PRINCESS: Knew it all?
He knew it all? He said that?

PAGE: And he asked
Me three times, four times, whether you yourself
Had really given me the letter.

PRINCESS: Whether
It was in truth from me? He used my name?

PAGE: The name—no, that he didn't do.—There might
Be spies, he said, who were about and who
Might tell it to the King.

PRINCESS *(surprised):*   Did he say that?

PAGE: The King would be extremely interested,
He said, particularly to receive
Some information telling of this letter.

PRINCESS: The King? You really heard him say the King?
That was the very word he used?

PAGE: It was!
He called the secret dangerous and gave
Me warning to be on my constant guard
With both my words and gestures, that the King
Might not become suspicious of me.

PRINCESS *(after some reflection, full of astonishment):* It
Is true.—This is how it must be—He must
Have heard of the affair.—Incredible!
Now who could possibly have told him?—Who?
I ask besides: Who sees so keenly—sees
So far, who but the eagle's eye of love?
But now continue with your tale: He read
The letter—

PAGE: It contained a happiness,
  He said, before which he must surely tremble;
  He never would have dared to dream of this.
  The Duke came at that moment in the room,
  A thing that forced us—
PRINCESS *(annoyed)*: What in all the world
  Would bring the Duke there then? But where, oh where
  Can he be now? What keeps him from me? Why
  Is he not here? You see how falsely you
  Have been advised! How happy he would be
  By now in just this time that it has taken
  For you to tell me that he would be happy.
PAGE: The Duke, I fear—
PRINCESS: It is again the Duke?
  What is the Duke to me? What does that man
  Of valor have to do with happiness
  Like mine? He could have simply left him there.
  He could have done the same to anyone.—
  Oh, truly, here's a prince who understands
  As little about love as about women.
  He does not know what minutes are.—Be still!
  I hear him come. Be gone. It is the Prince.
              (Page hurries out.)
  Away, away!—Where have I put my lute?
  I want him to surprise me, and my song
  Shall be a sign to him—

Scene 8

The Princesss. Immediately thereafter, Don Carlos.
PRINCESS *(has thrown herself down on an ottoman and plays)*:.
CARLOS *(rushes in. He recognizes the Princess and stands*
  there thunderstruck.): O God!
  Where am I?
PRINCESS *(lets the lute fall. To him)*:
              O Prince Carlos! It is you!
CARLOS: Where am I? Terrible trickery—I must
  Have entered the wrong room.

PRINCESS: I see how well
Don Carlos understands the way to find
The rooms where ladies are alone.
CARLOS: Princess—
Forgive, my Lady—I—I found the door
Was standing open.
PRINCESS: Is that possible?
I really think I locked the door myself.
CARLOS: You only think you did, but be assured
You are mistaken. That you wished it locked,
I will allow, I do believe—but locked?
Not locked, it truly was not locked! I heard
That someone played upon a lute—was it
A lute?
                    (He looks around uncertainly.)
            Yes, I am right, for there it is—
A lute—well, God in Heaven knows—I love
A lute insanely, and as always am
All ears. I think of nothing else. I rushed
Into the room that I might look into
The lovely eyes of the performer who
Enchanted me and moved me so intensely.
PRINCESS: A charming touch of curiosity
That you can quickly cure, as I could show you.
                    (after a pause, with meaning)
Oh, I must treasure someone so discreet,
Who will involve himself in such a lie
To save me from embarrassment.
CARLOS *(frankly)*:   Princess,
I feel that I am only making worse
What I would rectify. Release me from
A role that I am wholly unequipped
To play. You sought to find here in this room
A refuge and a shelter from the world.
Here unobserved by others you would try
To air the quiet wishes of your heart,
And I, misfortune's son, appear; forthwith
This lovely dream of yours is broken.—So
I needs must make a quick departure.—
                    (He starts to leave.)

PRINCESS (*surprised and taken aback, but immediately
regaining control of herself*):   Prince—
Oh, that was wicked.
CARLOS: I can understand,
Princess, what such a look in such a room
Could mean, and I respect your virtuous
Confusion here. Woe be it to the man
Whom maiden modesty makes bold. I must
Despair when women tremble in my presence.
PRINCESS: Is this then possible?—A young man and
A king's son, too, with an unrivaled conscience!
Yes, Prince—now you must really stay with me.
I ask you as a favor, for the fear
Of any maid is quickly calmed by such
Great virtue—but the song that I love best
Was interrupted by your sudden entrance.
     (*She leads him to the sofa and takes up her lute again.*)
That song, Prince Carlos, I most certainly
Will want to play again; your punishment
Will be to listen to me.
CARLOS (*sits down, not without constraint, next to the
Princess*):   Just as pleasant
Will be that punishment as my offense.
The content of your song was welcome to me—
It was so beautiful that I would be
Content to hear it even three times.
PRINCESS: What?
You have already heard it? That is frightful,
For I believe, indeed, it speaks of love?
CARLOS: And if I'm not mistaken, love that's happy—
Such lovely words from such a lovely mouth;
But certainly less true than they are fair.
PRINCESS: Indeed? You needs must doubt that they are true?
CARLOS (*earnestly*):
Perhaps I doubt that Carlos and Princess
Of Eboli can ever understand
Each other when they talk of love.
          (*The Princess is taken aback; he notices it and
          continues with an air of gentle gallantry.*)

For who,
When looking at these rosy cheeks, would think
That passion could be stirring in this breast?
Or could the Princess ever run the risk
Of fervent sighing all in vain? True love
He knows alone who loves without all hope.

PRINCESS (*with as much gaiety as previously*):
Oh, quiet! That sounds terrible.—And really,
It seems somehow this fate pursues you, Prince,
Above all men, today especially.

       (taking him by the hand, ingratiatingly)
You are not happy, O good Prince.—You suffer—
O God, you really suffer. Should this be?
For why, my Prince, why suffer, when you have
An open calling to enjoy the world,
With all the gifts that Nature can endow
And every claim on pleasures of this life?
When *you*—the son of a great king and *more*,
Far more than that—when you were in your cradle,
You were endowed with talents that indeed
Obscure the very radiance of your rank?
And *you*—who have bribed judges sitting there
In the strict council of the women who
Pass judgment without opposition on
A man's worth and his worldly reputation?
One who had only to *perceive* to conquer,
Enflames when he remains indifferent, when
He chooses to be ardent must bestow
The happiness of Paradise—the man
Whom Nature has adorned so he can be
The happiness of thousands not so blessed,
He should himself be wretched? Host of Heaven,
You who gave everything to him, then why,
Oh, why deny him just the eyes with which
To see his victory.

CARLOS (*who has been absorbed this whole time in the deepest
distraction, is suddenly brought to himself by
the Princess' silence and starts up*):
       That is superb!

Without compare, Princess! I beg you, sing
That part to me just one more time.
PRINCESS *(looks at him astonished):*   Don Carlos,
Where have you been the while?
CARLOS *(jumps up):*   Oh yes, God knows,
It's time that you remind me.—Now I must,
I must away—must quickly go.
PRINCESS *(holds him back):*   Where to?
CARLOS *(frightfully anxious):*
Out in the open—Let me go, Princess,
It is as if the world were burning up
Behind my back—
PRINCESS *(holds him by force):* What is the matter? Why
This very strange, unnatural behavior?
      *(Carlos stands still and becomes reflective. She
      seizes this moment to draw him to her on the sofa.)*
Now you must rest, dear Carlos, for your blood
Is in an uproar—just sit here by me—
Away with these black fever fantasies!
If you would ask yourself quite candidly,
If this head knows what stone lies on this heart?
And even if it knew the answer—then
Would any one of all this court's proud knights,
Of all the ladies any one, know how
To heal you, how to understand you—would
There be a single one?
CARLOS *(casually, without thinking):* Perhaps Princess
Of Eboli?
PRINCESS *(joyous and quick):* Indeed?
CARLOS: Just give me then
A written supplication to my father
To recommend me. Give me that! They say
You count for much.
PRINCESS: Who says it? (Ha, so that
Is what you think, that keeps you silent!)
CARLOS: Has
The story made the rounds already? I
Have got the notion to go to Brabant
Because—because I want to win my spurs.

My father does not wish it. My good father
Is apprehensive if I lead an army,
My singing might well suffer from it.
PRINCESS: Carlos!
You play a game. Now just admit you want
To lose me in these false meanderings.
Look here, dissembler! Face me eye to eye!
Who only dreams of knightly courage would—
Confess now!—would he ever stoop to this:
To count the ribbons that the ladies have
Let fall and steal away with them and—
You'll forgive me—
                    (as she flicks back the frill on his shirt with a
                    slight gesture of her finger and takes away a
                    ribbon that is hidden there)
                                    and preserve them with such care?
CARLOS *(in consternation steps back):*
Princess!—Oh, no, you go too far.—I am
Betrayed. I cannot fool you, for you are,
I think, in league with spirits and with demons.
PRINCESS: You seem to be surprised at this? But why?
What do you bet, my Prince, that I can call
Events back to your mind, and such events—
Why don't you try it, only question me.
If just a momentary mood, a sound
Breathed unclear in the air, a smile erased
Again by sudden earnestness, or if
Your aspect and your gestures, even, when
Your soul was far away, have not eluded
My notice, you may be the judge if I
Have understood what was to understand?
CARLOS: You really venture quite a lot.—I'll take
Your bet, Princess. You give a promise to me
To make discoveries within my heart
About things I have never known.
PRINCESS *(somewhat sensitive and serious):* What? Never?
Try to remember, Prince. Just look around.—
This little chamber is not like those large
Rooms of the Queen, wherein your masquerade

Was wont to be approved.—You are surprised?
You suddenly are all afire?—Of course,
For who would be so clever, so audacious,
So careless as to eavesdrop on Don Carlos
When Carlos thinks he is not heard?—Who saw
When at the last court ball he left the Queen,
His lady, in the middle of a dance,
To force himself upon another pair
And thus replace his royal partner by
Extending to the Princess Eboli
His hand, an error that our monarch saw
Himself just then as he came in the room!

CARLOS (*with an ironic smile*):
So even *he* saw? Well, my good Princess,
It was not for his benefit.

PRINCESS: As little
As was the scene there in the royal chapel
That certainly Don Carlos has forgotten
Himself by now. You were absorbed in prayer
Before the statue of the Holy Virgin,
When suddenly—were you to blame?—the clothes
Of certain ladies rustled at your back.
And then Don Philipp's one courageous son
Began to tremble like a heretic
Before the Host, and on his pallid lips
His spoiled prayer expired—a victim of
His passion—what a touching game was played
There, Prince—You seize the fingers of our Lord's
Own Mother, cold and holy fingers and
Then shower fiery kisses on the marble.

CARLOS: You are unfair, Princess, to my devotions.

PRINCESS: Well, there is something else, my Prince—for surely
It was alone the fear of loss that time
When Carlos and the Queen and I were sitting
At cards, and with a show of marvelous
Dexterity you robbed me of my glove—
                    (*Carlos jumps up, dismayed.*)
Which, it is true, you were polite enough
To deal to me in place of my next card.

CARLOS: O God, O God, O God, what did I do?
PRINCESS: Not something you would disavow, I hope.
  How happy and surprised I was to find
  So unexpectedly a note that you
  Had hidden cleverly within that glove.
  It was so moving and romantic, Prince,
  That I—
CARLOS *(interrupting her quickly):*
          'Twas poetry and nothing more.
  My mind is always blowing wondrous bubbles
  That, shortly after they are blown, will burst.
  And that is all it was. Don't talk about it.
PRINCESS *(moving away from him in astonishment and observing*
  him from the distance for a while):
  I am exhausted—everything I try
  Slides off this serpentine original.
              (She is silent for a moment.)
  But why?—Is it perhaps just manly pride
  That uses coyness as a mask? Perhaps?
          (She comes closer to the Prince and observes
          him uncertainly.)
  Now you enlighten me, Prince, for I stand
  Before a magic box that is tight locked,
  And all the keys I've tried have been the wrong ones.
CARLOS: I stand before you thus.
PRINCESS *(She turns away from him quickly, goes silently*
  back and forth in the room several times and seems
  to be thinking over something important. Finally,
  after a long pause, seriously and solemnly):
                          Then it is time—
  Now I must finally decide to speak.
  I choose you as my judge. You are a man—
  A noble man—you are a prince and knight.
  I throw myself upon your breast, and you
  Will save me, for if I cannot be saved,
  You will in sympathy weep over me.
      (The Prince moves closer in expectant, sympathetic
      astonishment.)
  A favorite of the King, the insolent

Ruy Gomez, Count of Silva, asks for me
In marriage, and the King agrees. They have
Made terms, and I am to be sold.
CARLOS *(intensely moved):*   Be sold?
  And then be sold again? And then again
  By that most famous, royal southern merchant?
PRINCESS: First hear me out, for it is not enough
  To sacrifice me to their politics;
  They also wish to steal my virtue. Here!
  This letter will unmask our holy man.
    (Carlos takes the paper and listens with impatience
    to her tale without taking the time to read it.)
  Where shall I find deliverance? Till now,
  O Prince, it was my pride that saved my virtue,
  But finally—
CARLOS: But finally you fell?
  You fell? Oh, no! For God's sake, no!
PRINCESS *(proud and noble):*   To *whom?*
  Such despicable sophistry! How weak
  These strong intelligences are! To think
  A woman's favor, luck in love, are like
  Some merchandise for which one bids! It is
  The only thing on this earth's round that will
  Permit no purchaser except itself.
  For love is always love's reward. It is
  The priceless diamond that I am free
  To give or else, eternally untouched,
  To hide away—just as that merchant did
  Who, unaffected by the market's gold
  And as an insult to the reigning kings,
  Preferred to give the ocean back its pearls,
  Too proud to sell them at a price too cheap.
CARLOS: (Beloved God! She is so beautiful!)
PRINCESS: Think it a whim or vanity: no matter.
  I will not parcel out my pleasures, but
  To one man, only one, that I have chosen,
  I'll give forever everything. I will
  Bestow myself but once eternally.
  My love will only make one person happy,

But this one it will make into a god.
Two souls' enchanting harmony—one kiss—
The pleasure of two lovers' hours together—
And beauty's lofty and celestial magic
Are the related colors of *one* beam,
Are just the petals of *one* flower. Should
I then, gone mad, bestow one petal torn
Asunder from this blossom's lovely chalice?
Should I defile the highest majesty
Of woman and the godhead's masterpiece
To make one night sweet for a profligate?

CARLOS: (It is incredible that such a maid
   Was living in Madrid and I first knew
   Of it today.)

PRINCESS: I should have left this court,
   I should have left this world long since, I should
   Have been entombed within some holy walls;
   But one bond holds me back; there is one bond,
   Which holds me powerfully to this world.
   It may be but a phantom, but to me
   Full worth! I love and am not loved.

CARLOS *(moving towards her full of ardor):* You are!
   As sure as there's a God in Heaven. I swear
   That you are loved ineffably.

PRINCESS: You swear?
   That was my angel's voice. Indeed, if you
   Can freely swear it, Carlos, I believe
   And I am loved.

CARLOS *(as he enfolds her tenderly in his arms):*
           O sweet and tender maiden!
   O creature most adorable!—I stand
   All ears—all eyes—enchanted—full of wonder.
   Who is there who has seen you, who can be
   Beneath this heaven and has seen you and
   Can say with pride—that he has never loved?—
   But at King Philipp's court? Why are you here?
   What, lovely angel, do you hope for here?
   Among such priests and all their rabble is
   No climate for such blossoms.—They might wish

To pluck you—I believe they might—But no!
As surely as I breathe, they will not! I
Will wrap you in my arms and carry you
Through Hell and all the devils there may be!
Oh, let me truly be your angel.

PRINCESS *(with the full gaze of love):*   Carlos!
How little I have known you! And how rich
And infinitely does your lovely heart
Reward the pains to understand it.
      (She grasps his hand and is about to kiss it.)

CARLOS *(draws it away):*   What,
Princess, are you about?

PRINCESS *(with delicacy and grace as she looks fixedly
at his hand):*   What beauty lies
In such a hand! How rich it is!—My Prince,
Two precious gifts may this hand give away—
A diadem and Carlos' heart—perhaps
One mortal woman will receive them both.
Just *one?* A gift sublime, it is almost
Too great for just *one* mortal. How then, Prince,
If you resolve upon a fair division?
For queens are not good lovers—but a woman
Who knows just how to love will then not know
About a crown: Thus a division were
Far better and right now. Or is it something
That you have done already?—Oh, you have!
And do I know this happy lady?

CARLOS: Yes,
You must, dear girl; I will disclose to you,
Thus to a nature pure and undefiled
I will disclose myself, for at this court
You are the worthiest, the only one
Who understands my soul.—Well then! I will
Not disavow my love!

PRINCESS: O wicked man!
Is that confession then so hard to make
And must I find myself lamentable
If you should think of me with love?

CARLOS *(taken aback):*   What's that?
What did you say?

PRINCESS: To carry on this game,
  Oh, truly, Prince, you have no shame. And to
  Deny you had the key!
CARLOS: The key! The key!
          (after deep reflection)
  Yes, it was so.—I understand—O God!
    *(His knees give way, he holds onto a chair,
    and covers his face.)*
PRINCESS *(A long silence. The Princess utters a loud cry and col-*
lapses.):
          Oh, horrible! What have I done?
CARLOS *(pulling himself up, in an outburst of deepest grief):*
          I am
  Completely, utterly cast out from all
  My heavens!—That is dreadful!
PRINCESS *(burying her face in the pillow):* O my God!
CARLOS *(throwing himself at her feet):*
  Princess, 'tis not my fault—this wild emotion—
  It is a total lack of understanding—
  I'm not to blame.
PRINCESS *(pushes him away):* Get out—out of my sight,
  For God's sake—
CARLOS: I will never do it! Leave
  You in this dreadful shock of disillusion.
PRINCESS *(thrusting him forcefully away):*
  Be generous, be merciful and get
  Out of my sight! Unless you want to kill me?
  I hate the very sight of you!
          (Carlos starts to leave.)
          But give
  My letter and my key to me again.
  Where have you put the other one?
CARLOS: What do
  You mean by that?
PRINCESS: The letter from the King.
CARLOS *(horrified):*
  From whom?
PRINCESS: The one I gave to you before.
CARLOS: 'Twas from the King? To whom? To you?
PRINCESS: O God!

How horribly am I entangled now!
The letter! Give it to me! I must have it.
CARLOS: A letter from the King to you?
PRINCESS: The letter!
By all the saints I beg!
CARLOS: The one that should
Disclose a certain person to me—this one?
PRINCESS: 'Twill mean my death!—Oh, give it here.
CARLOS: The letter—
PRINCESS (*wringing her hands in despair*):
What have I dared so thoughtlessly to do?
CARLOS: The letter—it was from the King?—Princess,
That quickly changes everything.—*That* is
                    (*holding the letter up joyfully*)
Invaluable—a letter without price,
That all King Philipp's crowns will be too light,
Too unimportant to redeem.—*That* letter
I'll keep.
                         (*He exits.*)
PRINCESS (*hurling herself in his path*):
Great God in Heaven, I am lost!

Scene 9

The Princess alone.

(*She is still stunned, distraught; after he has
left, she hurries after him and attempts to call him back.*)
PRINCESS: Just one more word, Prince! Listen!—Oh, he's gone!
Then that, too! He despises me.—I stand
In the most frightful solitude—cast off,
Discarded—
                    (*She sinks down upon a stool. After a pause*)
          No! Displaced is all, displaced
By someone who desires him, too. He loves.
No doubt of that. He has admitted it.
But *who* then is so fortunate?—So much
Is clear—he loves someone he should not love.

He fears discovery and from the King
He tries to hide his passion. But why just
From him who would desire it? Or is it
Not father that he fears in fearing father?
For when the King's lascivious intent
Was known to him—he clearly looked delighted,
Rejoiced like any happy man. . . How come
His strictness and his virtue were struck dumb?
But here? Just here?—What can there be that he
Should profit by, and even if the King
Would make the Queen a—

> *(She stops abruptly, taken by a sudden thought.
> —At the same time she snatches from her bosom
> the ribbon that she took from Don Carlos, looks
> at it for a second, and recognizes it.)*

                              Oh, I am insane!
Now finally—Where was my intuition?
Now, finally my eyes are open.—They
Had long loved one another when the King
Chose her. He never saw me without *her.*
So *she,* she was the one he meant when I
Believed I was so truly, warmly worshiped?
Oh, a deceit without a precedent!
And I betrayed my very weakness to her—

> *(silence)*

And can it be that he should love without
All hope! I do not think so.—Hopeless love
Cannot endure in such a battle. Thus
To grow and have the world's most brilliant prince
To pine—Now really! Such a sacrifice
Cannot prevail with hopeless love. His kiss—
It was like fire! How tender his embrace,
How tender near his pounding heart! This trial
Was almost too much for fidelity
That cannot ever be returned—He takes
A key, which, as he tries to tell himself,
The Queen herself has sent to him—and he
Believes it is a giant step of love—
He comes, he really comes!—So he believes

That Philipp's wife would make this mad decision.
How could he, if encouragement came not
Before? 'Tis out. She hears him, and she loves!
This saint, by Heaven, is so sensitive!
She is so fine! . . . I tremble, I myself,
Before this awesome totem of such virtue.
She towers next to me a higher being,
Her brilliance makes me pale. But to her beauty
I credited so grudgingly this peace,
So free from every turmoil of us mortals.
And was this peace appearance only? Had she
Desired to eat her cake and have it too?
Appeared to be divinely virtuous
And at the same time secretly to try
To take a taste of hidden, sinful pleasure?
And could she do that? Could hypocrisy
Be so successful and remain unknown?
Successful for the want of an avenger?
By Heaven, no! I worshiped her and that
Requires revenge! The King must know—the King?
　　　　　　　　(after some thought)
That's it—that is a way to reach his ear.
　　　　　　　　(She exits.)

A room in the royal palace

Scene 10

Duke of Alba. Father Domingo.
DOMINGO: What did you want to tell me?
ALBA:　　　　　　　　　　　　　An important
　Discovery I made today, about
　Which I would like to hear your thoughts.
DOMINGO:　　　　　　　　　　　　And what
　Discovery is that?
ALBA:　　　　　　　Today at noon,
　Before the antechamber of the Queen,
　I came upon Prince Carlos. I believed

Myself insulted. We became embroiled.
The fight was growing loud. We grabbed our swords.
Because of all the noise, the Queen appeared
And threw herself between us and then gave
One look, imperious and intimate.
It was a single look, but his arm froze.
He flew to me and then embraced my neck.
I feel a single red-hot kiss, and he
Is gone.

DOMINGO *(after a silence):*
                    That seems to me suspicious, Duke,
It makes me think of something else—There was
Another thought, I will confess, that sprouted
Sometime ago within my breast.—I flee
These dreams—I have told no one of it. There
Are two-edged blades, and some uncertain friends—
I am afraid of these. Hard to distinguish
And harder to be sure of are these persons.
Those words that do escape may make for insults
To those one trusts, and so I kept my secret,
Until the time to bring it to the light.
To offer certain services to kings
Is tricky, Duke, a calculated risk.
If it should miss its target, it could strike
The man who aimed it.—I could swear upon
The Host that what I said was true—but an
Eyewitness or a word that's overheard,
A piece of paper would weigh heavier,
Than my most active feeling.—'Tis a shame
That we stand here on Spanish soil.

ALBA: But why
Just here?

DOMINGO: At any other court one might
Forget to be so cautious with one's passions.
But here one is reminded by the laws.
The Spanish queens must make a special effort
To sin—I think so—but to our misfortune
'Tis *only* there—and just *there* only—where
We would be able to surprise them best.

ALBA: Now listen further—for today the King
  Received Don Carlos, and the audience
  Continued for an hour. He begged to be
  Made ruler of the Lowlands. Powerful
  His pleas were; I could hear him. But his eyes
  Were red with crying when I met him at
  The door. At noon thereafter he appeared;
  His attitude is one of triumph: it
  Delights him that the King has chosen to
  Reward me. He is thankful. Things have changed,
  He says, are better. He could not dissemble.
  How can I make sense of these contradictions?
  The Prince is overjoyed to be displaced;
  The King has granted me a favor, but
  With all the signs of anger!—What can I
  Believe? Indeed, this recent honor seems
  To be more similar to banishment
  Than to a favor.
DOMINGO: It has come to this
  Then? Come so far? And in a single moment
  All *that* is gone, which we took years to build?—
  And you complaisant and so calm?—And do
  You know this youth? Or even guess what will
  Await us, if he should gain power?—For
  The Prince—and I am not his enemy;
  The worries that disrupt my sleep concern
  The throne as well as God and Church—For the
  Infante (I can penetrate his soul)
  Does entertain a terrible design—
  The mad design to make himself the Regent
  And do away with our most Holy Church.—
  His heart is glowing with a newer virtue
  That, proud and certain and sufficient to
  Itself, will not be beggar to a faith.—
  He *thinks!* His head burns with a strange chimera—
  'Tis mankind that he worships—Duke, now do
  You think he will suffice as king?
ALBA: Ideas,
  That's all. Perhaps it is just youthful pride

That wants to play a part.—Is there perhaps
Another choice for him? That will soon pass
When it becomes his duty to command.
DOMINGO: I doubt it.—He is wary of his freedom
And unaccustomed to obey, whereby
One learns to buy obedience.—Will he
Suffice upon our throne? His strong, bold spirit
Will rip apart the fiber of our state.
I sought to moderate his stubborn courage
In vain by means of pleasures of the times;
But he withstood the test—'Tis frightening,
This spirit in this body—and to know
That Philipp will be sixty.
ALBA: You look far
Ahead.
DOMINGO: He and the Queen are of one mind.
Already does the poison of new things
Pervade both breasts, concealed, it's true, but soon
It will gain ground, if it can seize the throne.
I know these Valois.—We must fear complete
Revenge from such a quiet enemy,
If Philipp should prove weak. As yet our luck
Has proven favorable. If we win,
The two will fall in just one trap.—But now
To give the King a hint of this, and if
We know it to be proved or not—for much
Is won already, if he wavers. We
Ourselves, we have no doubts, and to convince
Is never hard for one who is convinced.
It cannot fail we will discover more,
If we are sure we must discover it.
ALBA: But now the most important of the questions!
Who takes it on himself to tell the King?
DOMINGO: Not you or I. Now I'll disclose to you
What I, consumed by this great plan, have done
With quiet industry to reach our goal.
The third and most important person is
Still missing to make our alliance whole.
The King loves the Princess of Eboli.

I nourish passions that encourage what
I wish. I am his messenger—I'll tell
Her of our plans.—In this young woman, if
My work succeeds, we ought to find an ally,
We ought to find a queen. And she herself
Has asked me to come to her room just now.
I have great hope for all. A Spanish maid
May soon displace the Lily of Valois,
Perhaps in just one midnight.
ALBA: What is this?
Can this be true, what I have heard? By Heaven!
That takes me by surprise. Yes, *that* will do
It! Brother Monk, I must admire your work.
Now we have triumphed—
DOMINGO: Quiet! Who is coming?—
'Tis she herself.
ALBA: I'll be in the next room.
If you—
DOMINGO: All right. I'll call for you.
                              (The Duke of Alba exits.)

Scene 11

The Princess. Domingo.
DOMINGO: At your
Command, my gracious Lady.
PRINCESS *(looking after the Duke curiously)*: Are we then
Not all alone? You have, as I can see,
A witness with you.
DOMINGO: What?
PRINCESS: Who was it,
Who was with you and just left?
DOMINGO: It was the Duke
Of Alba, gracious Lady, who requests
That after me he may have leave to speak
With you.
PRINCESS: What does the Duke of Alba want?

What can he want? Perhaps you know it and
Can tell me?
DOMINGO: I? Before I know what the
Occurrence of importance is that brings
A pleasure I have been deprived of to me,
A visit with Princess of Eboli?
              (a pause while he waits for an answer)
And have events then finally contrived
To speak in favor of the royal wishes?
Have I with reason hoped you'd reconcile
Yourself on further thought to a request
You had rejected out of stubbornness?
I have great expectations—
PRINCESS: Did you take
My previous answer to the King?
DOMINGO: I have
Delayed an answer that would wound him sore.
Still, gracious Lady, it is time. It is
Now up to you to make it gentler.
PRINCESS: Tell
The King I am expecting him.
DOMINGO: May I
Take this as truth, my beautiful Princess?
PRINCESS: 'Tis surely not a joke. My God! You make
Me very anxious.—Now, what have I done,
If even you—yes, you yourself—must blush?
DOMINGO: Princess, this is a great surprise, and I
Can scarcely comprehend it—
PRINCESS: Noble sir,
You do not need to do so. I would rather
Refrain from all the world's blessings than
To have you comprehend it, so just spare
Yourself the task of brooding over whose
Glib tongue you have to thank for this new twist.
And for your comfort I will add that *you*
Have no part in this sin, nor does the Church
Have any, though you proved to me there were
Some cases possible in which the Church

Knew how to use the very bodies of
Its youthful daughters for some higher goal.
But not that either.—Pious purposes
Like that are far above me, sir—

DOMINGO: Then I
Would gladly take them back as soon as they
Become unnecessary.

PRINCESS: Would you beg
His Royal Highness for my sake that he
Should not mistake my actions in this case.
That which I was, I am. The situation
Has altered only in the case since then.
When I rejected horrified his plea,
At that time I believed him *happy* as
The lord of the most beautiful of queens,
Believed his faithful wife was worthy of
My sacrifice, believed it then. But now,
Now I know better.

DOMINGO: Please, Princess, go on.
I think we understand each other.

PRINCESS: So,
She is found out. I will not spare her now.
The clever thief is caught. She has betrayed
The King of mighty Spain and me. She is
In love. I know this, that she loves. I bring
The evidence, and it will make you tremble.
The King has been betrayed—I swear by Heaven!
He shall not be unknowingly betrayed.
I'll snatch away her cloak of majesty,
Her superhuman resignation, so
That all the world can recognize the brow
Of one who sins. For me the price will be
Immense, but still—and that is what I savor,
What makes it victory for me—hers will
Be so much greater.

DOMINGO: Now the time is ripe.
Allow me to go out and call the Duke.
                                (He exits.)

PRINCESS (astonished): What's that?

Scene 12

The Princess. Duke Alba. Domingo.

DOMINGO *(conducting the Duke into the room):*
> The information that we had,
> Duke Alba, comes too late, for the Princess
> Has just disclosed the secret to us that
> She was to learn from us.

ALBA: Well then, my presence
> Will be much less unpleasant to her now.
> I cannot trust *my* eyes. Discoveries
> Like these require a woman's penetration.

PRINCESS: You speak about discoveries?—

DOMINGO: We want
> To know then, gracious Lady, where a place
> Is and a better time for you—

PRINCESS: That too!
> Tomorrow around noon I will await you.
> But there are reasons why I must not hide
> This punishable secret any more—
> No longer try to keep it from the King.

ALBA: That was what led me here. The King must know
> About it right away. And he must hear
> About it, my Princess, from you. Whom would
> He otherwise be likely to believe
> Than his wife's strict and vigilant companion?

DOMINGO: Whom more than you, who can, as soon as she
> Desires, command him absolutely?

ALBA: I
> Am Carlos' enemy; 'tis known.

DOMINGO: And they
> Do generally assume the same of me.
> Princess of Eboli is free. Where *we*
> Must hold our tongues, her duty forces her
> To speak, the duties of her post. The King
> Will not escape us, if your hints succeed,
> And then we can complete our work.

ALBA: But soon—

It must take place immediately. Moments
Are precious. Every coming hour can bring
Commands to set out on the march.—
DOMINGO *(turning to the Princess after some consideration):*
                                        And if
One could find letters? Letters coming from
The Prince, if intercepted, they would have
To get results.—Let's see.—It's true, you know.
And it occurs to me you sleep in the
Same room wherein the Queen sleeps?
PRINCESS: Next to it,
But why should that concern me?
DOMINGO: If we had
A person versed in locks!—Would you by chance
Have noticed where she is accustomed to
Conceal her private case's key?
PRINCESS *(considering):*   That could
Accomplish something.—Yes—the key might be,
I think, where we could find it.—
DOMINGO: Notes require
A messenger.—Her retinue is large.—
If only here we'd happen on a trace.
—And gold can manage much—
ALBA: Does no one know
If Carlos has a confidant?
DOMINGO: Not *one,*
In all Madrid he has not *one.*
ALBA: How strange.
DOMINGO: Be sure you can believe me. He despises
The people of the court; I have the proof.
ALBA: How then? It just occurs to me, as I
Was coming from the chambers of the Queen,
Don Carlos stood there with a page of hers,
They spoke together secretly—
PRINCESS *(quickly interrupting):* Oh, no,
That was—that was another matter.
DOMINGO: How
Can *we* know that?—The circumstances are
Suspicious.—

(to the Duke)
Do you know this page?
PRINCESS: This is
But foolishness. And what else could it be?
I know about these things. Now we will meet
Again before I see the King.—Meanwhile
A lot may happen.
DOMINGO *(drawing her aside)*: And the King may hope?
I may report this to him? As a fact?
And how fulfillment of his heart's desire
Will bring him many lovely hours? This too?
PRINCESS: In a few days I will be taken sick,
And they will separate me from the Queen—
That is the custom at this court, you know.
Then I will stay in my own room.
DOMINGO: Success!
Now our grand game is won, and may defiance
Become the lot of every queen—
PRINCESS: But listen!
They're asking for me—for the Queen requires me.
Farewell for now!
                    (She hurries off.)

Scene 13

Alba. Domingo.
DOMINGO *(after a pause, during which he follows the Princess
    with his eyes)*: Well, Duke, what of these roses
And all your battles—
ALBA: And your God—so I
Await the lightning that will finish us!
                    (They exit.)

In a Carthusian monastery

Scene 14

Don Carlos. The Prior.
CARLOS *(to the Prior, upon entering):*
　He has already been here?—I am sorry.
PRIOR: Three times already since this morning early.
　He went away an hour ago—
CARLOS: 　　　　　　　　　But he
　Will come again? Did he not leave a message?
PRIOR: Before the noontide; that he promised.
CARLOS *(at a window, looking around at the scenery):*
　　　　　　　　　　　　　　　　Here
　Your cloister lies far from the road. In that
　Direction one can see Madrid.—And by
　Us here the Mansanares flows—The view
　Is just as I would have it.—All around
　Is quiet as a mystery.
PRIOR: 　　　　　　　Just like
　The entrance to another life.
CARLOS: 　　　　　　　　　　I have
　Entrusted, Reverend Sir, those things that are
　Most holy and most precious to me to
　Your honesty. No living soul may know
　Nor even make a guess about the man
　With *whom* I speak here *secretly.* I have
　Important reasons to repudiate
　To the whole world the man I now await:
　I chose this cloister for that reason. Are
　We safe here from betrayal and surprise?
　Remember the assurances you gave?
PRIOR: Just trust us, gracious sir; for the suspicions
　Of kings do not extend to searching *graves.*
　The ear of curiosity is laid
　On doors where passion or good fortune wait.
　The world ends at this wall.

CARLOS: Perhaps you think
  Behind this caution and behind this fear
  A guilty conscience might conceal itself?
PRIOR: I have no thought.
CARLOS: You are mistaken, Father,
  You are most surely wrong. My secret trembles
  Before mankind, not before God.
PRIOR: My son,
  That troubles us so little. In this refuge
  The guilty and the innocent are welcome.
  And whether what you do is good or evil,
  And whether it is upright or depraved—
  That you must settle in your heart.
CARLOS (*warmly*):   What we
  Attempt to hide will not profane your God.
  It is His own, His finest work.—Indeed,
  To you I can disclose it.
PRIOR: To what end?
  Absolve me from this, my dear Prince. The world
  And its effects have lain for a long time
  With seal affixed on that long journey, and
  What reason is there, in the meager time
  Before I take my leave, to break it? There
  Is little that one needs to find salvation.
  The bell for hours rings. I must go pray.
                              (*The Prior exits.*)

Scene 15

Don Carlos. Marquis of Posa enters.
CARLOS: At last, at last—
MARQUIS: Oh, what a test this is
  For the impatience of a friend! The sun
  Rose twice and twice it set again, since they
  Decided what my Carlos' fate would be.
  And only now I'll hear it.—Speak, have you
  Been reconciled?
CARLOS: With whom?

MARQUIS: With Philipp; has
  A choice been made about the Lowlands?
CARLOS: That
  The Duke will leave for them tomorrow?—That
  Is the decision, yes.
MARQUIS: That cannot be.
  Is all Madrid deceived? They say you had
  A secret audience and that the King—
CARLOS: Remained unmoved. We are forever parted,
  And more than we have ever been—
MARQUIS: You do
  Not go to Flanders?
CARLOS: No! No! No!
MARQUIS: My hope!
CARLOS: Aside from that. O Roderick, since we
  Have parted, what have I lived through! But now
  Above all I need your advice. I must
  Communicate with her—
MARQUIS: Your mother? No!
CARLOS: I have some hope.—You blanch? You must be calm.
  I should be happy and I will be. But
  About that later. Now I need advice
  On how to see her—
MARQUIS: Oh, what does this mean?
  What new and feverish dream?
CARLOS: 'Tis not a dream!
  But by the God of miracles, 'tis true!
       (*Drawing forth the King's letter to the Princess
       of Eboli*)
  It is contained in this important paper!
  The Queen is *free* before the eyes of men
  As she is, too, before the eyes of Heaven.
  There, read and then stop wondering.
MARQUIS: Now what?
  What do I see? 'Tis written by the King?
                       (*after he has read it*)
  Who got this letter?
CARLOS: It came to Princess
  Of Eboli.—Two days ago the Queen's

Page brought a letter and a key to me
That came from unknown hands. Therein I read
That I should go to a small room that was
Located in the left wing of the palace,
There where the Queen dwells, and a lady would
Await me, whom I long had loved. I go
Directly after him—

MARQUIS: You're mad! You go?

CARLOS: I do not know the writing, and I know
But one such lady. Who is there but *she,*
Who would believe that Carlos worshiped her?
O'ercome by dizziness I reach the place;
A heavenly song reverberating from
Within the room does service as my guide—
I open up the chamber door—and whom
Do I discover?—You can feel my horror.

MARQUIS: I can divine it all.

CARLOS: O Roderick,
I would have been completely lost, if I
Had not been taken up by angel's hands.
It was unhappy chance. She was deceived
By what my eyes spoke carelessly and fell
A victim to the sweet delusion that
She was herself the idol of my eyes.
Affected by my quiet suffering,
Her gentle heart, both generous and rash,
Determined to return my love to me.
Respect for her seemed to demand my silence;
But she was bold enough to break it—laid
Her lovely soul before me bare—

MARQUIS: So calmly
Can you relate that tale?—But the Princess
Saw through you. There can be no doubt, she pierced
Into the inmost secret of your love.
You have offended her, and she controls
The King.

CARLOS *(confidently):* But she is virtuous.

MARQUIS: She is;
But from her love's self-interest.—I do fear

Such virtue greatly, for I know that it
Can never reach to that ideal which,
From out the soul's maternal ground, conceived
With grace both proud and beautiful, will sprout
Spontaneously and, without the help
Of gardeners, flourish unrestrained! It is
A foreign branch, pretense of a south wind,
Transplanted in a rawer atmosphere;
An essence, breeding, call it what you will,
A profitable innocence acquired
By cunning and a hard-fought battle with
Hot blood and credited with strictest care
To Heaven, which demands it and rewards it.
Now judge yourself! Will she be able to
Forgive the Queen now that she knows a man
Has swept past her own bitterly won virtue,
To be consumed by flames of hopeless love
He offers to Don Philipp's royal wife?
CARLOS: Do you know the Princess so well?
MARQUIS: No, not
At all. I've seen her maybe twice. Still, let
Me say just one more word: it seemed that she
Was careful to avoid exposure to
All vice and *knew* how virtuous she was.
And then I looked upon the Queen. What I
Perceived in her, O Carlos, was a thing
Quite different! There was inborn, quiet glory,
With carefree indiscretion, unaware
Of excess calculation of decorum,
As far from boldness as from fear, she trod
The narrow, middle road of what is *proper*,
Heroically, not knowing she drew worship
Where she had never dreamed to gain approval.
Now, Carlos, can you recognize the face
Of your Princess here in this mirror?—She
Was resolute because she loved you; love
Was part and parcel of her virtue. But
'Twas not returned—and she will fall.

CARLOS *(vehemently):* No! No!
(after walking furiously back and forth)
I tell you, no!—If Roderick but knew
How excellently it befits him to
Rob Carlos of his highest happiness,
That he has faith in human excellence!—

MARQUIS: Do I deserve that?—No, my dearest friend,
I did not mean that, God in Heaven knows!—
This Eboli—oh, she would be an angel,
And I would bow with reverence before
Her glory, as you do yourself, if she
Had not been privy to your secret.

CARLOS: See
How foolish this fear is! What proof has she
Except those things that would disgrace her and
She will not buy the satisfaction of
Revenge with her own honor.

MARQUIS: Many have
Already brought disgrace upon themselves
To cancel out a blush.

CARLOS *(reacting vehemently):* Oh, no, that is
Too harsh, too cruel! She is proud and noble;
I know her, and I do not fear her. You
Attempt in vain to frighten off my hopes.
I want to see my mother.

MARQUIS: Now? What for?

CARLOS: I have no reason to be careful now.
I want to know my fate. You need but see
That I can speak to her!

MARQUIS: You plan to show
This letter to her? That is what you want?

CARLOS: No questions about that. Just find the means
For me to see her now!

MARQUIS *(with significance):* Did you not say
You *loved* your mother?—Are you willing then
To show this letter to her?
(Carlos looks down and is silent.)
I can read

In your expression, Carlos, something new,
And foreign to me until now.—You turn
Your gaze away from me? *Why* do you turn
Your gaze away? So it is true?—And I
Have read you rightly then? Now let me see—
    (Carlos hands him the letter. The Marquis tears it up.)
CARLOS: Are you insane?
                            (with measured irritability)
                        Well, really, I'll admit—
A lot depended on that letter.
MARQUIS: That's
How it appeared. That's why I tore it up.
    (The Marquis rests a penetrating gaze on the Prince,
    who looks at him with doubt. A long silence.)
Now tell me what a violation of
The royal bed has got to do with you—
Your love? Did Philipp threaten you? What bond
Is there between the damaged duties of
A husband and your bolder hopes? And if
He sinned where you have loved? Now I confess
I understand you. Oh, how poorly I
Have understood about your love till now.
CARLOS: What, Roderick? What do you think?
MARQUIS: I see
How I must change my thoughts. Yes, once it was—
It was so different. Then you were so rich,
So warm, so rich! The circle of the world
Could find a place within your bosom. All
Of that is gone, devoured by *one* emotion,
The victim of one small and selfish interest.
Your heart has ceased to beat. There are no tears
Left over for the wretched fortune of
The province, not one single tear is left.
O Carlos, you are desperately poor
Since you love no one but yourself!
CARLOS *(throws himself into a chair. After a pause,*
    with scarcely suppressed sobs):   I know
That you do not respect me now.
MARQUIS: Not so!

I know these transports of emotion. They
Are aberrations of more worthy feelings.
The Queen belongs to you, the King stole her
Away from you—but until now you felt
A modest lack of trust in your own rights.
Perhaps the King was worthy of her. You
Could only quietly pass judgment here.
The letter changed that. You were worthier.
With pride and joy you saw how fate decided
Against a robber and a tyrant too.
You were exultant to be called the victim;
Great souls are honored to bear unjust wrong.
But here your fantasy began to wander,
Your pride was happy, with this *satisfaction*—
Your heart was promised *hope*. You see, I knew
You did not understand yourself this time.

CARLOS *(moved):*
No, Roderick, you are quite wrong. My thoughts
Were not so noble, not by far, as you
Would gladly like to make me think.

MARQUIS: Am I
So little known to you then? Only look,
Whenever you should wander, Carlos, I
Will seek that virtue among many to
Which I can charge your error. But now we
Can understand each other better. You
Will get to see the Queen, must see her now.—

CARLOS *(embracing him):*
Oh, how you make me blush!

MARQUIS: You have my word.
Now leave the rest to me. A wild and bold,
A happy thought is rising up in my
Imagination.—You must hear it, Carlos,
From out a mouth more beautiful than mine.
I'll hurry to the Queen, and it may be
That by tomorrow we will see the outcome.
Until then, Carlos, you must not forget:
"A stroke that higher reason bore and that
Humanity's affliction urges, though

Ten thousand times defeated, must endure."
Now listen, and remember Flanders!

CARLOS: All
That you and higher virtue bid me do!

MARQUIS (*goes to the window*):
The time is up. I hear your retinue.
> (*They embrace.*)
Again we are Crown Prince and vassal.

CARLOS: You
Head for the city?

MARQUIS: Yes.

CARLOS: Wait! One more word!
How easily it is forgotten!—News
Important to you:—"Letters from Brabant
Are opened by the King." Be on your guard!
The royal post—I know this—has had secret
Commands—

MARQUIS: How do you know it?

CARLOS: Don Ramón
Of Taxis is a friend.

MARQUIS (*after a silence*): That, too! So they
Will take the detour over Germany.
> (*They exit through different doors.*)

ACT 3

The bedroom of the King

Scene 1

On the night table two candles burn. Toward the back of the room several pages on their knees, fallen asleep. The King, partly disrobed, stands in front of a table, one arm over a chair, in a reflective posture. Before him are a locket and papers.

KING: She ever was a dreamer—who is there
Who can deny it? I could never give
Her love, and still—did she appear to need it?
But now here's proof that she is false.

(Here he makes a gesture that brings him to himself.
He looks up in dismay.)
                                        Where was I?
Is no one here awake except the King?
The candles are already low? But 'tis
Not day?—Well, I have lost my slumber. Take
It, Nature, as received. A king has not
The time to make up for the nights he's lost;
I am awake; let it be day.
        (He snuffs out the candles and opens the curtain
        at a window.—As he walks to and fro he notices
        the sleeping boys and stops for a moment silently
        before them; then he pulls the bell.)
                                        Is someone
Asleep there in the entrance chamber?

Scene 2

The King. Count Lerma.
LERMA *(dismayed as he becomes aware of the King):* Is
    Your Majesty not feeling well?
KING: There was
    A fire in the left wing. Did you not hear
    The frightful uproar?
LERMA: No, Your Majesty.
KING: What? No? Then have I only dreamed a dream?
    That cannot be pure chance. Does not the Queen
    Have her bedchamber in that very wing?
LERMA: She does, Your Majesty.
KING: The dream disturbs me.
    The watches shall be doubled there in future.
    You hear me? When 'tis evening—but be sure
    It is kept very quiet.—I would not—
    Why do you scrutinize me so?
LERMA: I see
    A burning eye that makes a plea for sleep.
    Now do I dare, Your Majesty, to try
    To make you think about your precious life,

To make you think about the people who
Would find the mark of nights when no sleep comes
In your appearance disconcerting?—If
You would sleep two short morning hours—
KING *(with a distraught look):*   To sleep?
I'll sleep when I am in my tomb.—As long
As kings do sleep, they do not wear their crowns.
The man who will for his wife's sake.—No, no!
It is but slander.—Was it not a woman?
A woman who has whispered in my ear?
The name of woman is but slander, and
This crime is not a certainty until
A man confirms it.
                (to the pages, who have meanwhile awakened)
                        Call Duke Alba!
                        (Pages exit.)
                                        Come
Here, Count! Now is it true? In one heartbeat
To know it all!—Now swear, if it is true?
Am I betrayed? Now is it true?
LERMA: My great,
My noble King—
KING *(recoiling):*   'Tis King! And only King
And King again! Is there no better answer
Than empty, hollow echoes? Here I beat
Upon this rock and ask for water, water
To ease my feverish thirst—and in return
He gives me gold.
LERMA: What should be true, my King?
KING: 'Tis nothing. Leave me now.
        *(The Count is about to leave; the King calls him
        back again.)*
                                You have a wife?
Are father? Are you?
LERMA: Yes, Your Majesty.
KING: You're married and you still can dare to spend
A night of watching by your Lord? Your hair
Is silver gray but still you do not blush
To have faith in your wife's integrity?

Go home now. There you're sure to find her in
Th' incestuous embrace of your own son.
Believe your King and go—You are dismayed?
You look at me with understanding?—for
I have myself some gray hair on my head?
Unhappy man, just keep in mind that queens
Do not defile their virtue. It would mean
Your death, if you should doubt—
LERMA *(with fervor):*   Who could do that?
  In all the lands belonging to my King,
  Who is there insolent enough to breathe
  With poisonous suspicion on a queen
  So angel pure, the best of queens—
KING: The best?
  And she is also best to you? She has
  So many friends around me here, I find.
  That must have cost her quite a lot—much more
  Than it was known to me that she could give.
  You are dismissed. Now let the Duke come in.
LERMA: I hear him in the anteroom.—
                    (starts to leave)
KING *(in a milder tone)*:   Count, what
  You said before, it is no doubt the truth.
  My head is burning from a night awake.
  What I have said as if in waking dream,
  Forget it. I remain your gracious King.
          *(He extends his hand to be kissed. Lerma exits
          and opens the door for the Duke of Alba.)*

Scene 3

The King and the Duke of Alba.
ALBA *(advances toward the King with uncertainty):*
  Your order was a most surprising one—
  At this most extraordinary hour!
      (He stops short as he observes the King more closely.)
  And your appearance—
KING *(has seated himself and grasps the locket on the*

*table. He looks at the Duke for a long time in
silence.):* Is it really true?
I have no servants I can trust?
DUKE *(stops, surprised):* What's that?
KING: Oh, I am sick to death—for it is known
And no one warns me of it!
ALBA *(with a look of astonishment):* An offense
That is aimed at my King and has escaped
My eye?
KING *(shows him the letters):*
Is this hand known to you?
ALBA: It is
Don Carlos' hand.—
KING *(after a pause, during which he carefully observes
the Duke):* Do not suspicions rise
Before your mind? You said he was ambitious?
And was it just ambition, only this,
That I should fear?
ALBA: Ambition is a large—
A spacious word in which an infinite
Amount can lie.
KING: And is there nothing special
You can disclose?
ALBA: Your Majesty entrusts
The Empire to my total vigilance.
And to the Empire I do fully pledge
My private knowledge and my judgment. What
I otherwise suspect or think or know
Belongs to me alone. These sacred things
That any bartered slave, no different from
The servant of the King of the whole earth,
Retains the right to keep—not everything
That seems apparent to *my* soul is ripe
Enough to tell my King. But if he must
Be satisfied, then I must beg that he
Not ask as master.
KING *(gives him the letters):*
Read these!
ALBA *(reads and turns to the King alarmed):*

                                        Who was this—
This madman, who would put this frightful piece
Of paper into my King's hand?
KING: What's that?
  You know, then, who is meant therein?—The name
  Is, as I know, not mentioned on the paper.
ALBA *(stepping back surprised)*:
  I was too quick.
KING: You know it?
ALBA *(after some consideration)*: It is out.
  My Lord commands and I cannot retreat—
  I cannot take it back, I know the one.
KING *(rising, with awful emotion)*:
  Oh, may that frightful god of vengeance help
  Me to discover a new death!—So clear,
  So world-renowned, so loud is this event
  That one divines it at first glance already,
  Without the trouble to investigate—
  That is too much! I did not know that! No!
  So I am then the last to find it out!
  The last one in my Empire—
ALBA *(throws himself at the King's feet)*: I admit
  That I am guilty, gracious King. I am
  Ashamed a coward's cunning told me to
  Be still, although the honor of my King
  And truth and justice importuned me loud
  That I should speak—although all men desire
  To keep their peace, and the enchantment of
  Great beauty does contrive to bind their tongues,
  Still let me dare these words, and if I know
  A son's ingratiating declarations
  Or the allurement of seductive kinds
  And tears and weeping of a wife—
KING *(quick and forceful)*:   Arise.
  You have my royal word—Arise and you
  May speak and never fear.
ALBA *(standing up)*:   Your Majesty
  Perhaps will think upon that incident
  There in the garden at Aranjuez.

You found the Queen had been deserted by
Her ladies—looking quite perturbed—alone
In a remotely lying bower.
KING: Ha!
What do I hear? Continue!
ALBA: The Marquise
Of Mondecar was exiled from the land
When she was generous and sacrificed
Herself unto her Queen—But now we are
Informed that the Marquise did nothing more
Than that which she was told to do and that
The Prince had been there.
KING (*starting up frightfully*): What? The Prince was there?
Then surely—
ALBA: In the sand the footprint of
A man who entered from the left side of
The bower, disappearing in a grotto.
A handkerchief was found there that the Prince
Had lost, awakening a suspicion, for
The gardener met the Prince there, and it was,
As if it had been reckoned to the minute,
Exactly when Your Royal Majesty
Appeared there in the bower.
KING (*coming out of a dark revery*): And she cried
When I showed my dismay! She made me blush
Before the gathering of my court and made
Me blush to mine own self—My God! I stood
As one condemned before her very virtue—
          (*a long and deep silence. He sits down and
          covers his face.*)
Yes, my Duke Alba—You are right—That could
Cause me to do a dreadful deed—Just leave
Me for a moment to myself.
ALBA: My King,
Not even that was all—
KING (*snatching up the papers*): Not even that?
And that? And even that besides? And this
Loud harmony of damning evidence?
Oh, it is brighter than the light—Those things

That I have known for a long time—The mischief
Had its beginning then when I received
Her in Madrid from your own hands—I still
Can see how her look dwelled in pallid fright
Upon my graying hair. That was the time
That it began, this base deceit!

ALBA: His bride
    Was lost forever to the Prince as mother.
    They had indulged already in vain hopes,
    Had come to know each other's fiery feelings,
    Which her position now forbade. The fear
    Had been o'ercome, the fear that does attend
    All first avowals, and seduction spoke
    Thus bolder in those confidential scenes
    Of things allowed in memory. Brought close
    Through harmony of thought and of their years,
    Made angry by the same compulsion, they
    Bowed to the turmoil of this daring passion.
    Here politics encroached upon their fancy;
    Can we believe, Your Majesty, that she
    Could recognize the power of the state?
    That it was lust compelled her to examine
    More carefully decisions of the council?
    She was prepared for love and she received—
    A crown.

KING (*offended and with bitterness*):
                    You can discriminate so very—
So wisely, Duke—I am amazed at your
Great eloquence. I thank you.
                    (*rising, cold and proud*):
                                        You are right;
The Queen was certainly remiss when she
Concealed from me the contents of these letters—
And kept a secret of the culpable
Appearance of Don Carlos in the garden.
She was remiss, but from false kindness I
Will find a punishment.
                    (*He pulls on the bell.*)
                                        Who else is there

Out in the anteroom?—I have, Duke Alba,
No further need for you. Dismissed.

ALBA: Have I
Displeased Your Majesty a second time
Because of excess zeal?

KING (to a page who enters): Domingo may
Come in.
                    (The page exits.)
        I will forgive you, even though
You spent almost two minutes of my time
In which you made *me* fearful of a crime
That can however fall instead on *you*.
                    (Alba withdraws.)

Scene 4

The King. Domingo.

KING (walks back and forth a couple of times to
collect himself):

DOMINGO (enters a few moments after the Duke leaves,
approaches the King, whom he watches for a
while in solemn stillness):
How happy, how astonished, Majesty,
Am I to see you so composed.

KING: Astonished—

DOMINGO: May Providence be thanked that all my fears
Had no foundation. I may hold that hope
Now even more.

KING: You were afraid? What need
Was there to be afraid?

DOMINGO: Your Majesty,
I do not dare conceal that I have known,
Already of a secret—

KING: Have I then
Expressed the wish to share a secret with you?
Who could be so impertinent to me?
It is extremely bold, I swear.

DOMINGO: My King,
   The place and the occasion where I heard it,
   The seal, whereunder I discovered it,
   At least will soon absolve me from impertinence.
   In the confessional it was entrusted—
   Entrusted to me as a sin that weighed
   Upon the conscience of the lady who
   Has found it out and seeks the grace of Heaven.
   The Princess weeps too late about a deed,
   For which she has good reason to expect
   Results most frightful for her Queen.
KING: In truth?
   Her heart is good—You guessed exactly right
   The reason why I had you called. You shall
   Now lead me through this dismal labyrinth,
   In which I have been tossed by my blind zeal.
   I will expect the truth from you. Speak out.
   What should I now believe and what conceal?
   I will demand the truth from you.
DOMINGO: My Lord,
   If in my calling I were not enjoined
   To practice the sweet duty of forbearance,
   I would implore Your Majesty no less,
   I would implore you for your peace of mind
   To silence this discovery—Forever
   Give up investigation of a secret
   That never can develop happily.
   What is now known can always be forgiven.
   The King need say one word alone—the Queen
   Has never erred. The will of majesty
   Grants virtue as it does good fortune—thus
   The constant calmness of my King alone
   Can fell the rumors that are sanctioned by
   This slander to a great extent.
KING: The rumors?
   Concerning me? Among my people?
DOMINGO: Lies!
   So damnable these lies! I swear it. But

There certainly will be some cases where
The people's credence, though 'tis never proved,
Becomes as weighty as the truth.
KING: My God,
And here it would be but—
DOMINGO: A name that's good
Is that one precious bit of property
For which the Queen must be in competition
With any common wife—
KING: For that, I hope,
There is no need for us to tremble?
          *(His gaze rests uncertainly on Domingo. After
          a silence)*
                                        Chaplain,
You are about to tell me something worse.
Do not delay it. I already read
It in your face, filled with misfortune's news.
Just out with it! No matter what it is!
Don't leave me to writhe longer on this rack!
What do the people think?
DOMINGO: Sire, once again
The people can be wrong—they must be wrong.
What they believe should not affect the King—
But that they have already gone so far
To claim such things is true—
KING: What? Must I beg
Of you so long to get this drop of poison?
DOMINGO: The people hold still in their memory
That month that brought Your Royal Majesty
Near unto death—and then they read in but
The space of thirty weeks about the happy
Confinement—
          *(The King rises and pulls the bell. The Duke
          of Alba enters. Domingo, taken aback)*
                    You surprise me, Sir!
KING *(advancing toward the Duke of Alba):* Toledo!
You are a man. Protect me from this priest.
DOMINGO *(He and the Duke look at each other in embarrass-
ment. After a pause):*

If there had been a way we could have known
This news would be suspected when they saw
The messenger—

KING: Did you say bastard? Did you?
I scarcely left a deathbed, so you said,
When, lo, she was with child?—Now, how was that?
It was, if I am not mistaken, then
That you required full praise be given in
The churches to Saint Dominic because
He had produced this miracle for me?—
What once was miracle, what is it now?
So you deceived me then or lie today.
What is it that you want me to believe?
Oh, I see through you. If the plot had been
Developed at that time, well, then the saint
Had done without the credit—

ALBA: Plot!

KING: And do
You two now meet with such unprecedented
Harmonious opinion and you still
Do not agree? And do you think you can
Convince me of it? Me? I should perhaps
Have not perceived how passionately and
How eagerly you threw yourselves into
This crime and gloated over every pain
Of mine and every rage so joyously?
Should I not note the Duke, consumed with zeal,
Advancing hastily towards favor, which
Should be allotted to my son? And how
This pious man defends a paltry grudge
By using royal anger's giant arm?
Am I the bow, or is that what you think,
Which you can bend and tighten at your pleasure?—
But still I have my will—and if I should
Begin to doubt, allow me to begin
With you.

ALBA: We did not think our loyalty
Would be thus understood.

KING: Your loyalty!

With loyalty one warns of threatening wrongs,
But vengeance speaks of things already done.
Now tell me what I've won through your desire
To serve me!—Still, if what you say is true,
What is there but the pain of parting and
The dismal triumph of revenge?—But no,
You only are afraid, you give me vague
Insinuations—on the edge of Hell
You bid me stay and you depart.

DOMINGO: Then is
It possible to give you proof when what
You see does not convince you?

KING (*after a long pause, turning to Domingo with
gravity and solemnity*):   I will bring
Together all the nobles of my land
And sit myself on the tribunal. You
Will stand before them all—have you the courage?—
Accuse her of illicit intercourse!
And she shall be condemned—no mercy—she
And the Infante both shall die—but—mark
You! If she proves her innocence—you die!
Will you make such a sacrifice to find
The truth? Decide! You cannot? You grow dumb?
You cannot choose? That is a liar's zeal.

ALBA (*who has stood silently at a distance, coldly
and calmly*):
I will.

KING (*turns around surprised and looks at the Duke
fixedly for a time*):
         Oh, that is bold! But it occurs
To me that you have risked your life upon
The field of battle for far lesser things—
Have risked it as one plays a game of dice,
For the absurdity of fame—And what
Is life to you?—I will not sacrifice
The royal blood to such a madman, who
Has nothing more to hope for than to give
His trifling life up nobly—I reject

Your sacrifice. Now go—just go—and wait
In my reception room for further orders.
              (Both exit.)

Scene 5

The King alone.
KING: Give me a man, O my good Providence—
  You have already given me so much.
  Now give me but a man. You are alone,
  Your eye examines what is hidden to me,
  I ask you for a friend; for I am not,
  As you, omniscient. The assistants, whom
  You have appointed for me, you know well
  What they are to me. What they earn from me
  They have deserved. Their tame iniquities,
  Kept well in check, have served my purposes,
  Just as your storms can purify the earth.
  I need the truth—to dig its silent source
  Out from the gloomy rubble of what's false
  Is not the lot of kings. But give me just
  That one unusual man with heart both pure
  And open, with a spirit bright and eyes
  Unbiased, who can help me find it—I'll
  Shake out the lots; among the thousands that
  Will flutter round the sphere of majesty,
  Oh, let me find the one.
           (He opens a case and takes out a tablet. After
           he has turned the pages for a while)
                     They are but names—
  'Tis only names stand here, no mention of
  The services for which they owe their place
  Upon this sheet—and what can be forgotten
  More easily than gratitude? But here
  Upon this other sheet I read precisely
  Appended every small offense. But why?
  That is not good. Does memory of vengeance

Require, perhaps, assistance?
                              (reads on)
                                        Here's Count Egmont?
Why is he here?—The victory at Saint Quentin
Was long ago. I'll put him with the dead.
            (He erases the name and writes it on the other
            sheet. After he has read some more)
Marquis of Posa?—Posa?—Posa?—I
Can scarcely call this man to mind at all!
And underlined three times—that is to show
I had intended something great for him!
And is it possible this man withdrew,
Avoiding contact with his royal debtor?
He is, by God, the only man in the
Whole circle of my colonies who does
Not need me! But if he were greedy or
Ambitious, he had long since come before me.
Then shall I take a chance with this strange man?
Who does not need me he will have truth for me.
                              (Exits.)

The reception room

Scene 6

Don Carlos in conversation with the Prince of Parma. The Dukes
of Alba, Feria, and Medina Sidonia. Court of Lerma and other
grandees with papers in their hands. All await the King.
MEDINA SIDONIA *(visibly avoided by all the others, turns to the*
    Duke of Alba who, alone and brooding, walks back and forth):
    You've spoken with Our Lord just now, my Duke.—
    How did you find his humor?
ALBA: Very bad
    For you and for the news you bring.
MEDINA SIDONIA: It was
    For me far better under English fire
    Than on this paving here.

(Carlos, who has been looking at him with sympathy, approaches now and presses his hand.)
                                        My warmest thanks,
My Prince, for these most generous tears. You see
How everyone avoids me here. Now has
My downfall been determined on.
CARLOS: Hope for
The best. You have my father's mercy, friend,
And your own innocence.
MEDINA SIDONIA: I lost a fleet
For him, like none that ever sailed the sea—
Compared to seventy sunken galleons, what
Can be the value of this head?—But, Prince—
Five sons, as promising as you—that breaks
My heart—

Scene 7

The King enters fully clothed. The same persons. (All remove their hats and make way on both sides, thus forming a half circle around him. Silence.)
KING *(glancing over the whole circle):*
                    Now cover all your heads.
        *(Don Carlos and the Prince of Parma approach first
        and kiss the King's hand. He turns to the latter
        with some friendliness without seeming to notice
        his son.)*
                                        Your mother
Desires to know, Nephew, if we are pleased
With you here in Madrid.
PARMA: She should not ask
Before I have done service in a battle.
KING: Just be content. Your turn is bound to come
At last, when this crop has been harvested.
                    (to the Duke of Feria)
What do you bring?
FERIA *(kneeling before the King):* The Grand Commander of

The Calatrava order died this morning.
I bring his knight's cross back to you.

KING (*takes the decoration and looks around the whole
circle*): Who will
Be worthiest of all to wear it?
> (*He beckons Alba, who kneels down before him, and
> hangs the order around his neck.*)
> Duke,
You are my first commander—be no *more*,
And then my favor will be with you ever.
> (*He notices the Duke of Medina Sidonia.*)
Behold, my Admiral!

MEDINA SIDONIA (*approaches unsteadily and kneels before
the King with bowed head*): This, my great King,
Is all of the Armada and the youth
Of Spain I do bring back again.

KING (*after a long silence*): Our God
Is over me.—I sent you forth against
Mere mortals, not a storm and hidden reefs—
I welcome you back to Madrid.
> (*He extends his hand to be kissed.*)
> My thanks
That you preserved a worthy servant for me.
For this, my grandees, I do recognize him
And want to know that he is recognized.
> (*He signals him to stand up and put on his hat—
> then he turns to the others.*)
Now what is left to do?
> (*to Don Carlos and the Prince of Parma*)
> I thank you, Princes.
> (*They exit. The remaining grandees approach and,
> kneeling, hand the King their papers. He thumbs
> through them and hands them to the Duke of Alba.*)
Lay these before me later—Am I done?
> (*No one answers.*)
How does it happen that among my nobles
Marquis of Posa never shows himself?
I know quite well that this Marquis has served

Me with great honor. Is he still alive?
Why is he never here?
LERMA: The Chevalier
Has recently returned from journeys, which
He undertook to make through all of Europe.
He is now in Madrid and only waits
Upon your public day in order to
Prostrate himself before his Lord and King.
ALBA: Marquis of Posa?—Right! He is that knight
Of Malta who, Your Majesty, is said
To have accomplished bold and wondrous deeds.
When at the summons of the order's master
The knights all took their places on the island
That Suliman lay siege to, it was then
The eighteen-year-old youth abruptly left
His studies in Alcala's halls and, though
Not called, he stood before Valetta, and
He cried, "The cross was bought for me; now I
Will earn it." He was one of forty knights
Who held the castle of St. Elmo at
High noon against Piali, Ulucciali,
Mustafa, and Hassim as they attacked
The walls three times. But when they had been scaled
At last and all the knights had fallen there
Around him, then he threw himself into
The sea and came, the lone survivor, to
Valetta. When the enemy two months
Thereafter left the island, he returned
To end the studies that he had begun.
FERIA: And this Marquis of Posa later made
Discovery of that notorious plot
In Catalonia and it was by
His skill alone that he preserved this most
Important province for the Crown.
KING: I am
Astonished. For what kind of man is this
Who's done so much, and of the three who spoke
Not one has any envy? It is certain

The character of this man is uncommon
Or nonexistent—I must talk to him
Because it is so strange.
                              (to Duke Alba)
                              When mass is over,
Direct him to my private room.
                    (The Duke exits. The King calls Feria.)
                              And you
Will take my place here at the council meeting.
                              (He exits.)
FERIA: Today our Lord is very gracious.
MEDINA SIDONIA: You
    Might say: He is a god!—He was to me.
FERIA: How much you do deserve your fortune. I
    Can sympathize most heartily.
ONE OF THE GRANDEES: I, too.
A SECOND: And truly, I as well.
A THIRD: My heart swells for you.
    You are deserving, Admiral.
THE FIRST: The King
    Dealt not just graciously with you—but justly.
LERMA *(to Medina Sidonia as they exit)*:
    With just two words you suddenly are rich!
                              (All exit.)

The King's private chamber

Scene 8

Marquis of Posa and the Duke of Alba.
MARQUIS *(entering)*:
    He wants to see me? Me?—That cannot be.
    You are mistaken in the name—What should
    He want with me?
ALBA: He wants to get to know you.
MARQUIS: From idle curiosity.—Oh, then
    It is a shame to lose the moment—Life
    Is gone astonishingly soon.

ALBA: I leave
You to your lucky star. You can command
The King. This moment is for you to use
As well as possible, and you will have
Yourself, and just yourself, to blame, if it
Is lost.

                    (He leaves.)

Scene 9

The Marquis alone.

MARQUIS: That is well spoken, Duke. A man
  Must seize the moment, for it comes but *once*.
  In truth, this courtier does give me good
  Advice—and though in his interpretation
  Perhaps it may not be, it is in mine.
                    (He walks back and forth.)
  How do I come to be here?—Can it be
  Coincidence's whimsical caprice
  That shows me my reflection in *this* mirror?
  Among a million others, why just me,
  The most unlikely one, it grasped and then
  Revived me in the memory of the King?
  It was but chance? Perhaps 'twas more—and what
  Is chance except the unwrought stone that can
  Be brought to life beneath the sculptor's hand?
  But chance is only Providence—and man
  Must shape it to his ends.—Now, what the King
  May want with me is all the same! I know
  What I—what I want with the King—and if
  I can throw boldly but a spark of truth
  Into this despot's soul—how fruitful that
  Might be in Providence's hand. So what
  At first was whimsical to me might be
  Both sensible and useful. Be or not be—
  No matter. I will act in this belief.
        (He walks back and forth in the room a few times
        and finally pauses in quiet contemplation before

*a painting. The King appears in the neighboring
room, where he gives some commands. Thereupon
he enters, stops by the door, and observes the
Marquis for a while without being noticed.)*

Scene 10

The King and the Marquis of Posa.
KING *(regards him with a look of surprise)*:
  You've talked with me before?
MARQUIS: No.
KING: You have made
  Yourself deserving to the Crown. But why
  Do you avoid my thanks? There are so many
  Who crowd into my thoughts. There is but one
  Who can know everything. It was your right
  To seek attention from the King. Wherefore
  Have you not done so?
MARQUIS: There have passed but two
  Days, Sire, since I have made my way back to
  The kingdom.
KING: I do not intend to be
  Indebted to my servants. Now you may
  Request a favor.
MARQUIS: I have benefit of law.
KING: Well, even murderers have that.
MARQUIS: How much more then
  A proper citizen. But I'm content.
KING *(to himself)*:
  Self-confidence and courage here, by God!
  That was to be expected. I will have
  My Spaniards proud. I rather like it when
  The goblet's foaming over.—I have heard
  That you have left my service.
MARQUIS: Only to
  Make room for someone better, do I leave.
KING: That is too bad. When heads like yours are idle,
  How great the loss is for my state.—Perhaps

You are afraid that you will miss the sphere
Your intellect is worthy of.
MARQUIS: Oh, no!
For I am certain that the expert judge,
Well trained in human spirits and their substance,
Will understand with just a single glance
What I can do for him, what not. And I
Perceive with humble gratitude the kindness
Your Royal Majesty attempts to heap
Upon me with your fine opinions of me,
Still—

                    (He pauses.)

KING: You deliberate.
MARQUIS: I am—I must
Confess, my Lord, not wholly ready now
To clothe in words of servitude what I
As citizen of this wide world have thought.—
For at that time when I dissolved forever
Allegiance to the Crown, I thought that I
Was liberated from the need to give
Accounting for the reasons for this step.
KING: And are these reasons then so poor? And do
You fear they are a risk to you?
MARQUIS: If I
Should have the time to tell them all, my life
At most. But I'll expose the truth, if you'll
Deny this favor to me, for the choice
Remains to me between incurring your
Disfavor and your scorn—Must I decide,
Then I would rather be a criminal,
Sire, in your eyes, than be a fool.
KING *(with an expectant air):*   Well, then?
MARQUIS: —I cannot be a courtier.
             (The King regards him with surprise.)
                                        I do
Not want to cheat the purchaser, Sire.—If
You deem me worthy of employment, you
Will only want my actions in the main.
You'll want my arm and courage in the field.

You'll want my head in council. But my deeds
And their approval by the Crown will not
Become the purpose of my deeds. For me,
However, virtue is its own reward.
The happiness the King may plant through me
I will create myself, and it will be
My pleasure and my choice when it should be
But duty. Can that be your view? Can you
Endure a strange creator in your own
Creations? Should I stoop to be a chisel,
When I can be the sculptor?—I do love
Humanity, but in a monarchy
I dare love no one but myself.

KING: Your ardor
Is laudable. You might initiate
Much good, and how you do it can mean much
To patriot as well as wise man. Seek
That office in my kingdom that will most
Enable you to satisfy at will
This noble urge.

MARQUIS: There is not one.

KING: How's that?

MARQUIS: The things Your Majesty distributes through
My hand—can that bring human happiness?—
Is that the same as happinesss that my
Pure love can grant to humankind?—Before
Such happiness the Crown would tremble—No!
The royal policy created this
Anew—a happiness that *it* is rich
Enough to share, and in the hearts of men
It stills new forces with this happiness.
It strikes its coinage with the truth, *that* truth
That it can bear. Repudiated is
Each impress that does not resemble it.
But what is profit to the Crown—is that
Enough for me? Can my fraternal love
Redeem itself diminishing my brother?
How do I know he's happy—when he may
Not think? So do not choose me, Sire, to spread

That happiness that *you* will stamp for us.
I must decline to spread your mark about.
I cannot be a courtier.
KING *(rather quickly):*   You are
   A Protestant.
MARQUIS *(after some thought):* Your faith, Sire, is the same
   As mine.
                     (after a pause)
   I am misunderstood. That is
What I had feared. And when you see me draw
The veil of majesty with my own hand,
Who can assure you that what I have ceased
To fear will still be holy to me. I
Am dangerous because I thought about
Myself. I am not that. My wishes, Sire,
Die here.
              (laying his hand on his breast)
              The foolish madness of these times
Of innovation, which can only make
The burden of those chains they cannot break
The greater, will not heat my blood. The age
Has not matured enough for my ideal.
I am a citizen of times to come.
Why should an image spoil your rest, when but
Your breath obliterates it?
KING: Am I then
   The first to know you from this side?
MARQUIS: From this
   One—yes!
KING *(rises, takes a few steps, and stops across from the*
   Marquis): At least this tone is something new!
And flattery can pale while imitation
Humiliates an able man.—This once
To take a sample of the opposite.
Why not? Surprises can end happily.—
If that is what you want, then I'll prepare
A different service to the Crown—
A spirit that is strong.
MARQUIS: I hear you do

Not think too much of human dignity
And even in the speech of free men see,
My Lord, the art of flattery. It seems
To me I know who makes this possible.
'Tis Man himself compels you to it; he
Has willingly renounced nobility,
And willingly has placed himself upon
A lower level. In alarm he flees
Before the ghosts of his own inner value,
Is happy with his poverty and with
His timid wisdom decorates his chains
And calls it virtue if he bears them well.
Thus you could overcome the world and thus
Man was delivered to your noble father.
How could you have respect for man in such
A sad, maimed state as this?

KING: A bit of truth,
 I find, is in these words.

MARQUIS: But what a shame!
 For when you turned the work of our Creator
 Into the work of your own hands and gave
 Yourself to this new-molded living creature
 As God—then did you only overlook
 One thing: You had yourself remained a man—
 A man from our Creator's Hand. And *you*
 As mortal had to suffer, to desire;
 You need compassion—and before a God
 A man can only sacrifice and pray
 And tremble! A regrettable exchange!
 Unhappy twist of Nature!—When you cast
 Mankind away to music of your lyre,
 Who then could share your harmony?

KING: (By God,
 He strikes me to the soul!)

MARQUIS: But yet to you
 This sacrifice is meaningless. In this
 You likewise are unique—a class alone—
 At such a price you are a god.—How dreadful
 If that were *not* the case—if for this price,

The happiness of millions trampled by
Your foot, you had gained nothing! If the freedom
You were destroying was the one thing
Alone that could mature your wishes? Let
Me go, I beg you; my emotion draws
Me on. My heart is full, and the temptation
Is great to stand before the only one
To whom I wish to open it.

> (*Count Lerma enters and speaks a few words quietly
> with the King, who motions him to leave and remains
> sitting in his previous position.*)

KING: (*to the Marquis, after Lerma has gone*): Speak freely!
MARQUIS (*after a silence*):
I feel, Sire—the importance—
KING: Finish speaking!
You had still more to say to me.
MARQUIS: My Lord!
Most recently I came from Flanders and
Brabant.—Such rich and blooming provinces!
A vigorous, a noble people—and
A good one—to be father of this people
That must, I thought, be godlike!—Then I saw
A pile of human bones consumed by fire—

> (*At this point he becomes silent; his eyes rest
> upon the King, who tries to return the gaze but,
> disconcerted and embarrassed, looks down.*)

But you are right. You must do this. And that
You *can* do what you understand you must
Has filled me full of dreadful wonder. What
A shame that, as he welters in his blood,
The victim cannot really sing a hymn
Of praise to him who does the sacrificing!
That only men—not creatures of a higher
Variety—create world history!—
More gentle times will drive out Philipp's era
And bring a milder scene where citizens'
Prosperity abides in peace with princes,
A miser state will use its children well,
Necessity will then become humane.

KING: When, do you think, that this humane time would
    Have come, if I had trembled at the evil
    Of this one? Look around my Spain. Here blooms
    The fortune of the citizens in peace,
    And I do grant *this very peace* to Flanders.
MARQUIS *(quickly):*
    It is the peace of graveyards! Do you hope
    To end what you began? And do you hope
    To put a stop to Christianity's
    Most timely change, the universal spring
    That renovates the world's appearance? *You,*
    Alone in all of Europe, will yourself
    Obstruct the wheel of destiny that rolls
    At its top speed and never stops? You will
    Insert a human arm into its spokes?
    You will not! Thousands have already fled,
    Though poor, still happy, from these lands. You've lost
    For their beliefs those citizens who were
    Most noble. Queen Elizabeth receives
    These fugitives with open arms, and Britain
    Is blossoming most fruitfully with our
    Land's arts. Granada lies deserted by
    The industry of the new Christians and
    All Europe does rejoice to see its foe
    Lie bleeding from its self-inflicted wounds.
        (The King is moved; the Marquis notices this and
        moves a few steps closer.)
    You mean to plant seeds for eternity
    And sow but death? An action so contrived
    Lasts not beyond the life of its creator.
    You cultivate for man's ingratitude—
    In vain contend with Nature in harsh strife,
    Have offered up your great and noble life
    In vain to these most devastating schemes.
    But man is more than you have held him for;
    For he will break the bonds of his long slumber
    And reassert what is his holy right.
    To join a *Nero,* a *Busiris* will

He relegate your name, which pains me, for
I know that you were good.

KING: What has made you
So certain of these things?

MARQUIS *(with passion):*   By the Almighty!
Yes—yes—I will repeat it. Give us what
You took from us again! And generous,
As strong, let happiness flow from your horn
Of plenty—let men's souls mature within
This universe of yours. Oh, give us what
You took from us again, and you will be,
Among a million other kings, the King.
> *(He approaches him boldly, all the while directing
> his gaze fixedly and ardently upon him.)*
If only all the eloquence of those,
The thousands who participate in this
Great hour, could hover on my lips, that it
Might fan the flicker that I notice in
Those eyes into a flame! Relinquish now
This most incongruous idolatry
That will destroy us. Be to us a model
Of what is true and endless. Never has
One mortal ever owned so much that he
Could use in such a godlike way. The kings
Of Europe swear allegiance to the House
Of Spain. Then lead the way for Europe's kings.
A single stroke done by your pen and newly
Created is the earth. Give us the right
To think with freedom.—
> *(throwing himself at the King's feet)*
KING *(surprised, turning his face away and then fixing
his eyes on him again):* Strange and wondrous dreamer!
But still—arise—I—

MARQUIS: Look around yourself
In His most heavenly Nature. It is founded
In freedom—and how rich it is because
Of freedom! He, the Great Creator, casts
A worm into a drop of dew and lets,

Within the dead confines of putrefaction,
Free will prevail—*your* creation is
So narrow and so poor! The rustle of
One leaf alarms the lord of Christendom—
For *you* must tremble before virtue. *He*—
That He might not intrude on freedom's joyous
Appearance—rather lets the awful host
Of evil rage within His universe—
Of Him, the Artist, one is not aware,
Discreetly veiled within eternal laws;
A man whose thoughts are free sees them instead
Of Him. Why God? he says. The world's enough.
And prayers of Christians do not glorify
Him more than these free thinkers' blasphemy.

KING: And will you undertake to reproduce
Within my lands such an exalted model
That shows our mortal state?

MARQUIS: You are the one
To do it. Who besides? And to the people's
Well-being dedicate your royal strength,
Which has so long employed the Throne's great power
For its own profit—reestablish then
The lost nobility of humankind.
The common man may be again what he
Has been, the purpose of the Crown—no duty
Confines him but his brother's sacred rights.
Now if man has come to himself again,
Awakened to the feeling of his worth—
Sublime and proud the virtues that increase
With freedom—Then, my Lord, when you have made
Your realm into the happiest on earth—
Then 'tis your duty to control the world.

KING (*after a long silence*):
I let you finish what you had to say—
I realize the world that's in this head
Is different than in other heads—then, too,
I will not measure you by foreign rules.
I am the first to whom you have disclosed
Your inner self. I think so, for I know it.

For this restraint, that you have kept in silence
Up to this day these views, although they are
So ardently embraced—because of this
Most modest prudence, I will promise to
Forget, young man, that I have heard them and
How I have heard them. Now you may arise.
I would refute the youth who acts too rashly
From venerable age and not as King.
I would because I want to—even what
Is deadly can, I find, in milder natures
Be purified to something better.—But
You must avoid my Inquisition.—I
Would be so sorry—
MARQUIS: Really? Would you?
KING *(lost in contemplating his appearance):* I
Have never seen a man like you.—Oh, no,
Marquis! You touch me much too much. I do
Not want to be a Nero—will not be
One—not to you. And every happiness
Shall not in my rule wither and dry up.
But you yourself, you shall have leave to be
A man within my sight.
MARQUIS *(quickly):*   And what of all
My fellow citizens?—O Sire! it was
Not for myself, I did not want to plead
My cause. What of your subjects, Sire?—
KING: Now if
You know so well how times to come will judge
Me, then you must learn from yourself how I
Will take the part of men when I have found
A man.
MARQUIS: Oh! The most righteous of all kings
Should not become so suddenly the most
Unrighteous—In your Flanders thousands are
Much better men than I. 'Tis just that *you*—
May I speak frankly here, my noble King?—
In this more placid picture *you* now see
What freedom is for the first time.
KING *(with tempered severity):*   No more

Upon this subject, my young man.—I know
You will think differently when you have learned
To know mankind as I.—But still I would
Not like to say farewell to you. How shall
I start to bind you to myself?

MARQUIS: Just leave
Me as I am. What would I be to you,
If you could bribe me, Sire?

KING: This pride I will
Not tolerate. From this day on you are
In my employ.—Make no objection! I
Will have it so.

                         (after a pause)
                         But how? What did I want?
The truth, was that not what I wanted then?
And here, I find, is something more—for you
Have found me out upon my throne, Marquis.
Not also in my house?

                    (as the Marquis appears to reflect on this)
                                        I understand
You. But—if I were the least fortunate
Of fathers, could I not be fortunate
As husband still?

MARQUIS: A son who's promising,
Possessed of the most charming consort, if
Those things can give the right to any mortal
To own his name, Sire, then you are in both
Most fortunate.

KING *(with a sad expression)* No, I am not, Marquis!
And that I am not, I have never felt
More deeply than just now—

                    (his melancholy gaze lingering on the Marquis)
MARQUIS: The Prince's thoughts
Are noble. I have ever found it thus.

KING: But I have not—and that which he has taken
From me no crown can give me back again—
A virtuous queen!

MARQUIS: Who can there be who dares
To say that, Sire?

KING: The world! The gossips! I

Myself!—There are here witnesses who do
Condemn her undeniably; there are
Still others in existence who have let
Me fear the worst.—But, oh, how difficult
It is for me to think this is the truth.
Who can accuse her?—For if *she*, if she
Should find it possible to so degrade
Herself, how much more possible it is
For me to think an Eboli defames
Her? Does the priest not hate her and my son?
Is Alba not intent upon revenge?
My wife is worth more than the lot.
MARQUIS: My Lord,
There is still something in that woman's soul
That is sublime beyond appearances,
Beyond all calumny—and it goes by
The name of woman's virtue.
KING: Yes, I say
That, too. As much as one berates the Queen,
To sink so low would cost me dear. Though they
Would have me think so, honor's holy bonds
Are not so freely rent. You are a judge
Of men, Marquis. Long have I needed such
A man, and you are good and cheerful and
You still can be a judge of men.—For that
I've chosen you—
MARQUIS (*surprised and alarmed*): You've chosen me?
KING: You stand
Before your lord and ask for nothing for
Yourself. Now that is new to me—You will
Be just. Your eye will not be led astray
By passion.—Find your way close to my son.
Examine the Queen's heart. You will receive
My full authority to speak with her
Alone. Now leave me!
                    (*He pulls the bell.*)
MARQUIS: If I go with only
One hope fulfilled—then this day is the best
Of my whole life.
KING (*extends his hand to be kissed*):

It is not one that I
Consider wasted in my own.
(The Marquis rises and exits. Count Lerma enters.)
The knight
Will henceforth be admitted unannounced.

ACT 4

Hall in the Queen's chambers

Scene 1

The Queen. The Duchess Olivarez. The Princess of Eboli. The Countess Fuentes and other ladies.

QUEEN *(to the Chief Stewardess, as she rises):*
  The key could not be found, then? You will have
  To break the cabinet's lock for me, and do
  It right away—
                    (As she notices the Princess of Eboli, who
                    approaches her and kisses her hand)
                    Princess, we welcome you!
  I'm happy that you are recovered now—
  A little pale—
FUENTES *(somewhat spitefully):*
                    The fault of the high fever
  That grips the nerves with such amazing strength.
  Is that not so, Princess?
QUEEN: I have so wished
  To visit you, my dear.—But I was not
  Allowed to.
OLIVAREZ: The Princess of Eboli,
  At least, was not in need of company.
QUEEN: That I believe. What is it? You are trembling.
EBOLI: 'Tis nothing—nothing. May I beg, my Queen,
  For your permission to depart—
QUEEN: You are
  Concealing from us that you are more ill

Than you would like for us to think. To stand
Is even hard for you. Please help her, Countess,
To take a seat upon this cushion here.
EBOLI: Outside I will be better.
                    (She exits.)
QUEEN: Follow her
Please, Countess—Such a seizure!
        *(A page enters and speaks with the Duchess, who
        then turns to the Queen.)*
OLIVAREZ: The Marquis
Of Posa comes, Your Majesty, and he
Comes from His Majesty, the King.
QUEEN: I will
Await him.

Scene 2

Marquis of Posa. The others as before.
(The Marquis kneels before the Queen, who motions him to rise.)
QUEEN: Tell me what my Lord commands.
May I hear publicly—
MARQUIS: My message is
Addressed to you, Your Majesty, alone.
        (The ladies withdraw at a gesture from the Queen.)

Scene 3

The Queen. Marquis of Posa.
QUEEN *(in surprise)*:
What is this? Can I trust my eyes, Marquis?
The King has sent you here to me?
MARQUIS: Does that
Appear, Your Majesty, so strange to you?
'Tis not at all to me.
QUEEN: Now has the world
Relinquished its accustomed orbit. You
And he—I must admit—

MARQUIS: That it sounds strange?
    That certainly may be.—The present time
    Has yielded many other wondrous things.
QUEEN: No greater, surely.
MARQUIS: Say that I have been,
    At last, converted.—Was it just that I
    Was tired of playing the original?
    Original! What does that mean? A man
    Who wants to make himself of service must
    Attempt to make himself an equal first.
    What is the use of ostentatious dress?
    Say—Who is there so free of vanity
    That he will not seek to solicit for
    His faith?—Or say I have in mind to put
    My choice upon the throne?
QUEEN: No!—No! Marquis.
    I will not, even as a joke, accuse
    You of this immature conceit. You are
    No dreamer who would undertake to do
    What cannot be completed.
MARQUIS: That, I think,
    Was just the question.
QUEEN: What at most I might
    Accuse you of, Marquis—what could perhaps
    Cause me to be displeased with you would be—
MARQUIS: My ambiguity. May be.
QUEEN: At least
    Your insincerity. The King most surely
    Did not intend for me to hear what you
    Will say to me.
MARQUIS: He did not.
QUEEN: Then can what
    Is good ennoble evil methods? And—
    Forgive my doubt—but can your noble pride
    Then lend itself to such employment?
    I scarcely think so—
MARQUIS: Nor would I, if it
    Were just a method to deceive the King.
    But that is not my aim. I think this time

That I will serve him more sincerely than
His orders would have done.
QUEEN: I credit you
With that, and now enough! What is he doing?
MARQUIS: The King?—It seems to me I'll have revenge
Quite soon on my most stringent judge. The things
That I saw fit to take my time to tell
It seemed to me Your Majesty was in
Far, far less haste to hear.—But still, it must
Be heard, in any case! Our monarch bids
Me ask Your Majesty to grant this day
No audience to the ambassador
Of France. That was the mission that he gave
To me. Now that is done with.
QUEEN: Is that all,
Marquis, that you have to report to me
From him?
MARQUIS: Well, it is nearly everything
That justifies my being here.
QUEEN: I will
Be satisfied, Marquis, if I am not
To know what must remain a secret from me—
MARQUIS: And that it *must*, my Queen.—Indeed, if you
Were not yourself, then I would hasten to
Apprise you of some things and caution you
About some certain people—but there is
No need to handle matters thus with you.
For dangers may arise and fall around
You, you will never know it. All of this
Is certainly not worth enough to drive
The golden slumber from an angel's brow.
It was not that, however, brought me here.
Prince Carlos—
QUEEN: Tell me, how is he?
MARQUIS: Just like
The only wise man of his time for whom
'Tis made a crime to worship truth—and still
In such brave spirits is he, that he would
Die for his love of you as you for his.

I bring you but few words—still here he is
Himself.
                    (*He gives the Queen a letter.*)
QUEEN (*after she has read it*):
                    He says he has to speak to me.
MARQUIS: I say that, too.
QUEEN: And will it make him happy,
    If he can see with his own eyes that I
    Am also not?
MARQUIS: Oh, no, but it will make
    Him more determined, more aggressive.
QUEEN: How?
MARQUIS: The Duke of Alba has been named for Flanders.
QUEEN: I heard that he was named.
MARQUIS: The King will not
    Withdraw his name. Indeed, we know the King.
    And it is true. The Prince dare not remain—
    Not here, now not at all—and Flanders must
    Not be a sacrifice.
QUEEN: Do you know how
    We can prevent it?
MARQUIS: Yes—perhaps. The means
    Is almost worse than is the danger. It
    Is just as rash as it is desperate.—
    I know no other.
QUEEN: Tell me of it.
MARQUIS: You
    And only you I dare to tell, my Queen.
    And only from your lips can Carlos hear
    It, hear without detesting it. The name
    That it will bear indeed sounds somewhat harsh,
    It's true—
QUEEN: Rebellion—
MARQUIS: He will have to go
    Against the wishes of the King; he shall
    Proceed to Brussels secretly, and there
    With open arms the Flemish will await
    Him. At his signal all the Netherlands
    Will rise. The beneficial action gets
    Its strength from royal blood. Oh, let him use

His weapons to induce the Spanish throne
To tremble. What his father would not grant
Him in Madrid, he will in Brussels.
QUEEN: You
Think thus and spoke with him today?
MARQUIS: Because
I spoke with him today.
QUEEN *(after a pause):*   The plan that you
Describe repels me and attracts me both.
I cannot think that you are wrong.—The thought
Is bold, and for that very reason it
Appeals to me. I want to think about
It. Is the Prince aware of it?
MARQUIS: My plan
Is he should hear it first from your own lips.
QUEEN: Without a doubt! The plan is sound.—And yet
The Prince is still so young—
MARQUIS: No harm done. He
Will find an Egmont and an Orange there,
The worthy warriors of Emperor Karl,
As smart in council as in warfare feared.
QUEEN *(with vivacity):*
No! This idea is good and fair.—The Prince
Must now assume command. That much is clear.
The part one sees him play here in Madrid
Would, in his place, depress me deeply. I
Can promise France to him and Savoy. I
Hold your opinion, Marquis, he must take
The lead.—But this attempt needs money.
MARQUIS: That
Is there already—
QUEEN: I will help.
MARQUIS: So may
I give him hope about the rendezvous?
QUEEN: I'll have to think about it.
MARQUIS: Carlos is
Insistent on an answer, Majesty.
I promised not to come back empty handed.
          (handing the Queen his writing materials)
Two lines would be enough for now—

QUEEN *(after she has written):*   Will I
See you again?
MARQUIS: As much as you require.
QUEEN: As much—as much as I require? Marquis!
How am I able to explain this freedom?
MARQUIS: As innocently as *you* ever could.
It is ours to enjoy. That is enough—
That is, my Queen, enough for you.
QUEEN *(interrupting):*   How great
Would be my joy, Marquis, if after all
This refuge for our freedom still remained
In Europe!—And remained because of *him.*
Rely upon my quiet aid—
MARQUIS *(passionately):*   I knew it,
I knew I would be understood—
       (Olivarez appears at the doors.)
QUEEN *(distantly to the Marquis):* I will
Respect the wishes of my lord, the King,
As if they were the law. Now you may go
And give him my assurance of compliance!
     (She gives a sign. The Marquis exits.)

A gallery

Scene 4

Don Carlos and Count Lerma.
CARLOS: No one will interrupt us here. What is
It that you wish to tell me?
LERMA: At this court
Your Highness had a friend.
CARLOS *(taken aback):*   One whom I did
Not know!—How so? What do you mean by that?
LERMA: So I must ask forgiveness that I came
To know more than I was supposed to know.
But that Your Highness may be reassured,
I have it from a loyal source at least,
In short, I have it from myself.

CARLOS: Who do
  You mean?
LERMA: I mean Marquis of Posa—
CARLOS: Well?
LERMA: If somewhat more than anyone should know
  About Your Highness should be known to him,
  As I do almost fear—
CARLOS: As you do fear?
LERMA: —He went to see the King.
CARLOS: So?
LERMA: Two full hours.
  And in a secret conversation.
CARLOS: Really?
LERMA: The conversation dealt with nothing small.
CARLOS: I will believe that.
LERMA: Your name, Prince, I heard
  Repeatedly.
CARLOS: I hope that that is not
  A sign of something bad.
LERMA: This morning in
  The bedroom of the King, a puzzling mention
  Was made about Her Majesty, the Queen.
CARLOS *(steps back dismayed):*
  Count Lerma?
LERMA: After the Marquis was gone,
  Then I received commands that he would be
  Henceforth admitted unannounced.
CARLOS: Now that
  Is quite a lot.
LERMA: There is no precedent
  For it as long as I have served the King.
CARLOS: 'Tis much! 'Tis truly much!—And how was it,
  You said, the Queen was mentioned?
LERMA *(steps back):*   No, my Prince.
  Oh, no! The ties of duty bind me.
CARLOS: Strange!
  You tell me one thing and you then conceal
  The other from me.
LERMA: I owed you the first,
  The second I do owe my lord, the King.

CARLOS: —I must agree.
LERMA: That the Marquis can be
  Relied upon, I know.
CARLOS: Then you do know
  Him very well.
LERMA: And each and every virtue
  Remains unblemished to the very time
  Of this new test.
CARLOS: And here and far beyond.
LERMA: It seems to me a great king's favor does
  Deserve this query. Many virtues caught
  Upon this golden hook have bled to death.
CARLOS: Oh, yes.
LERMA: It is oft wise to make disclosure
  Of what can never be kept secret.
CARLOS: Wise!
  But, as you say, you have known the Marquis
  To be a man of honor ever?
LERMA: If
  He is that *still*, my doubt makes him no worse,
  And you have profited twofold.
CARLOS: Threefold
  I profit, noble, worthy man—I am
  Now richer by a friend and still I do
  Not lose the one whom I possessed.
                    (Lerma exits.)

Scene 5

Marquis of Posa enters through the gallery. Carlos.
MARQUIS: Don Carlos!
CARLOS: Who calls? Ah, it is you. 'Tis good. I'll go
  Into the cloister. You come after.
                    (He starts to leave.)
MARQUIS: Just
  Two minutes—wait.
CARLOS: If they should find us here—
MARQUIS: They will not. It is instantly resolved.
  The Queen—

CARLOS:　　　　You went to see the King, my father?
MARQUIS: He bade me come; yes.
CARLOS *(full of expectation)*:　　　Well?
MARQUIS:　　　　　　　　It is all right.
　For you to speak to her.
CARLOS:　　　　　　　The King? What does
　The King want, then?
MARQUIS:　　　　　　　The King? Not much. He is
　But curious about me. Or a good,
　Though unknown, friend attempts to serve me. How
　Should I know? He extends his favor.
CARLOS:　　　　　　　　　　Which
　You have refused?
MARQUIS:　　　　Of course.
CARLOS:　　　　　　　And how were things
　When you departed?
MARQUIS:　　　　Fairly good.
CARLOS:　　　　　　　The talk
　Must not have had to do with me.
MARQUIS:　　　　　　　　With you?
　Well, yes. It did in general.
　　(He takes out his memento and gives it to the Prince.)
　But two words from the Queen and then tomorrow
　I will find out both where and how—
CARLOS *(reads distractedly, puts the sheet in his pocket,*
　and starts to leave):　　　　You'll meet
　Me at the Prior's.
MARQUIS:　　　Wait, what is the hurry?
　Indeed, no one is coming.
CARLOS *(with a feigned smile)*: Have we then
　In truth reversed our roles? Today you are
　Extremely sure.
MARQUIS:　　　Today? Why just today?
CARLOS: What was it that the Queen wrote me?
MARQUIS:　　　　　　　　Did you
　Not read it just this very moment?
CARLOS:　　　　　　　I?
　Oh, yes.
MARQUIS: What ails you? What is wrong?
CARLOS *(reads the message again. Enraptured and overjoyed)*:

                                    O angel
Of Heaven! Yes, I want to be—I want—
Want to be worthy of you. Great souls make
Their love the greater. Be it as it may,
I will obey whatever *you* command.—
She writes that I should now prepare myself
For an important resolution. What
Can be her meaning? Do you know?
MARQUIS: And if
I knew it, Carlos—are you now inclined
To listen to it?
CARLOS: Have I hurt your feelings?
I was distracted. Roderick, forgive.
MARQUIS: Distracted? Why?
CARLOS: I do not know myself.
Is this memento mine?
MARQUIS: Well, not entirely.
But rather, I have come to beg you—give
Me yours.
CARLOS: Why should I give you one?
MARQUIS: And also
Whatever other trifles you might have
That should not fall into another's hands,
Like letters or some plans you might have sketched
And carry with you—briefly, all that's in
Your letter case—
CARLOS: But why?
MARQUIS: For all events.
Who can be sure about surprises? Me
No one will ever search. Give here.
CARLOS (*very uneasy*):   This is
So strange. Why suddenly this—
MARQUIS: Just be calm.
I do not mean to hint at anything.
Most surely not. It is but caution that
Precedes all danger. To alarm you was
Most certainly not what I meant to do.
CARLOS (*gives him the portfolio*):
Take care of them.

MARQUIS: I will.
CARLOS *(looks at him meaningfully):*   O Roderick!
  I gave you much.
MARQUIS: But nowhere near as much
  As I already have of you—So there's
  The rest, and now I bid farewell—farewell!
                    (He is about to exit.)
CARLOS *(struggles irresolutely with himself—finally calls
  him back):*
  Give me the letters once again. There is
  Among them one from her that she wrote to
  Alcala at that time when I lay near
  To death. I carried it since that time next
  My heart most constantly, and it is hard
  For me to tear myself away from it.
  Leave me that letter—just the one—the rest
  You can have all of.
      (He takes out the portfolio and gives it back to him.)
MARQUIS: This I hate to do.
  It was this letter that I want.
CARLOS: Farewell!
    *(He goes slowly and quietly away, stops at the door
    for a moment, turns around, and brings him the letter.)*
  You have it here.
      *(His hand trembles, tears course from his eyes, he
      embraces the Marquis and presses his face on his
      chest.)*
            My father cannot do this.
  Is that not true, my Roderick? He cannot?
            (He exits quickly.)

Scene 6

The Marquis looks after him, astonished.
MARQUIS: Now is it possible? And do I still
  Not know him? Not entirely? In his heart
  This wrinkle has in truth eluded me?
  Distrustful toward his friend! Oh, no! This is

But calumny!—What has he done to me
That weakest of the weak I should indict him?
What I accuse him of, I am myself—
Surprise—it may be that, I like to think.
But when would he have acted with such strange
Reserve toward his dear friend?—And this distress!
I cannot save you from it, Carlos, and
I must still longer torment your good soul.
The King has placed belief in this one vessel
To which he charges his most holy secret,
And this belief requires his gratitude.
Why be loquacious when my silence will
Not bring you harm? Perhaps will spare you? Why
Point out the storm clouds hanging overhead
To one who sleeps?—It is enough that I
Should lead them quietly away from you,
And when you wake, the sky will be bright blue.
                    (He exits.)

The King's private room

Scene 7

The King, seated in a chair—beside him the Infanta Clara Eugenia.
KING *(after a profound silence):*
  But no! She is my daughter for all that—
  Could Nature tell a lie so truthfully?
  These eyes of blue are mine indeed! Do I
  Not find myself again in every feature?
  You are my love's child, yes, you are. I press
  You to my breast—you are my blood.
                    (He hesitates and stops.)
                                        My blood!
  What can I fear that's worse? My features here,
  Are they not also his?
      *(He has taken up the locket and looks alternately
      at the picture and in a mirror opposite—finally*

*he throws it to the floor, stands up abruptly, and
pushes the Infanta away.)*

Away! Away!

For I am lost in this abyss.

Scene 8

Count Lerma. The King.

LERMA: Just now
Her Royal Majesty, the Queen, has come
Into the antechamber.
KING: Now?
LERMA: And asks
You for an audience—
KING: But now? Just now?
At this most unaccustomed hour? Oh, no!
I cannot talk to her just now—not now—
LERMA: Here is Her Majesty herself.

(He exits.)

Scene 9

The King. The Queen enters. The Infanta.

*(The Infanta rushes to the Queen and clings to her. She falls at
the feet of the King, who stands speechless and confused.)*

QUEEN: My
Lord
And husband—I—I must—I am compelled
To look for justice here before your throne.
KING: For justice?
QUEEN: I am held in poor esteem
Here at this court. Someone has broken into
My private case—
KING: Your what?
QUEEN: And things that are
Extremely valuable to me are gone—
KING: Extremely valuable to you—

QUEEN: Important
  Because the impudence of those who are
  Unknowing might allow—
KING: The impudence—
  Important—You may rise.
QUEEN: I will not, Sire,
  Will not until you make a solemn promise
  To use the power of your royal arm
  To bring the culprit to me face to face,
  If not, to let me leave this household, where
  The thief conceals himself—
KING: You must arise—
  In this position—please arise—
QUEEN *(rises):*   That he
  Must be of the nobility, I know,
  For there were pearls and diamonds in the case
  Worth far more than a million, and he was
  Content to take the letters—
KING: May I ask—
QUEEN: Of course, my husband. They were letters and
  A locket that I got from the Infante.
KING: From—
QUEEN: The Infante, from your son.
KING: To you?
QUEEN: To me.
KING: From the Infante? And you tell
  Me that?
QUEEN: And why not tell you that, my husband?
KING: So brazenly!
QUEEN: But why does that disturb you?
  I think you will recall the letters that
  Don Carlos wrote to me at St. Germain
  With the permission of both ruling heads.
  And if the picture that he sent with them
  Was not a part of what he was allowed,
  And if his hopes were rash and took upon
  Themselves this step so bold—I do not want
  To even venture to decide. So if
  It was construed as overzealous, 'twas

Still most forgivable—I'll vouch for that.
For at the time he did not know, of course,
That I would be his mother—
                              (notices the King's agitation)
                                        What is this?
What is the matter?
INFANTA *(who has meanwhile found the locket on the floor
and has been playing with it, brings it to the
Queen):*   Mother, look at this!
The pretty picture—
QUEEN: What do you—
        *(She recognizes the locket and stands speechless,
        as if frozen. They look at each other fixedly.
        After a long silence)*
                                        My Lord,
In truth, *this* way to test a woman's heart,
I think, is very kingly, very noble—
Still, I'll permit myself to ask one question.
KING: It is *my* turn to ask.
QUEEN: Because of my
Suspicion, innocence shall not be blamed.—
For if this theft was the result of your
Command—
KING: It was.
QUEEN: Then I have no one whom
I can accuse and no one to deplore—
No one but you, for whom *your* wife has not
Shown herself worth the effort of such methods.
KING: I know *this* kind of talk.—But you, Madam,
Will not be able to deceive me twice
As you deceived me in Aranjuez.
That Queen so angel pure who could defend
Herself with so much dignity back then—
I know her better now.
QUEEN: What's that?
KING: In short,
Madam, and now without reserve!—Does it
Still hold true that you spoke with no one there?
With no one? Is that really true?

QUEEN: I spoke
With the Infante. Yes.
KING: Yes? Well, now it
Is out. It is now plain. How impudent!
Such small regard for my own honor!
QUEEN: Honor?
If there was honor to offend, I fear
There was a greater one at stake than brought
Castile to me, which was a bridegroom's gift.
KING: Why did you disavow it to me?
QUEEN: I
Am not accustomed, Sire, when in the presence
Of courtiers, to be interrogated
As if I were a criminal. The truth
Will never be denied by me, if it
Is asked for with respect and kindness.—And
Was that, indeed, the tone Your Majesty
Assumed with me there in Aranjuez?
Is then perhaps a gathering of nobles
The seat of judgment where your queens are brought
And made to give accounting for those deeds
That they have done in private? I allowed
The Prince to have this rendezvous, which he
So urgently requested. This I did
Because I wanted to—because I do
Not want to let mere custom judge those things
That I consider faultless—and I did
Conceal it from you, for I did not want
To quarrel with Your Majesty about
This freedom with your courtiers around.
KING: Your words are daring, Madam, very—
QUEEN: Let
Me add thereto, because Don Carlos scarce
Is able to enjoy the fairness that
He well deserves within his father's heart—
KING: The fairness he deserves?
QUEEN: For why should I
Conceal it, Sire?—I greatly value him
And love him as my dearest kin, who once

Was thought full worthy to assume a name
That was far more important to me—I
Have not been able rightly to perceive
That he should therefore be more strange to me
Than any other, just because he once
Was dearer to me than any other was.
Your principle of government ties bonds
Where it thinks proper, but they will become
A little harder for it to unbind.
I do not want to hate him whom I should—
And since I am at last compelled to speak,
I do not want—I will not see my choice
Restricted anymore—

KING: Elizabeth!
In my weak moments you have seen me. This
Remembrance makes you bold. You base your trust
In an omnipotence that you have tested
Enough against my firmness.—But you should
Fear that much more. Those things that made me weak
Can also lead me to insanity.

QUEEN: What crime have I committed?

KING *(takes her hand):*   If it's true,
Is *really*—is there any doubt?—If all
The heaped-up measure of your guilt should grow,
And were it only by the weight of one
Short breath—if I have been deceived—
                        (He drops her hand.)
                                        I can
Still overcome this one last weakness, too.
I can and will.—Then woe to me and you,
Elizabeth!

QUEEN: What crime have I committed?

KING: Then blood may flow, for all I care—

QUEEN: This thing
Has gone so far—O God!

KING: I do not know
My own self anymore—I care no more
For customs or the voice of Nature or
The nation's contracts anymore.

QUEEN: How much
I pity you, Your Majesty—
KING *(beside himself)*: You pity!
A harlot's sympathy—
INFANTA *(clings to her mother frightened)*:
The King is angry,
And now my pretty mother cries.
(The King shoves the child away from the Queen roughly.)
QUEEN *(gently and with dignity, but with a trembling voice)*:
I must
See that this child receives protection from
Abuse. Come with me, Daughter.
(She takes the child in her arms.)
If the King
Will not acknowledge you, then I must ask
Beyond the Pyrenees for guarantors
Prepared to take our cause in hand.
(She is about to exit.)
KING *(overwhelmed)*: My Queen?
QUEEN: Now I can do no more—that is too much.
*(She tries to reach the door, but at the threshold
she falls to the floor with the child.)*
KING *(hurrying to her, alarmed)*:
O God! What is this?
INFANTA *(cries out, frightened)*: Oh, my mother bleeds!
(She exits quickly.)
KING *(anxiously attempting to take care of her)*:
A dreadful accident! Here's blood! Do I
Deserve such punishment from you? Get up!
Come to yourself! Get up! Someone is coming!
They will surprise us!—Please get up. Or shall
My courtiers all revel in this show?
Oh, must I beg you to get up?
(She gets up, supported by the King.)

Scene 10

The same. Alba, Domingo enter alarmed. Ladies follow.
KING: Escort
   The Queen to her abode. She is not well.
            (The Queen exits, accompanied by the ladies.
            Alba and Domingo approach.)
ALBA: The Queen was crying, and upon her face
   Is blood—
KING: Should that surprise those devils who
   Led me astray?
ALBA, DOMINGO *(together)*: You speak of us?
KING: Who said
   Enough to me to drive me almost mad,
   But nothing to convince me.
ALBA: We produced
   What we possessed—
KING: And Hell may thank you for it.
   I did what I am sorry for. Was what
   She said the answer of a guilty conscience?
MARQUIS *(offstage)*:
   I wish to see the King.

Scene 11

The Marquis of Posa. The former.
KING *(starting up briskly at the sound of this voice*
   and taking a few steps toward the Marquis):
                              Ah, there he is!
   Marquis, you are quite welcome. Duke, your presence
Is now no longer needed. Leave us.
         (Alba and Domingo look at each other in mute
         surprise and exit.)

Scene 12

The King and the Marquis of Posa.

MARQUIS: Sire!
  It is quite hard on that old man who has
  Faced death for you on twenty battlefields
  To find himself removed this way!

KING: It is
  Quite right for you to think, for me to act,
  This way. What in just hours you have become
  To me, *he* was not in a generation.
  I will not make my satisfaction secret;
  The seal of my most royal favor shall
  Appear illuminated on your brow.
  I want to see that he whom I have made
  My friend is envied.

MARQUIS: Even if the cloak
  Of darkness is the only way he can
  Be worthy of the name?

KING: What do you bring
  To me?

MARQUIS: When I went through the antechamber,
  I heard about a frightful rumor there
  That seems incredible to me—There was
  A violent dispute—and blood—the Queen—

KING: You come from there?

MARQUIS: I should be horrified,
  If that report were not entirely false,
  If anything had meanwhile happened to
  Your Majesty.—Discoveries that I
  Have made are of great import, and they change
  The state of the whole matter.

KING: Well?

MARQUIS: I found
  An opportunity to take the Prince's
  Portfolio with many papers in it
  That will, I hope, shed light upon—
      (*He gives Don Carlos' briefcase to the King.*)

KING *(searches through it eagerly)*:   A letter—
　'Tis from the King, my father—What is this?
　I do not think I ever knew of this.
　　　　(He reads it through, puts it aside, and hurries
　　　　on to other papers.)
　The ground plan of a fortress—Disconnected
　Ideas out of Tacitus—And here—
　What can this be? I surely ought to know
　This hand? It is a lady's hand.
　　　　(He reads it attentively, now loud, now softly.)
　　　　　　　　　　　　　　　　"This key
　Will open the rear door of the pavilion
　Belonging to the Queen"—What's this? "Here love
　May freely—favor now awaits—rewards"—
　Satanic treachery! I know it now,
　She is the one. It is her hand!
MARQUIS:　　　　　　　　　　The Queen's?
　It cannot be the Queen's hand—
KING:　　　　　　　　　　The Princess.
　Of Eboli—
MARQUIS:　　So it is true what once
　Not long ago the Page Henárez swore,
　Who brought the letter and the key.
KING *(grasping the Marquis' hand with strong emotion)*:
　　　　　　　　　　　　　　　　Marquis!
　I've fallen into frightful hands, I see.
　This woman—I must now admit—Marquis,
　She broke into the Queen's own private case,
　And the first warning came from her. Who knows
　How much the Monk is implicated—I
　Have been betrayed by heinous villainy.
MARQUIS: Then it was fortunate—
KING:　　　　　　　　　　Marquis! Marquis!
　I have begun to fear that I have done
　My Queen far too much harm—
MARQUIS:　　　　　　　　If there has been
　A secret understanding made between
　Don Carlos and the Queen, it surely was
　Concerning far, far different subjects than

The ones they are accused of. I have heard
Through certain information that the Prince's
Desire to travel to the Lowlands was
The Queen's idea.

KING: I have always thought so.

MARQUIS: The Queen has her ambitions. Do I need
To say much more?—With sensitivity
She sees her proudest hopes are dashed, and she
Herself excluded from a royal share.
The Prince's reckless youth holds out to her
Extensive schemes and plans—as for her heart,
I doubt if she knows how to love.

KING: I am
Not wont to tremble at her politics.

MARQUIS: And whether she is loved?—Could there then be
Worse things to fear from the Infante? This
Appears to me to be worth questioning.
A stricter vigilance is necessary—

KING: You answer for him.

MARQUIS (*after some thought*): If Your Majesty
Thinks I am fit to undertake this office,
Then I must ask to have it totally,
Unlimited and wholly in my hands.

KING: It shall be so.

MARQUIS: At least I do not want
To be disturbed in any undertaking
That seems to me quite necessary by
Assistants or however they are called—

KING: By none. I give my promise to you. You
Have been my guardian angel. How much thanks
I owe you for this evidence!

        (*to Lerma, who enters at these last words*)
                    How did
You leave the Queen?

LERMA: She was still weak and faint.
    (*He looks at the Marquis dubiously and exits.*)

MARQUIS (*after a pause, to the King*):
One more precaution seems advisable.
The Prince, I fear, may well be given warning.

There are around him many friends—perhaps
He has in Ghent connections with the rebels.
And fear could lead him to make desperate
Decisions—Therefore, I advise you to
Take steps to meet this kind of situation
Immediately with some remedy.
KING: You are quite right. But how—
MARQUIS: Your Majesty
Could place a secret warrant of arrest
Into my hands so that I could make use
Of it myself immediately in
The danger of a moment—and—
                    (as the King appears to consider)
                                        It can
Remain a secret for the time—
KING *(going to the desk and writing out the warrant
of arrest):*   The Empire
Is now at stake and extraordinary
Means are now sanctioned by this danger. Here,
Marquis, I need not bid you to take care.
MARQUIS *(takes the warrant of arrest):*
Our backs are to the wall, my King.
KING *(putting his hand on the Marquis' shoulder):*
                                        Now go.
Go, dear Marquis—to bring peace back into
My heart and to restore sleep to my nights.
                    (They exit to opposite sides.)

Gallery

Scene 13

Carlos enters in great anxiety. Count Lerma comes toward him.
CARLOS: I looked for you.
LERMA: And I for you.
CARLOS: Can it
Be true? For God's sake, is it true?
LERMA: What, then?

CARLOS: They say he pulled a dagger and that she
  Was carried from his room with blood upon her.
  I call upon the saints! Please answer me!
  What must I think? What is the truth?
LERMA: She fell
  Into a faint and cut herself falling.
  'Tis nothing more.
CARLOS: There is no other danger?
  'Tis nothing? On your honor, Count?
LERMA: Not for
  The Queen—but for that reason, more for you.
CARLOS: No danger for my mother! God be thanked!
  There was a frightful rumor reached my ears:
  The King was raging against child and mother,
  And that a secret was unearthed.
LERMA: The last
  May well be true—
CARLOS: Be true? But how?
LERMA: My Prince, I gave a warning *once* to you
  Today that you ignored. But utilize
  The second better.
CARLOS: What?
LERMA: If I am not
  Mistaken, Prince, a day or two ago
  I saw you holding a portfólio
  Of sky-blue velvet worked with gold—
CARLOS (*somewhat perplexed*):   I own
  Just such a one. Yes—well?
LERMA: And on the cover
  A silhouette, I think, with pearls around—
CARLOS: That's right.
LERMA: As I just now quite unexpected
  Stepped in the private chamber of the King,
  I thought I saw the same one in his hand,
  And the Marquis stood right beside him.
CARLOS (*after a short, paralyzing silence, vehemently*):
                             That
  Cannot be true.
LERMA (*his feelings hurt*):   Then I aim to deceive you.

CARLOS (*looking at him for a long time*):
  You do indeed.
LERMA: Oh, I forgive you that.
CARLOS (*strides back and forth in frightful agitation
  and finally stops in front of him*):
  What has he ever done to you? What has
  Our innocent attachment done to you,
  That you should strive with such satanic zeal
  To break these bonds?
LERMA: O Prince, I do respect
  The pain that makes you be unjust.
CARLOS: O God!
  God!—God! Protect me from distrust!
LERMA: I can
  Remember even the King's very words,
  Just as I entered: How much thanks, he said,
  That I do owe you for this evidence.
CARLOS: Oh, quiet! Quiet!
LERMA: The Duke Alba has
  Been put aside and the great seal recalled
  And taken from Prince Ruy Gomez and has
  Been handed on to the Marquis—
CARLOS (*lost in deep brooding*):   He kept
  It secret from *me!* Why from *me?*
LERMA: The court
  Admires him as omnipotent already,
  As favorite unlimited—
CARLOS: He loved
  Me once, he loved me very much. I was
  As dear as his own soul. Oh that I know—
  A thousand proofs of that were given me.
  But should the millions, should his fatherland
  Not be still dearer to him than just *one?*
  His heart was far too great for just one friend,
  And my own happiness too small for him.
  He sacrificed me to his virtue. Dare
  I then reproach him for that?—It is true!
  It must be true. And now I know I've lost him.
          (*He turns to the side and covers his face.*)

LERMA (*after a silence*):
Oh, my dear Prince, what can I do for you?
CARLOS (*without looking at him*):
Just as you must—betray me to the King.
For I have nought to offer.
LERMA: Do you wish
To wait and see what may transpire?
CARLOS (*leans on the balustrade and stares into space*):
                                    I've lost
Him. Oh! Now am I totally forsaken!
LERMA (*approaches with compassion*):
But you will not consider your escape?
CARLOS: Escape? O my good man!
LERMA: And otherwise
Need you be fearful for no one besides?
CARLOS (*starts up*):
Oh, what must you remind me of!—My mother!
The letter that I gave to him! At first
I would not, but I finally did!
          (*He walks back and forth furiously,
          wringing his hands.*)
                              What has
She done to merit this from him? He should
At least have spared *her*. Lerma, should he not?
          (*hastily decided*)
Then I must go to her—must warn her—must
Prepare her—Lerma, Lerma, my dear friend—
Who can I send then? Is there no one left?
Praise God! I still have one friend left—and there
Is nothing to make worse.
          (*Exits quickly*)
LERMA (*follows and calls after him*):   My Prince! Where to?
          (*Exits*)

One of the Queen's rooms

Scene 14

The Queen. Alba. Domingo.

ALBA: If we may be permitted, noble Queen—
QUEEN: What will you ask of me?
DOMINGO: Sincere concern
  Regarding our most Royal Majesty's
  Illustrious self will not allow us to
  Keep idly silent when an incident
  Is threatening your safety.
ALBA: We make haste
  Now by our timely warning to defeat
  A plot that is played out against you here—
DOMINGO: To lay our fervor—and our service—at
  The feet of our most Royal Majesty.
QUEEN *(looks at them in amazement)*:
  Right reverend sir, and you, my noble Duke,
  You really do surprise me, for I was
  Quite unaware of such devotion from
  Domingo, and from you, Duke Alba—though
  I know how I must value you. You tell
  Me of a plot that's said to threaten me.
  May I be told who is—
ALBA: We beg of you
  To be on guard against the Marquis Posa,
  Who now conducts the private business of
  His Royal Majesty.
QUEEN: It is with pleasure
  I hear our monarch chooses well. I had
  Long since been told that the Marquis was said
  To be a man of greatness. Never was
  The favor of the King more justly given—
DOMINGO: More justly given? We know better there.
ALBA: For long ago it ceased to be a secret,
  The reason why this man is used.

QUEEN: Indeed?
  And what would that be then? With this you rouse
  My curiosity.
DOMINGO: —Has it been long
  Since for the last time you, my Queen, looked in
  Your private case?
QUEEN: What's that?
DOMINGO: And have you chanced
  To note some precious items missing there?
QUEEN: Why do you ask? What I am missing, my
  Whole court knows well.—But the Marquis of Posa?
  Now what has this to do with the Marquis?
ALBA: Oh, quite a lot, Your Majesty.—The Prince
  As well is missing some important papers,
  And these were seen this morning in the King's
  Own hands—just at the time the Chevalier
  Was given private audience.
QUEEN (*after some thought*):   That's strange,
  Indeed, yes, it is very odd!—I find
  I have an enemy I never dreamed of,
  And on the other hand I have two friends
  I never thought that I possessed. For truly,
       (*as she fixes a penetrating gaze on both of them*)
  I must admit I was just now in danger
  Of offering to you forgiveness for
  That wicked service someone gave the King.
ALBA: To us?
QUEEN: To you.
DOMINGO: Duke Alba! Us!
QUEEN (*with her gaze still fixed firmly upon them*):
                                   How nice
  It is for me then to become aware
  So quickly of my hastiness. Besides,
  I had decided still today to ask
  His Majesty to put before me my
  Accuser. Now so much the better! I
  Can call upon Duke Alba's evidence.
ALBA: On me? You really would do that?
QUEEN: Why not?

DOMINGO: And undermine this way the services
  We gave to you in secret?
QUEEN: Gave in secret?
              (with dignity and severity)
  Now I would like to know, Duke Alba, what
  The wife of your great king would have to settle
  With you, or likewise, Priest, with you, that her
  Exalted husband ought not know. Am I
  Judged innocent or guilty?
DOMINGO: What a question!
ALBA: But if the King were not so very just?
  At least were not so at this time?
QUEEN: Then I
  Would have to wait until he was. And happy
  The one who will prevail when that time comes!
        (She bows to them and exits; they leave
        on the other side.)

Room of the Princess of Eboli

Scene 15

Princess of Eboli. Immediately thereupon, Carlos.
EBOLI: The extraordinary news that fills
  This court—can it be true?
CARLOS *(enters):*   Do not be frightened,
  Princess, I will be gentle, like a child.
EBOLI: The Prince—how unexpected.
CARLOS: Are you still
  Offended?
EBOLI: Prince!
CARLOS *(more urgently):* Are you offended still?
  I beg of you to tell me.
EBOLI: What is this?
  It seems you have forgotten, Prince. What do
  You want from me?

CARLOS (*seizing her hand with ardor*):
                                    O maiden, will you hate
  Forever? Never to forgive?
EBOLI (*tries to release herself*): Oh, what
  Do you remind me of?
CARLOS: Of your own goodness
  And my ingratitude. Oh, well I know!
  Severely I offended you, O maiden,
  And broke your gentle heart, and I drew tears
  Out of those dear, angelic eyes. Oh, me!
  And even now I am not here to rue it.
EBOLI: Release me, Prince—I—
CARLOS: I have come here now
  Because you are a gentle maiden and
  Because I count upon your lovely soul.
  Look, maiden, look, I do not have a friend
  Upon this earth, not one but you. Once you
  Were good to me—you will not always hate
  And will not be implacable.
EBOLI (*turns her face away*):   Oh, still!
  Say nothing more, for God's sake, Prince—
CARLOS: Let me
  Remind you of that golden time now past—
  Remind you of that love you had for me.
  Your love for me, O maiden, that I did
  So shamefully transgress upon. Let me
  Once more assert what I have been to you,
  And what the visions of your heart gave me—
  Once more—and just—yes, just once more, place me,
  As once I was, before your very soul
  And offer to this shadow what to me
  You cannot ever ever offer!
EBOLI: Carlos!
  How horribly you play with me!
CARLOS: Rise up
  Above your sex. Forget the many wrongs,
  Do what no woman did before you—what
  No woman will do after you. What I
  Demand is still unheard of—Let me—on

My knees I beg you—let me, let me speak,
Speak one word with my mother.
                    (He throws himself at her feet.)

Scene 16

*The previous. Marquis of Posa rushes in, behind him two
officers of the royal bodyguard.*
MARQUIS *(out of breath, stepping between them, beside himself)*:
                              What has he
Confessed? Do not believe him.
CARLOS *(still on his knees, raising his voice)*:
                              Now, by all
That's holy—
MARQUIS *(interrupts him vehemently)*:
                    He is raving. You must pay
His ravings no attention.
CARLOS *(louder, more urgently)*: 'Tis a case
Of life and death. Now take me to her.
MARQUIS *(pulls the Princess away from him by force)*:
                                        I
Will kill you, if you listen to him.
                    (to one of the officers)
                              Count
Of Cordua. Now, in our monarch's name.
                    (He presents the warrant of arrest.)
Don Carlos is your prisoner.
                    *(Carlos stands frozen as if thunderstruck. The
                    Princess screams and is about to flee, the officers
                    are astonished. A long, deep pause. The Marquis
                    appears to tremble violently and retains his control
                    with difficulty. To the Prince)*
                              I ask
You for your sword—Princess of Eboli,
You will remain; and
                    (to the officer)
                    you will see to it

His Highness speaks to no one—no one—even
To you, at peril of your head!
> *(He speaks quietly with the officer, then turns
> to the other one.)*
>> I go
To throw myself before our Monarch's feet,
To give accounting to him—
>> *(to Carlos)*
>>> And I will
To you, Prince, too—await me in an hour.
> *(Carlos allows himself to be led away without a
> sign of awareness.—Only in passing he lets a
> feeble, dying glance fall upon the Marquis, who
> covers his face. The Princess attempts once more
> to flee; the Marquis conducts her back by the arm.)*

Scene 17

Princess of Eboli. Marquis of Posa.

EBOLI: By all the blessed saints in Heaven, let
Me leave this place—

MARQUIS *(brings her all the way forward, in dead earnest)*:
>> What did he say to you,
Unlucky person?

EBOLI: Nothing—let me go—

MARQUIS *(holds her back by force. With severity)*:
How much have you discovered? Here there is
No more escape. You will not tell it to
Another soul upon this earth.

EBOLI *(looks him in the face, frightened)*: Great God!
What do you mean by that? You surely will
Not murder me!

MARQUIS *(pulls his sword)*: In very fact, I am
Disposed to do it. Make it brief.

EBOLI: Me? Me?
Oh, everlasting mercy! What have I
Then done?

MARQUIS *(looking up to Heaven, placing the sword on her breast)*:

There is still time. The poison has
Not issued over these fair lips. I can
Destroy the vessel and all things remain
As they have been. It is the fate of Spain
Or else one woman's life!
        (He remains in this position, irresolute.)
EBOLI *(has collapsed against him and looks fixedly into
    his face):*   Why hesitate?
I ask not to be spared. Oh, no! I have
Deserved to die and want to.
MARQUIS *(lets his hand sink slowly. After brief reflection):*
                        That would be
As cowardly as it is cruel. No, no!
Thank God! There still remains another way!
        *(He lets the sword fall and hurries out. The
        Princess rushes out through another door.)*

One of the Queen's rooms

Scene 18

The Queen to Countess Fuentes.
QUEEN: What is the clamor in the palace? Each
    New turmoil, Countess, frightens me today.
    Oh, please investigate and tell me then
    What it can mean.
                *(The Countess Fuentes exits, and the
                Princess of Eboli rushes in.)*

Scene 19

Queen. Princess of Eboli.
EBOLI *(breathless, her face pale and distorted, collapses
    at the Queen's feet):* My Queen! O Madam, help!
    He is a prisoner.

QUEEN: Who is?

EBOLI: Marquis
Of Posa took him at the King's command.

QUEEN: But whom? Whom did he take?

EBOLI: The Prince.

QUEEN: You're mad.

EBOLI: They're taking him away just now.

QUEEN: And who
Was it who took him?

EBOLI: The Marquis.

QUEEN: Well, now!
We can thank God that it was the Marquis
Who took him prisoner!

EBOLI: How can you say
That quietly, my Queen? So calm?—O God!
You do not understand—or know—

QUEEN: Why he
Was taken captive?—'Twas some small misconduct,
I think, that was quite natural to the youth's
Impetuous behavior.

EBOLI: No, oh, no!
I know the cause much better—no—O Queen!
Accursed, most satanic deed!—For him
There is no rescue. He will die!

QUEEN: He'll die?

EBOLI: And I will be his murderer!

QUEEN: He'll die!
That's madness. Stop and think that over!

EBOLI: Why?
Why will he die?—Oh, if I had but known
That it would ever come to this!

QUEEN (*taking her graciously by the hand*): Princess!
You've lost your self-control. Now, first of all,
You must collect your thoughts so that you can
Relate this to me quietly without
These horrors that do fill my soul with dread.
What do you know and what has happened?

EBOLI: Oh!
I cannot stand angelic kindness,

Nor bear your graciousness, my Queen! They are
Like flames from Hell that strike and sting my conscience.
I am not worthy to lift up these eyes,
So desecrated, to gaze on your glory.
So trample 'neath your foot this wretch, who here
Lies crumpled in the dust, weighed down by her
Remorse, her shame, her self-contempt.

QUEEN: Poor girl!
What is it that you want to tell me?

EBOLI: Angel
Of light! O saintly Lady! You are still
Without suspicion of the devil that
You have so sweetly smiled upon. Today
You'll recognize her. I—I was the thief
Who robbed you.

QUEEN: You?

EBOLI: And handed over all
Your letters to the King.

QUEEN: 'Twas you?

EBOLI: I was
The one who dared accuse you—

QUEEN: It was you.
You could—

EBOLI: Revenge—and love—insanity—
I hated you and I loved the Infante—

QUEEN: Because you loved him—?

EBOLI: And I told him so
And found he did not love me.

QUEEN *(after a silence):*   Oh, you have
Explained it all to me!—Now do arise.
You loved him—I already have forgiven.
It is forgotten now.—Arise.
                    (She extends her arm.)

EBOLI: No! No!
I have another terrible confession.
And not before, O noble Queen—

QUEEN: What is
There still that I must hear? But speak—

EBOLI: The King—

Seduction—Oh, you look away—I read
Rejection on your countenance. The crime
I accused you of—it was the one
I did myself.

> (She presses her feverish face onto the floor.
> The Queen exits. Long pause. The Duchess of
> Olivarez comes, after a few moments, out of the
> private chamber into which the Queen had gone,
> and finds the Princess still lying in the previous
> position. She approaches her quietly; at the
> sound the Princess straightens up and jumps to
> her feet frantically when she sees the Queen is
> no longer there.)

Scene 20

Princess of Eboli. Duchess of Olivarez.

EBOLI: She has forsaken me!
   Now it is done.

OLIVAREZ *(comes closer):* Princess of Eboli—

EBOLI: I am aware of why you've come, O Duchess.
   The Queen has sent you here to notify
   Me of her verdict. Quickly!

OLIVAREZ: I've received
   An order from Her Majesty to take
   Your cross from you and also take your key—

EBOLI *(takes the golden cross of an order from her breast
   and puts it in the hands of the Duchess):*
   Just *once* more will it be allowed to me
   That I may kiss the best Queen's hand?

OLIVAREZ: You will
   Go to St. Mary's cloister and will learn
   What is decided about you.

EBOLI *(amidst sudden tears):*   I will
   Not see the Queen again?

OLIVAREZ *(embraces her with her face averted):*
                      May you be happy!
      (She leaves quickly. The Princess follows to the

*door of the private chamber, which is immediately
closed behind the Duchess. For a few moments she
remains speechless and motionless on her knees
there, then she pulls herself together and hurries
away with her face covered.)*

Scene 21

The Queen. Marquis of Posa.

QUEEN: Oh, finally, Marquis, I'm glad you've come!

MARQUIS *(pale, his face distorted, voice trembling, and
 through the whole scene with solemn, deep emotion):*
Now is Your Majesty alone, and is
There no one in the other room to hear?

QUEEN: No, no one—Why? What do you bring?
 *(as she looks at him more closely and steps back,
 alarmed)*
                                            And why
Are you so changed? What is it? You do make
Me tremble, O Marquis—your countenance
Is changed, like someone dying—

MARQUIS: You most surely
Already know—

QUEEN: That Carlos has been taken,
And they have added that it was by you.
And is it true? For I would not believe
A soul but you.

MARQUIS: Yes, it is true.

QUEEN: By you?

MARQUIS: By me.

QUEEN *(looks at him for a few moments uncertainly):*
I will respect the things you've done,
Although I do not understand. But this
Time, please forgive a timid woman. For
I fear you play a daring game.

MARQUIS: I have
Already lost it.

QUEEN: God in Heaven!

MARQUIS: You
  Must be quite calm, my Queen! For *him* I have
  Provided. I have only lost myself.
QUEEN: What must I hear! O God above!
MARQUIS: For who,
  Who bade me wager all upon just one
  Uncertain throw? Yes, all? Such insolence,
  To challenge Heaven with such confidence!
  Who is the man who will presume to take
  The heavy rates of chance upon himself,
  Although he does not claim to be omniscient?
  Oh, it is fair!—But why must it be now
  For *me?* The moment is a precious one,
  Just as a human life! And who is there
  Who knows, if from the judge's stingy hand
  The last drops fall for me already?
QUEEN: From
  The judge's hand? That is a solemn note!
  I do not grasp the meaning of this speech,
  But it does frighten me—
MARQUIS: He has been saved!
  And what the price was is no matter! Still,
  'Tis for today alone, and there remains
  But little time. He should be sparing. He
  Must leave Madrid tonight.
QUEEN: Must leave tonight?
MARQUIS: The preparations have been made. In that
  Carthusian cloister where we have been wont
  Long since to find a refuge for our friendship,
  He will receive the news. Here in exchange
  Is what my fortune left me on this earth.
  What's lacking, *you* can add. Indeed, I had
  For Carlos many things still in my heart,
  Still much that he should know; but it could be
  That I shall find the time is lacking me
  To take it up with him in person—You
  Will speak with him this evening, so I turn
  To you—
QUEEN: To put my mind at rest, Marquis,

You must explain to me more clearly—not
Converse this way with me in frightening riddles.
Just tell me what has happened.
MARQUIS: I have still
One weighty declaration to submit;
I put it in your hands. For me there was
One piece of fortune such as few may have:
I loved a sovereign's son—My heart, in that
I dedicated it to only one,
Included the whole world! In Carlos' soul
Through me a paradise for millions was
Created. Oh, my dreams were beautiful—
But Providence decided to recall
Me when my lovely seedling was not grown.
Soon he will have his Roderick no more.
The friend will cease in the beloved. Here,
Here—here—on this most holy of all altars,
Within the heart of his dear Queen, I lay
My last, most precious legacy, and here
He'll find it when I am no more—
            (He turns away, his voice choked with tears.)
QUEEN: This is
The speech of someone who is dying. Still,
I hope it is but melancholy—or
Do these words have a meaning?
MARQUIS *(attempts to compose himself, and continues with
a firmer tone):*   You shall tell
The Prince that he must think about that oath
That in those wild, enthusiastic days
We swore together on the Host we shared.
The oath I swore that time I have kept well,
I have been true to it until my death—
Now it is time for him—
QUEEN: Till death?
MARQUIS: He shall—
Oh, tell him that!—shall make the vision true,
That daring vision of a brand new state,
The godlike offspring of our friendship. He
Shall be the first to touch the unwrought stone.

And if he finishes it or succumbs—
Is all the same to him! He touched it. When
The centuries have flown away, then will
Some Providence repeat again a prince,
Like him, upon a throne, like his, and will
Inflame with that enthusiasm its
New favorite. And you shall tell him that
For these grand visions of his youth he shall
Be treated with esteem when he is older.
He shall not open up the heart of this
Most tender blossom to the deadly bug
Of celebrated better judgment—that
He might not be misled if dusty wisdom
Should slander heavenly enthusiasm.
I said it to him once before—

QUEEN: Marquis?
Where does that lead?

MARQUIS: And you must tell him that
I lay the fate of humankind upon
His soul, that dying I demanded—
Demanded! *That* I am entitled to.
It would have been my chance to cause a whole
New dawn to break above the Spanish Empire.
The King bestowed his heart upon me. He
Addressed me as his son—I bear his seal,
And all his Albas are no more.

> (*He stops and for a few moments looks silently
> at the Queen.*)

                                    You weep—
These tears are known to me, you lovely soul,
'Tis joy that makes them flow. But that is past,
All past. 'Twas Carlos or myself. The choice
Was quick and frightful. One was to be lost,
And I want to be *that one*—I would rather—
Do not require more information.

QUEEN: Now,
Now I begin to understand at last—
Unhappy man, what is it you have done?

MARQUIS: A sacrifice of two short evening hours

To save the sunshine of a summer's day.
I will give up the King. What can I be
Then to the King?—In this unyielding land
No rose will bloom for me again—the fate
Of Europe ripens with my noble friend!
I hand Spain now to him, for it will lie
And bleed 'neath Philipp's hand till then!—Oh woe
To me and him, if I should rue this act!
Perhaps I've chosen what was worse! But no!
I know my Carlos—that will never be
The case—and my security, O Queen,
Is you!
                    (after a silence)
            I saw it stir, this love, I saw
The most unfortunate of passions take
A hold upon his heart—Still then it was
Within my strength to offer opposition.
I did not, no, I nourished it, it did
Not seem unfortunate to me. The world
May judge it differently. I'll not repent.
My heart does not accuse me. I saw life,
Where they saw death—I recognized within
These hopeless flames the golden rays of hope.
I meant to lead him into excellence,
To elevate him to the utmost beauty;
Our moral state denies an image to me,
Our language words—so I committed him
To this—my only guidance for him was
An explanation of his love.
QUEEN: Marquis,
Your friend filled up your thoughts entirely, so
You have forgotten me. Did you believe
I was absolved from woman's frailty
When I was designated as an angel
And he was given virtue as his weapon?
You did not ponder very long upon
How much there is our hearts must dare, when we
Seek to ennoble passion with such names.
MARQUIS: For other women, only not for *one*.

Of *one* I'm confident—Or can it be
You are ashamed of this most noble longing,
To be the author of heroic virtue?
What is it to King Philipp, if in the
Escorial the artist grasps from the
Transfiguration all eternity?
And does the lovely harmony that sleeps
Within the lyre belong to one who buys
It and who guards it with deaf ears? He has
Bought up the right to smash it into pieces,
But not the art to summon silvery tones
And melt away into the song's delight.
For truth is in existence for the wise
And beauty for a feeling heart. The two
Belong to one another. And this faith
Cannot be shattered for me by some biased
Belief. Now promise me to love him ever,
Nor tempted by the fear of men or by
Some pseudo-valor to a vain denial,
To love him ever and unchangingly,
Can you give me this promise?—O my Queen—
Give it to me here in my hand.

QUEEN: My heart,
  I promise you, shall be alone and always
  The judge of love for me.

MARQUIS (*draws back his hand*): Now I can die
  In peace—My work has been completed now.
        (*He bows to the Queen and is about to leave.*)

QUEEN (*in silence follows him with her eyes*):
  So you will leave, Marquis—and not advise
  When we—how soon—we'll meet again.

MARQUIS (*he comes back but turns his face away*):
                                    Of course!
  We'll meet again.

QUEEN: I understand you, Posa—
  I understand you well—Why have you done
  This thing to me?

MARQUIS: 'Twas he or I.

QUEEN: No! No!

You threw yourself into this deed that you
Call noble. You cannot deny it now.
I know you. You have thirsted for this chance.
May hearts break by the thousands, what is it
To you as long as you can feed your pride.
Oh, now—now I can understand you! You
Were seeking veneration.

MARQUIS *(taken aback, to himself):* No! Oh, I
  Was not prepared for that—

QUEEN *(after a silence):*   Marquis! Is there
  No chance at all of an escape?

MARQUIS: None.

QUEEN: None?
  Consider carefully. Is there no chance?
  Not with my help?

MARQUIS: Not with your help.

QUEEN: You know
  Me only partly—I am brave.

MARQUIS: I know.

QUEEN: And there is no escape?

MARQUIS: No, none.

QUEEN *(moves away from him and covers her face):*
                              Then go!
  I will esteem no man again.

MARQUIS *(throwing himself at her feet with intense emotion):*
                              My Queen!
  —O God! But life is beautiful!
    *(He jumps up and leaves quickly. The Queen goes
    into her private chamber.)*

The King's antechamber

Scene 22

*Duke of Alba and Domingo walk back and forth in silence and
separately. Count Lerma comes out of the King's private chamber,
thereupon Don Raimund of Taxis, the chief postmaster.*

LERMA: Has the Marquis still not made his appearance?
ALBA: Not yet.
     (Lerma is about to go back in.)
TAXIS *(comes forward)*: Count Lerma, please announce me now.
LERMA: The King sees no one.
TAXIS: If you would but say
 That I *must* speak with him. His Majesty's
 Concerns are here at stake. You must make haste.
 The matter is extremely urgent.
    (Lerma goes into the private chamber.)
ALBA *(approaches the Chief Postmaster)*: Taxis,
 You must learn to have patience. You will not
 Speak with the King
TAXIS: I won't? And why?
ALBA: You should
 Have had the foresight to secure permission
 Ahead of time from the Marquis of Posa,
 Who holds both son and father prisoner.
TAXIS: Marquis of Posa? So? That's right! He is
 The person from whom I received this letter—
ALBA: What letter is that?
TAXIS: One I was to send
 To Brussels—
ALBA *(alert)*: Brussels?
TAXIS: 'Twas the one I was
 Just bringing to the King—
ALBA: To Brussels! Did
 You hear that, Chaplain? Brussels!
DOMINGO *(joins them)*:   That might be
 Suspicious.
TAXIS: He was anxious and self-conscious
 When he was giving it to me.
DOMINGO: So! Anxious?
ALBA: To whom is it addressed then?
TAXIS: The Prince
 Of Nassau and of Orange.
ALBA: To William?—That,
 O Chaplain! that is treason!
DOMINGO: What else could
 It be?—Yes, certainly, this letter must

Immediately be transmitted to
The King. Such merit, worthy man, from you,
To be so firm in service to the King!
TAXIS: O noble sir, I only did my duty.
ALBA: You did it well.
LERMA *(comes out of the private chamber. To the Chief
Postmaster):*   The King will speak with you.
                    (Taxis goes in.)
Is the Marquis not here yet?
DOMINGO: They are looking
All over for him.
ALBA: Strange and wonderful.
The Prince a captive of the State, the King
Himself uncertain still just why.
DOMINGO: He has
Not even come to give him an account?
ALBA: How did the King receive the news?
LERMA: The King
Spoke not a word.
              (noise in the private chamber)
ALBA: Hark! What was that?
TAXIS *(comes out of the private chamber):* Count Lerma!
                 (Both go in.)
ALBA *(to Domingo):*
What's happening?
DOMINGO: What is this note of fear?
Perhaps this intercepted letter? I
Suspect no good, my Duke.
ALBA: He calls for Lerma!
And certainly must know that we are in
The antechamber—
DOMINGO: Well, our time is past.
ALBA: And am I not the man for whom all doors
Were opened wide before? How everything
Has changed around me now—how strange—
DOMINGO *(has approached the door to the private room and
stands there listening):*   Hark!
ALBA *(after a pause):*   All
Is quiet as the tomb. You hear them breathe.
DOMINGO: The sound is muffled by the tapestries.

ALBA: Away! They come.

DOMINGO (*moves away from the door*):
I feel so solemn now,
So fearful, just as if this moment should
Decide great destinies.

Scene 23

The Prince of Parma, the Dukes of Feria and Medina Sidonia enter with still other grandees. The previous.

PARMA: Now, is the King
Receiving?

ALBA: No.

PARMA: No? Who is with him?

FERIA: The
Marquis of Posa doubtless.

ALBA: They await
Him momentarily.

PARMA: This very minute
We have arrived from Saragossa. All
Madrid is seized by the same fear. Is it
Then true?

DOMINGO: Yes, sad to say!

FERIA: It's true? He has
Been taken prisoner by the Maltese?

ALBA: Yes, it is so.

PARMA: But why? What happened?

ALBA: Why?
That no one knows except His Majesty
And the Marquis.

PARMA: Without consulting with
The kingdom's Cortes first?

FERIA: A curse upon
The man who shared in this state injury.

ALBA: A curse on him, I add.

MEDINA SIDONIA: I, too.

THE OTHER GRANDEES: We all.

ALBA: Who goes into the chamber with me? I
Will grovel at his feet.

LERMA (*rushes out of the chamber*): Duke Alba!
DOMINGO: Now!
  May God be praised!
                (*Alba hurries in.*)
LERMA (*breathless, greatly agitated*):
                When the Maltese arrives,
  Our Lord will now not be alone, and he
  Will have him summoned.
DOMINGO (*to Lerma, as all the others gather around him full
  of curious expectation*): What has happened, Count?
  You are as pale as any corpse.
LERMA (*about to hurry off*):   It is
  The devil's work!
PARMA AND FERIA: What is? What is?
MEDINA SIDONIA: What has
  The King done?
DOMINGO (*at the same time*): The devil's work? What is it, then?
LERMA: The King
  Has wept.
DOMINGO: Has wept?
ALL (*at the same time, with mounting astonishment*):
                Has wept? The King has wept?
    (*A bell can be heard in the private chamber. Count
    Lerma rushes in.*)
DOMINGO (*after him, tries to hold him back*):
  Count, just one word—Forgive me—He is gone!
  We stand here rooted to the floor in dread.

Scene 24

*Princess of Eboli. Feria. Medina Sidonia. Parma. Domingo and
other grandees.*
EBOLI (*in a hurry, beside herself*):
  Where is the King? Where is he? I must speak
  With him.
              (*to Feria*)
      Duke, you can take me to him.
FERIA: There

Are weighty problems now before the King.
And no one can go in.

EBOLI: Has he subscribed
The frightful sentence yet? He is deceived.
I have the proof to bring to him that he
Has been deceived.

DOMINGO (*gives her a meaningful signal from the distance*):
Princess of Eboli!

EBOLI (*approaches him*):
You, too, are here, Priest? Good! I need you now.
You shall confirm my word.
(*She grabs his hand and tries to pull him into
the private chamber.*)

DOMINGO: I shall?—Are you
Insane, Princess?

FERIA: You must stay back. The King
Will not receive you now. He must receive
Me. He must hear the truth—the truth! Were he
Ten times himself a god!

DOMINGO: Away! Away!
You will risk everything. You must stay back.

EBOLI: Before your graven idols, tremble, Priest.
There's nothing that I have to risk.
(*As she is about to go into the chamber, out rushes
Duke Alba.*)

ALBA (*His eyes are gleaming, his carriage is triumphant.
He hurries to Domingo and embraces him.*):
Require
A Te Deum to sound in every church.
The victory is ours.

DOMINGO: Is ours?

ALBA (*to Domingo and the other grandees*):
Now come
In to our Lord. You'll hear the rest from me.

ACT 5

A room in the royal palace, separated by a door with an iron grate from a courtyard in which guards pace back and forth.

Scene 1

Carlos sitting at a table, his head on his arms, as if he were sleeping. In the back of the room some officers who have been locked up with him. Marquis of Posa enters, without being noticed by him, and speaks quickly with the officers, who immediately move away. He himself moves very close to Carlos and watches him for a few moments sadly in silence. Finally he makes a movement that arouses the Prince from his stupor.

CARLOS *(stands up, becomes aware of the Marquis, and winces*
in fear. Then he gazes at him for a while with big,
staring eyes and rubs his forehead with his hand, as
if he were trying to think of something):
MARQUIS: 'Tis I.
CARLOS *(holds out his hand):*
             You've really come to see me, then?
That's very kind of you.
MARQUIS: I took it in
My head that you could make use of a friend.
CARLOS: In truth? You really thought that? Well, now look!
I am so pleased—it pleases me immensely.
I thought for certain you were still my friend.
MARQUIS: That I deserved from you.
CARLOS: Is it not true?
We understand each other totally.
I like that well. Consideration, mildness
Become such noble souls as you and me.
No matter that I was unreasonable
In my demands, have you then also to
Deny me reasonable ones? For stern
Is virtue, but it is not ever cruel,
Not ever barbarous. It cost you much!

Oh, yes, I think I know quite well how much
Your gentle heart did bleed as you adorned
Your victim for the sacrifice.

MARQUIS: O Carlos!
How do you mean that?

CARLOS: You will now achieve
What I should have and could not. You will give
To Spaniards as a gift the golden days
That they had hoped in vain to get from me.
For me 'tis over now forever! You
Had recognized that. Oh, this frightful love
Has carried off the early blossoms of
My spirit irretrievably. For all
Your noble hopes I am as good as dead.
But Providence or chance has led you to
The King. My secret is all it requires,
And he is yours—and you can be his angel.
For me there is no rescue—but perhaps
For Spain. Oh, there is nothing to condemn,
Not anything except my own delusion
That kept me till this day from comprehending
You are—as great as you are tender.

MARQUIS: No!
That was not something I foresaw—I could
Not see that my friend's generosity
Would have more ingenuity than would
My prudent care. The structure that I built
Comes tumbling down—for I forgot your heart.

CARLOS: If you had only found it possible
To save *her* from this fate—I would have been
Unutterably thankful to you. Could
I then not bear it all alone? Had she
To be a second sacrifice?—Enough
Of that! I will not burden you with blame.
What is the Queen to *you?* Did *you* love her?
And should your austere virtue answer to
The unimportant worries of my love?
Forgive me—I have been unfair.

MARQUIS: You are.

But—not because of this rebuke. If I
Deserved the *one,* then I deserved them all—
And I would not stand *thus* before you.
           (He takes out his portfolio.)
                                     Here
Are letters from among the ones that you
Have given to me to look after. Take
Them back again.
CARLOS *(looks with astonishment, first at the letters, then at the Marquis):* What?
MARQUIS: I return them to you
Because they would be safer in your hands
Now than they'd be in mine.
CARLOS: How can this be?
The King has never read them then? He did
Not even take a look at them?
MARQUIS: At *these?*
CARLOS: You did not show them all to him?
MARQUIS: Who told
You that I showed him one?
CARLOS *(extremely astonished):* Can that be so?
Count Lerma.
MARQUIS: He's the one who told you? Oh,
Now everything, yes, everything is clear!
Who could have guessed it? It was Lerma then?
No, *that* man never learned to lie. Quite right,
The other letters are in the King's hands.
CARLOS *(looks at him for a long time in speechless astonishment):*
What is the reason I am here?
MARQUIS: Precaution—
So if you should attempt a second time
Perhaps to choose an Eboli to be
Your trusted friend—
CARLOS *(as if waking from a dream):* Aha! Now finally!
I see now—everything is clear—
MARQUIS *(goes to the door):*
                    Who comes?

Scene 2

Duke Alba. The previous.

ALBA (*approaches the Prince respectfully, his back turned
to the Marquis through this whole scene*):
Prince, you are free. The King dispatched me here
So that I might inform you.
> (*Carlos looks at the Marquis in surprise. All are
> silent.*)
>   In addition,
I think myself quite fortunate to be
The first to have the honor—

CARLOS (*looks at both with extreme astonishment. After a
pause, to the Duke*):   I have been
Imprisoned, and now I have been released,
And I have not been told the reason why
Both things were done.

ALBA: Just a precaution, Prince,
From what I know, to which the King was led
By someone who was practicing—deceit.

CARLOS: But was it then upon the King's command
That I am here?

ALBA: Yes, it was the result
Of a mistake our monarch made.

CARLOS: I am
Extremely sorry. Still, it would befit
The King, when he has made an error, to
Correct the wrong that he has done in person.
> (*He tries to catch the eye of the Marquis and observes
> a proud look of disparagement toward the Duke.*)
Here I am called Don Philipp's son. They treat
Me with both curiosity and lies.
So what His Majesty finds he must do,
I do not want to seem to owe their favor.
And otherwise I am prepared to go
Before the Cortes' judgment. I will not
Accept my sword from hands like those.

ALBA: The King

Will certainly not hesitate to grant
Your Highness such a just request. If you
Will just allow me to accompany
You, we will go to him.
CARLOS: I will stay here
Until the King or all of his Madrid
Shall lead me out of this confinement. Take
That answer to him.
> *(Alba departs. He can be seen still for a time,*
> *tarrying in the courtyard and issuing orders.)*

Scene 3

Carlos and Marquis of Posa.
CARLOS *(after the Duke has gone, full of expectation*
and surprise, to the Marquis):
                              Now what can this be?
Explain it. Are you not the minister?
MARQUIS: As you can see, I have been one.
> *(walking toward him, with great emotion)*
                                        O Carlos,
It worked. It really did succeed. Now it
Is done, and glory be the power that did
Allow it to succeed.
CARLOS: Succeed? How's that?
I do not understand your words.
MARQUIS *(seizes his hand):*   You have
Been rescued—you are free—and I—
> *(He stops short.)*
CARLOS: And you?
MARQUIS: And I—I now can press you to my breast
For the first time with full and total right;
For I have purchased this with everything—
O Carlos, everything that's dear. How sweet,
How great this moment is! Now I can well
Be satisfied with what I've done.
CARLOS: What are
These sudden changes in your features? I

Have never seen you so. More proudly do
You stand with head held high and shining eyes.
MARQUIS: Now, Carlos, we must part, but do not fear.
Oh, be a man. Please promise me you will
Not make this separation difficult
Because of overwhelming grief, unworthy
Of noble souls, no matter what you hear—
For many years you'll love me, Carlos. Fools
Call it forever.
            (*Carlos pulls his hand away, stares at him fixedly,
            and does not answer.*)
                        Be a man. I have
Depended on you, have not hesitated
To suffer through these dreaded hours with you,
The ones so frighteningly called the *last*—
Indeed, shall I admit it, Carlos? I
Found pleasure in it.—Come, let us sit down.
I feel quite tired and weak.
            (*He moves close to Carlos, who is still stiff
            and lifeless and allows himself to be
            involuntarily drawn down.*)
                        Where do you bide?
You do not answer me?—I will be brief.
The next day after we for the last time
Had seen each other at the monastery,
The King required my presence. My success
You know as does all of Madrid. But you
Do not know that your secret was betrayed
To him, that letters found within the Queen's
Own case bore evidence against you, that
I learned about this from his very mouth,
And that—I was his confidant.
            (*He stops to hear Carlos' answer; he persists
            in his silence.*)
                        Yes, Carlos!
I broke my loyalty to you with my
Own lips. I steered the plot myself that brought
About your downfall. What was done already

Was too apparent, and it was too late
To clear you of it. To assure myself
Of his revenge was what was left—and so
I was your enemy to serve you better.
—Do you not hear?

CARLOS: I hear. Go on. Go on.

MARQUIS: To this point I am guiltless. But too soon
The unaccustomed rays of royal favor
Betray me, and my reputation comes
To you just as I had foreseen. Then I,
Infected by misled affection and
Deceived by proud illusion that I could
Conclude this daring venture without you,
Conceal my risky secret from my friend.
That was the great rashness on my part!
I was so wrong. I know it. Confidence
Was my undoing. Pardon me—It was
Based on your friendship's perpetuity.

> (*Here he becomes silent. Carlos' expression changes from
> a petrified stare into one of extreme mobility.*)

What I had feared then happens, and you are
Alarmed by fabricated dangers. Here
The Queen lies in her blood—the frightfulness
Of the reverberating palace—Lerma's
Unfortunate desire to serve you—my
Incomprehensible reserve, these all
Assault your heart so unaware. You waver—
And think your friend is lost. But in your own
Nobility you deck his disaffection
With greatness; then you dare to call him faithless
When, though he's faithless, you can still admire
Him. So deserted by the one, you throw
Yourself into the arms of the Princess—
Unhappy man! into a devil's arms;
For she it was who had betrayed you.

> (*Carlos rises.*)

I espy you going there. An awful thought
Flies through my mind. I follow you. Too late.

You lie there at her feet. And o'er your lips
Already has passed your confession. Now
For you there is no rescue—

CARLOS: No! No! She
Was moved. You are so wrong. I know that she
Was moved.

MARQUIS: It turns to night within my mind!
There's nothing—nothing—no way out—no help—
Not in the whole extent of Nature! And
Despair makes me a beast, a fury. I
Then place my dagger on a woman's breast—
But then a ray of light gleams in my soul.
"If I could but delude the King? If I
Myself could seem to be the guilty one?
A possibility or not!—For him
Enough, for Philipp probably enough,
Since it was bad. So be it! I will try.
Perhaps a thunderbolt, which unforeseen
Should strike, will stop the tyrant—and what more
Is needed? He considers, and the time
Is gained for Carlos to flee to Brabant."

CARLOS: And that—that is what you have done?

MARQUIS: I write
A letter to the Prince of Orange that says
I loved the Queen and have succeeded in
Escaping the suspicion of the King
Through the mistrust that falsely lay on you—
That through the King himself I found a way
To freely come in contact with the Queen.
I add that I am fearful of detection,
That you, advised about my passion, have
Gone quickly to Princess of Eboli,
Perhaps through her to warn the Queen—that I
Have taken you a captive here, and now,
Since everything is doubtless lost, I am
Prepared to come to Brussels.—In this letter—

CARLOS (*interrupts him, frightened*):
But you have not relied upon the mail!
You know all letters to the Netherlands—

MARQUIS: Are handed over to the King. So as
 The situation stands Taxis will have
 Already done his job.
CARLOS: Then I am lost!
MARQUIS: You lost? Why you?
CARLOS: Unhappy man, and you
 Are lost with me. My father never will
 Forgive you this whole monstrous trickery.
 No! He cannot forgive!
MARQUIS: What trickery?
 You are distracted. Think! Who tells him then
 That it was trickery?
CARLOS *(stares fixedly at him)*: *Who,* do you ask?
 I do myself.

     (He starts to leave.)
MARQUIS: You're mad. Stay here!
CARLOS: Away!
 For God's sake! Do not stop me now. For while
 I tarry here, he will already have
 Engaged his killers.
MARQUIS: So the time is precious.
 We still have much to tell each other.
CARLOS: What?
 Before he has—
   (He starts to leave again. The Marquis takes him
   by the arm and looks at him meaningfully.)
MARQUIS: Now listen, Carlos. Was
 I in such haste, was I so conscience-stricken
 That time you bled for me—when still a boy?
CARLOS *(stands before him, moved and full of admiration)*:
 'Tis Providence!
MARQUIS: Oh, save yourself for Flanders!
 The kingdom is your calling, and to die
 For you was mine.
CARLOS *(goes to him and takes him by the hand, full of*
 the most ardent emotion): Oh, no! Oh, no! He will—
 He cannot possibly resist! Cannot
 Resist so much nobility!—I will
 Lead you to him. We will go to him arm

In arm. And I will say to him: My father,
You see, a friend has done this for his friend.
Oh, that will move him. Just believe me, he
Is not without humanity, my father.
Yes, certainly, he will be moved. His eyes
Will overflow with kindly tears, and he
Will pardon you and me—

> *(A shot comes through the barred door.*
> *Carlos jumps up.)*

Who was that for?

MARQUIS: I think—for me.

> *(He sinks to the floor.)*

CARLOS *(falls with a cry of pain next to him on the floor)*:

O heavenly
Compassion!

MARQUIS *(his voice breaking)*:

He is very quick—this King—
I hoped—for more—Consider your escape—
You hear?—Consider your escape. The Queen
Knows everything. I can no more—

> *(Carlos remains by the corpse, lying as if dead.*
> *After a time the King enters, accompanied by many*
> *grandees, and recoils at the sight. A general, deep*
> *pause. The grandees place themselves in a half-circle*
> *around the two and look alternately at the King and*
> *at his son. The latter still lies without a trace of*
> *life. —The King looks at him in meditative silence.)*

Scene 4

The King. Carlos. The Dukes of Alba, Feria, and Medina Sidonia.
The Prince of Parma. Count Lerma. Domingo and many gran-
dees.

KING *(in a benevolent tone)*: I have
Acceded to your plea, my Prince. I come
Myself with all the nobles of my land
To notify you of your freedom.

> *(Carlos looks up and glances around like one who has*

awakened from a dream. He looks first at the
King, then at the dead Marquis. He does not answer.)
Take

Your sword again. These things were done too rashly.
   (He approaches, extends his hand, and helps him rise.)
This is no place to find my son. Arise
And come into your father's arms.

CARLOS *(Receives the King's embrace unconsciously—but*
suddenly remembers himself, stops, and looks at
him more closely.):   You smell
Of murder. I cannot embrace you now.
   (He pushes him away; the grandees are all agitated.)
Oh, no! Do not be so distraught. What have
I done that is so monstrous then? Attacked
The Heaven's own anointed? Do not fear.
I will not lay a hand on him. Do you
Not see the mark upon his forehead? God
Has branded him.

KING *(moving away quickly):* Now, follow me, my grandees.

CARLOS: Where to? Not from this spot, Sire—
   (He holds him by force with both hands and
   with one gets hold of the sword that the King
   has brought. It comes out of the sheath.)

KING: Will you draw
A sword against your father?
        (All the grandees draw theirs)
             Regicide!

CARLOS *(holding the King firmly with one hand, the bare sword*
with the other):
Now sheathe your swords. What do you want? Do you
Believe I am insane? No, I am not
Insane. Were I, *you* ought not to remind
Me that his life depends upon my sword's
Sharp point. So, please, I ask you to keep back,
For dispositions of my kind need to
Be flattered—therefore, keep away. What I
Intend to settle with this king has nought
To do with your oath of allegiance. Look,
His fingers bleed! Look carefully at him.

Just look! And look here, too! *That* is what he
Has done, this great performer!

KING (*to the grandees, who attempt to press close around
him*):   You must all
Move back. Why do you tremble? Are we not
A son and father? I will but await
Whatever shameful deed that Nature—

CARLOS: Nature?
I know of none, for murder is the watchword.
All human bonds are torn asunder. You
Yourself have rent them, Sire, in all your lands.
Shall I respect what you are scornful of?
Oh, look, look here! No murder has occurred
Except today.—Is there no God? What? Can
Within His universe kings wreak such havoc?
I ask, is there no God? As long as mothers
Have given birth, there is but *one*—just *one*
Who died so undeservedly.—Do you
Know *what* you've done? Oh, no, he does not know,
Knows not that he has stolen from this world
A life that was far more important and
Was nobler and more precious than he was
With his whole century.

KING (*in a mild tone*):   If I have been
Too rash, does it befit you to call me
To answer *for* whom I have erred?

CARLOS: What's that?
Now can that be? You do not guess what this
Dead man has been to me—oh, tell him—help
His all-inclusive knowledge solve this riddle.
The dead man was my friend. And do you want
To know why he is dead? He died for me.

KING: Aha! I had a feeling!

CARLOS: You who died,
Forgive that I profane this for such ears!
But this great judge of human nature should
Sink down for shame that his gray wisdom was
Outwitted by the cleverness of youth.
Yes, Sire! For we were brothers! Brothers through

A nobler bond than Nature ever fashioned.
The story of his life was love. His love
For me, his fair and noble death. He was
My own when *you* did brag about his interest
And when his playful eloquence made sport
Of your most haughty giant intellect.
You fancied you controlled him—but you were
A docile implement of his designs.
That I was taken captive was a plan
Drawn out of friendship. Then to save me he
Composed the letter to the Prince of Orange—
O God! It was the first lie of his life!
To save me he propelled himself toward death,
Which he endured. Your favor was conferred
Upon him—but he died for me. Your heart,
Your friendship you forced him to take. He made
Your scepter to a plaything in his hand;
He threw it down and died for me!

> *(The King stands motionless, his eyes glued to
> the floor. All the grandees look at him
> disconcerted and nervous.)*
> And was

This possible? That you could place your faith
In this crude lie? How little must he have
Respected you when he endeavored to
Approach you with this clumsy trickery!
You dared to strive to win his friendship and
You had already failed this easy test!
Oh, no—no, that was not for you. That was
No man for you! He knew it well himself,
When he rejected you with all your crowns.
This delicate stringed instrument was crushed
By your iron hand. For all that you could do
Was murder him.

ALBA *(till now has not let the King out of his sight
and has watched the commotion with obvious
uneasiness that appears on his face. Now he
approaches him timidly):* Sire—not this deathly silence.
Just look around you. Speak with us.

CARLOS: He was
   Concerned about you. You had long since had
   His sympathy. Maybe! He could have made
   You happy, for his heart was full enough
   To satisfy you with its ample surplus.
   The fragments of his spirit would have made
   Of you a god. But you have robbed us of
   His very self—
   What can you offer to replace a soul
   Like this one?
      (A deep silence. Many of the grandees look away
      or cover their faces with their cloaks.)
   Oh, you who gather here, struck dumb by horror
   And admiration—you must not condemn
   The youth who makes this speech attacking his
   Own father and the King.—Just look at him!
   Yes, he has died for me! Do you have tears?
   Does blood, not glowing bronze, flow in your veins?
   Look here and you will not condemn me!
      (He turns to the King with more composure
      and self-possession.)
   Perhaps you wait to see how this unnatural
   Affair will end? Here is my sword. You are
   My King again. Now do you think I tremble
   Before your vengeance? You can murder me
   As you have murdered this most noble man.
   My life is forfeit, I know that. What is
   My life to me? I will renounce all that
   Which might await me in this world. And you
   May look at strangers searching for a son—
   There lies my kingdom.
      (He sinks down upon the corpse and takes no more
      part in the following. Meanwhile there can be
      heard in the distance the disordered noise of
      voices and a crowd of people. There is a deep
      silence around the King. He looks about the whole
      circle, but no one meets his gaze.)
KING: Well? Does no one want
   To answer?—Every eye is on the floor—

Each face is veiled! My sentence has been passed.
In these mute countenances I can read
The proclamation—that my subjects do
Condemn me.
> *(The same silence as before. —The tumult comes*
> *nearer and becomes louder. A murmur moves through*
> *the nobles standing there; they make gestures of*
> *embarrassment to one another. Finally Count Lerma*
> *touches the Duke of Alba gently.)*

LERMA: That is an assault!
ALBA *(softly):*   I fear so.
LERMA: They're forcing their way through. They come.

Scene 5

An officer of the bodyguard. The foregoing.
OFFICER *(urgently):*   Rebellion!
Where is the King?
> *(He works his way through the throng and forces his*
> *way through to the King.)*
                    Madrid is up in arms!
The frenzied soldiers and the people ring
The palace by the thousands. It is said
Prince Carlos has been taken prisoner,
His life in danger. And the people want
To see that he's alive or they will let
Madrid go up in flames.
ALL THE GRANDEES *(agitated):* Oh, save—oh, save
The King!
ALBA *(to the King, who stands calm and motionless):*
          You must take refuge, Sire—there is
A risk. We do not know as yet just who
Has armed the people—
KING *(wakens from his stupor, pulls himself together,*
and strides majestically among them):
                    Does my throne still stand?
Am I still Monarch in this Kingdom?—No.
I am not any more. These cowards weep,

Made weaklings by a boy. They only wait
Upon the signal to desert me now.
I am betrayed by rebels.

ALBA: O my Lord,
That is but frightful fantasy!

KING: Down there!
Fall prostrate on the ground! Before this young,
This budding king throw yourself down. For I
Am but a powerless old man!

ALBA: Now has
It come to this!—Up, Spaniards!
    (All crowd around the King and kneel with drawn
    swords before him. Carlos remains by the corpse,
    alone and deserted by all.)

KING *(pulls off his cloak and throws it down):*
          Cover *him*
With royal finery—and carry him
Upon my trampled body—
    (He falls unconscious into Alba's and Lerma's arms.)

LERMA: Help! O God!

FERIA: O God! How strange!

LERMA: He is unconscious—

ALBA *(leaves the King in Lerma's and Feria's hands):*
          Take
Him to his bed. And in the meanwhile I
Will bring peace to Madrid.
    (He exits. The King is carried off, and all the
    grandees accompany him.)

Scene 6

Carlos remains alone by the corpse. After a few moments Luis
Mercado appears, looks around timidly, and stands silently for a
while behind the Prince, who does not notice him.

MERCADO: I have been sent
Here by Her Royal Majesty, the Queen.
    (Carlos looks away and does not answer.)
My name's Mercado—and I am the doctor

Who waits upon the Queen—and here is my
Authority.
> *(He shows the Prince a seal ring—the latter maintains
> his silence.)*
The Queen desires to speak
With you today, my Prince—important matters
Are pending—

CARLOS: Nothing is important to
Me in this world.

MERCADO: She said there is a message
That the Marquis of Posa left—

CARLOS *(gets up quickly):* What's that?
Immediately.
> *(He starts to leave with him.)*

MERCADO: No! Not now. You must
Await the night. For every entrance is
Watched carefully, and every guard is doubled.
It is impossible now unobserved
To enter this wing of the palace. You
Would hazard everything—

CARLOS: But—

MERCADO: Only one
Means, Prince, is there that still exists at all—
The Queen has thought it out. She wants to put
It to you—it is bold, unusual, and
Adventurous.

CARLOS: It is—?

MERCADO: There has long been
A legend, as you know, that says at midnight
The ghost of the departed emperor
Does walk the royal castle's vaulted halls,
Dressed as a monk. The common people do
Believe this story, so that sentries will
Serve at this post with dread. If you can make
Your mind up to use this disguise, you can
Succeed in going by the men on watch
Entirely free and safe up to the room
In which the Queen resides and which this key
Will open. In this saintly guise you will

Be well protected from attack. But your
Decision must be made upon the spot.
The necessary garment and the mask
Are in your room. I must make haste to bring
Your answer to the Queen.

CARLOS: What time?

MERCADO: The time
Is twelve o'clock.

CARLOS: Just tell her that she can
Await me.

> *(Mercado exits.)*

Scene 7

Carlos. Count Lerma.

LERMA: Up and save yourself, my Prince.
The King is raging at you. An attempt
Upon your freedom—or perhaps your life.
Do not interrogate me further. I
Have stolen off to warn you. You must flee
Without delay.

CARLOS: But I am in the hands
Of the Almighty.

LERMA: As the Queen observed
To me herself, you ought to leave Madrid
Today still, and then flee to Brussels. Do
Not put it off, oh, not at all. The riot
Will aid your flight. The Queen brought it about
With this intention. Now no one will venture
To practice force against you. There awaits
A carriage at the monastery; here
Are weapons, if you should be forced—

> *(gives him a dagger and a pocket pistol)*

CARLOS: My thanks,
Count Lerma!

LERMA: The events today have touched
Me to the quick. No friend will ever love
Like that again! All patriots must weep
For you. I can say nothing more just now.

CARLOS: Our dear departed said of you, Count Lerma,
　You were a noble man.
LERMA: 　　　　　　　　　Once more, my Prince!
　A good trip to you. Better times will come;
　But then I will not be here anymore.
　You shall receive my homage now.
　　　　　　(*He goes down at his feet on one knee.*)
CARLOS (*tries to prevent him from this. Very moved*):
　　　　　　　　　　　　Oh, don't.
　Please don't, Count. You affect me so—I do
　Not want to be so weak—
LERMA (*kisses his hand with emotion*):
　　　　　　　　　　My children's king!
　My children will be able to give up
　Their lives for you. I may not. In my children
　Remember me.—Oh, that you may return
　To Spain in peace—that you may be humane
　Upon King Philipp's throne, for you have learned
　The art of suffering. Do not attempt
　A bloody deed against your father! No—
　No bloody deed, my Prince! King Philipp used
　Coercion to remove his father from
　The throne—this Philipp must today be fearful
　Of *his* own son! Be mindful then of this,
　My Prince—and so may Heaven be your guide!
　　　　(*He leaves quickly. Carlos is about to hurry off
　　　　in another direction, turns around suddenly, and
　　　　throws himself down before the corpse, which he
　　　　embraces once more. Then he quickly leaves the room.*)

The King's antechamber

Scene 8

The Duke of Alba and the Duke of Feria are conversing.
ALBA: The city is at peace. How did you leave
　The King?
FERIA: 　　　In the most terrible of moods.
　He is in strict seclusion—and no matter

What should occur, he will allow no one
To come before him. His whole nature has
So suddenly been altered by Marquis
Of Posa's treachery. We do not know
Him anymore.

ALBA: I must go to him. This
Time I just cannot spare him. An important
Discovery has just been made.

FERIA: A new
Discovery?

ALBA: A monk from the Carthusian
Community, who secretly stole into
The Prince's rooms and caused suspicion with
His curiosity about the death
Of the Marquis, was noticed by my guards.
They held him, questioned him, and fear of death
Forced a confession from him that he had
With him some papers of great worth that the
Deceased had ordered him to give into
The Prince's hand alone—if he had not
Appeared to him himself before the sun
Went down.

FERIA: And so?

ALBA: The letters read as follows:
That Carlos between midnight and the dawn
Will leave Madrid.

FERIA: What's that?

ALBA: And that a ship
Is lying ready in Cadiz to take
Him off to Vlissingen and that the Lowlands
Are only waiting for him to arrive
To cast aside the Spanish chains.

FERIA: Aha!
What is this then?

ALBA: And other letters tell
That Suliman has put a fleet to sea
From Rhodes already—thus, according to
The terms of the agreement, to attack
The King of Spain upon the Inland Sea.

FERIA: Can that be possible?

ALBA: The letters make
  The trips that the Maltese was taking through
  All Europe recently more clear to me.
  'Twas nothing less than to equip with arms
  The northern powers to fight for Flemish freedom.

FERIA: So that was it!

ALBA: And to these letters was
  Attached a detailed plan of the whole war
  That was to separate the Netherlands
  Forever from the Spanish Kingdom. There
  Is nothing overlooked, all opposition
  And strengths are reckoned, all the sources and
  The country's strengths are accurate, and all
  The principles that should be followed, all
  Alliances to be concluded. The
  Design is fiendish, but in truth—divine!

FERIA: Incomprehensible betrayal!

ALBA: Further,
  There is referred to in a letter here
  A secret conversation to take place
  Between his mother and the Prince upon
  The evening of his flight.

FERIA: What? That would be
  Today.

ALBA: Tonight at midnight. So I have
  Already given orders for this instance.
  You see that it is urgent, I cannot
  Afford to lose a moment. Open up
  The King's room.

FERIA: No, for entrance is forbidden.

ALBA: Then I must open it—the growing danger
  Will justify this boldness—

> *(As he goes toward the door, it is opened, and
> the King enters.)*
>
>   It is he!

Scene 9

The King and those present.

(All are alarmed by his appearance, fall back, and respectfully let him through their middle. He moves in a waking dream, like a sleepwalker. His garments and his person still show the disorder that is the result of his having fainted. He walks with slow steps past those grandees who are present, looks fixedly at each one without really seeing any one of them. Finally he stops deep in thought, his eyes fixed on the floor, until his agitation finally becomes audible.)

KING: Deliver up the dead to me. I must
　　Have him again.
DOMINGO *(quietly to the Duke of Alba):*
　　　　　　　　　　Go on and speak to him.
KING *(as above):*
　　He thought of me as insignificant
　　And died. I must have him again. He must
　　Think better of me.
ALBA *(approaches timidly):* Sire—
KING:　　　　　　　　　　　　Who speaks?
　　　　　　(He looks slowly around the circle.)
　　　　　　　　　　　　　　　　　　　　Have you
　　Forgotten who I am? Why are you not
　　Upon your knees before me, vassal? I
　　Am still the King. Submission will I have.
　　Will all of you neglect me just because
　　That *one* disdained me?
ALBA:　　　　　　　　　Nothing more of him,
　　My King. An enemy more consequent
　　Than he arises in your land—
FERIA:　　　　　　　　　Prince Carlos—
KING: He had a friend, a friend who suffered death
　　For him—for him! With me he would have shared
　　My kingdom! Oh, how he looked down upon
　　Me! Even from a throne one does not look
　　So proudly down. Was it not clear how much

He had in mind with such a conquest? What
He lost, his grief acknowledged. And such tears
Are not for something transient. Had he lived!
I'd give an India for that. O cheerless
Omnipotence, that cannot even stretch
Its arm into the grave, cannot amend
A little overhaste with human life!
The dead do not rise up again. Who dares
To tell me I am fortunate? There in
The grave there dwells one who kept his esteem
From me. What do I care about the living?
One soul, just *one* free man, stood up in this
Whole century. That one—he scorned me and
He died.

ALBA: Then we have lived in vain! Let us
Go to our graves, O Spaniards. Even now
In death this man can rob us of our King's
Affection.

KING *(He sits down, his head supported by his arm.):*
          Had he only died for *me!*
I loved him, loved him very much. He was
As dear to me as my own son. A new
And better morning dawned for me in this
Young man. Who knows what I had planned for him!
Oh, he was my first love. May Europe call
Its curses down on me. Let Europe curse.
From him I had earned thanks.

DOMINGO: What was the spell
He used—

KING: He made this sacrifice for whom?
For that mere boy, my son? Oh, not at all.
I will not credit that. A Posa does
Not die for a mere boy. The meager flame
Of friendship will not fill a Posa's heart.
It beat for all mankind. His taste was for
The world with all its coming generations.
To gratify it he secured a throne—
And let it go. Should Posa then forgive
Himself for this high treason to his own

Humanity? Oh, no. I know him better.
Not Philipp to Don Carlos but instead
He sacrificed an old man to a youth,
His pupil, for the father's setting sun
Was not worth the day's work. That is put off
Till his son's coming rise. Oh, it is clear!
They wait for my departure.

ALBA: Will you read
The full corroboration in these letters?

KING *(rises):*
He could have been mistaken. I am still—
Still here. And thanks to Nature. I can feel
The strength of youth throughout my sinews. I
Will make of him a laughingstock, and let
His virtue have been only a chimera.
Let him have died a fool, and may his fall
Depreciate his era and his friend!
Let's see how they can do without me. For
One evening more the world is mine. I want
To use it, this one evening, so that when
I'm gone, no planter for ten generations
Will harvest anything from this scorched earth.
He sacrificed me to humanity,
Humanity shall make atonement! Now
His puppet shall be first.
                    (to the Duke of Alba)
                         What did you say
About the Prince? Repeat it to me. What
Is in these letters for me?

ALBA: Sire, these letters
Contain the legacy of the Marquis
Of Posa to Prince Carlos.

KING *(reads quickly through the papers, while all the
bystanders watch him carefully. After he has been
reading for a while, he puts them aside and walks
silently through the room):* Call to me
The Grand Inquisitor. I will request
Him to present me with an hour's time.
          (One of the grandees exits. The King takes up

the papers again, goes on reading, then puts them
aside again.)
And so this very night?
TAXIS: At two o'clock
The coach will stop before the monastery.
ALBA: The people whom I have sent out have seen
Some travel gear marked by the royal arms
And being carried to the monastery.
FERIA: And also it has been reported that
In Brussels great amounts of money have
Reportedly been raised in the Queen's name
By Masons.
KING: Where did you last see the Prince?
ALBA: By the Maltese's corpse.
KING: Is there still light
In the Queen's room?
ALBA: There all is quiet. She
Dismissed her maids-in-waiting earlier
Than she is usually accustomed to.
The Duchess of Arcos, who was the last
To go out of her room, left her by then
In a deep sleep.
(An officer of the bodyguard enters, draws the
Duke of Feria to one side, and speaks quietly
with him. The latter turns surprised to the Duke
of Alba, others press around, and a murmur arises.)
FERIA, TAXIS, DOMINGO *(together)*: How strange!
KING: What is it?
FERIA: A report, my Lord, that is
Not easy to believe—
DOMINGO: Two Swiss guards, who
Come just now from their posts, report—it is
Too laughable to be repeated.
KING: Yes?
ALBA: That in the left wing of the palace they
Beheld the ghost of the late emperor—
And that with bold and solemn step it passed
Beside them. And this same report has been
Confirmed by all the watches that are spread

Through the pavilion, and they add to this,
The apparition disappeared into
The Queen's apartment.
KING: And what was the shape
That he appeared in?
OFFICER: In the same apparel
That he was clothed in when he last appeared
In Justi as a monk of St. Jerome.
KING: He was a monk? Well, did the sentries know
Him when he lived? If not, how did they know
Then that it was the emperor?
OFFICER: That it
Must be the emperor his scepter showed.
'Twas carried in his hands.
DOMINGO: And also he
Has often been observed, the story goes,
In such a form.
KING: Did no one try to speak
A word with him?
OFFICER: No, no one dared to do it.
The sentries said their prayers and let him pass
With reverence between them.
KING: And the figure
Was lost within the chambers of the Queen?
OFFICER: The antechamber of the Queen.
                    (general silence)
KING *(turns around quickly):*   What think you?
ALBA: We are quite speechless, Sire.
KING *(to the officer, after some thought):*
                                    Now under arms
My guards shall barricade each entrance to
That wing. I am desirous of a chance
Of meeting with this apparition.
              (The officer exits. Immediately after, a page)
PAGE: Sire!
The Grand Inquisitor.
KING *(to those present):* You will depart.
              (The Grand Inquisitor, an old man of ninety years,
              and blind, leaning on a staff and led by two

*Dominicans. As he walks through their ranks, all
the grandees throw themselves down before him and
touch the hem of his garment. He bestows his
blessing on them. All withdraw.)*

Scene 10

The King and the Grand Inquisitor.
                              (a long silence)

GRAND INQUISITOR: Do
  I stand before the King?
KING: You do.
GRAND INQUISITOR: I could
  No longer tell.
KING: I will renew a scene
  From years gone by, as Crown Prince Philipp asks
  His teacher for advice.
GRAND INQUISITOR: My pupil Karl,
  Your noble father, never asked advice.
KING: The happier was he. I have committed
  A murder, Cardinal, and know no rest—
GRAND INQUISITOR: Why have you done a murder then?
KING: It was
  Deceit beyond example—
GRAND INQUISITOR: I know him.
KING: What do you know? Through whom? Since when?
GRAND INQUISITOR: For years
  What *you* have known since sunset.
KING *(in consternation)*:   You had known
  About this man before?
GRAND INQUISITOR: His life lies as
  It started and it terminated in
  The holy registers of Santa Casa.
KING: And he was free to walk about?
GRAND INQUISITOR: The tether
  He dangled on was long but would not break.
KING: He was outside the borders of my kingdom.
GRAND INQUISITOR: Where he was, I was, too.

KING (*walks back and forth indignantly*): Then it was known
    Whose hands I'd fallen into.—Why did you
    Neglect to tell me of it?

GRAND INQUISITOR: I will give
    This question back to you—why did you not
    Inquire, since you had thrown yourself into
    His arms? You knew him! Just one look unmasked
    The heretic.—What gave you then the right
    To rob the Holy Office of its victim?
    Thus do you trifle with us? And if kings
    Stoop to receiving stolen goods—behind
    Our backs make concord with our enemies,
    What will become of us? If *one* finds mercy,
    Why would we have the right to sacrifice
    Ten thousand?

KING: He was sacrificed.

GRAND INQUISITOR: But no!
    He has been murdered—wantonly! unknown!—
    The blood that should be flowing for our glory
    Was shed by an assassin's hand. The man
    Was ours—What gave *you* then the right to lay
    A finger on the Holy Order's goods?
    For he was there to die through us, and God
    Sent him for the requirement of this age,
    To make a show of ostentatious reason
    In solemn desecration of his spirit.
    That was my well-weighed plan. But now it lies
    Laid low, and gone the work of many years.
    We have been robbed, and you have nothing left
    But bloody hands.

KING: A passion seized and forced
    Me to it. I do ask forgiveness.

GRAND INQUISITOR: Passion?
    Does Philipp, the Infante, answer me?
    Have I alone become an old man?—Passion?
        (*shaking his head indignantly*)
    Let consciences be free in this, your land,
    If you would still retain your chains.

KING: I am

As yet an amateur in things like this.
Have patience with me.
GRAND INQUISITOR: No! I am not pleased
With you.—*So* to defame the whole course of
Your sovereignty! Where was that Philipp then
Whose constant soul was like the polar star
In Heaven that, unchanged eternally,
Is orbiting itself? Had this whole past
Been lost behind you, then, and was the world
No longer at that moment just the same
One as when you held out your hand to him?
Was poison no more poison? Was the wall
Dividing good from evil, true from false,
Destroyed? What is a plan? stability?
Fidelity?—if in a moment's mildness
A principle of sixty years can melt
Away just as a woman's mood can change?
KING: I looked into his eyes—Be lenient in
Your views on my relapse into a mortal's
Fragility. The world has one less door
Into your heart. Your eyes have ceased to see.
GRAND INQUISITOR:
What has this man to do with you? What is
There new that he can show to you that you
Were not aware of? Do you know so little
About the minds of innovators and
Of dreamers? Did the boastful speech of world
Reformers sound so unaccustomed to
Your ear? Now, if the structure of belief
Can tumble for you and through words alone,
What was the face that you assumed to sentence
One hundred thousand feeble souls to death,
Who climbed that pile of wood for nothing worse?
KING: I looked around to find a man; for this
Domingo—
GRAND INQUISITOR: Why a man? What are, then, men
To you but numbers, nothing more. Must I
Now hear the lessons of my gray-haired pupil
About the elements of princely skill?

Now let the earth's great god insist he has
A need for what can be withheld from him.
If *you* should whine and ask for sympathy,
Have you not granted that the world is of
Your kind? What right have you, I'd like to know,
To point out what you think is of your kind?
KING (*throws himself into a chair*):
 I am a little man; I feel it—You
 Demand a creature be like his Creator.
GRAND INQUISITOR:
 My Lord, I cannot be deceived. We have
 Seen through you—that you wanted to escape
 Us, that the Holy Order's chains had weighed
 You down; you wanted to be free, unique.
            (*He stops. The King is silent.*)
 So, we are understood.—Now thank the Church,
 Which is content to punish like a mother.
 The choice that you so blindly had to make
 Was your chastisement. You have been corrected.
 Return to us now.—If I did not stand
 Before you now—then by the living God!
 You would have stood before me on the morrow.
KING: Speak not so, Priest! You must restrain yourself!
 I will not suffer it. I cannot let
 You use this tone to me.
GRAND INQUISITOR: Why do you call
 The shade of Samuel up? I have bestowed
 The Spanish throne upon two kings and hoped
 To leave a firmly founded work behind.
 I see the harvest of a lifetime lost.
 Don Philipp has himself attacked my structure,
 And now, Sire—for what reason am I called?
 Why am I here?—I am not willing to
 Repeat this visit.
KING: Just one effort more,
 The last—then you may take your leave in peace.
 The past may be the past, and peace may be
 Preserved between us.—Are we reconciled?

GRAND INQUISITOR:
  If Philipp humbly kneels.
KING *(after a pause):*   My son has plans
  To lead the rebels.
GRAND INQUISITOR: What is to be done?
KING: Not anything—or all.
GRAND INQUISITOR: And what is all?
KING: I'll let him flee, if I cannot decide
  To let him die.
GRAND INQUISITOR: Well then, Your Majesty?
KING: Can you establish a new faith for me
  That will defend the murder of a child?
GRAND INQUISITOR:
  The Son of God died on the Tree to make
  Atonement to eternal justice.
KING: You
  Will spread this view throughout the whole of Europe?
GRAND INQUISITOR:
  Wher'er the Cross is worshiped.
KING: I offend
  The voice of Nature—can you also silence
  This mighty voice?
GRAND INQUISITOR: No voice of Nature is
  Of any worth before our Faith.
KING: I put
  My office as a judge into your hands—
  Can I withdraw completely from it?
GRAND INQUISITOR: Give
  It me.
KING: He is my only son.—For whom
  Have I then gathered?
GRAND INQUISITOR: Better to destroy
  Than to make free.
KING *(rises):*   Agreed. Now come.
GRAND INQUISITOR: Where to?
KING: Where you may take your victim from my hand.

The Queen's room

Last Scene

Carlos. The Queen. In the end the King and his retinue.
CARLOS *(in a monk's robe, a mask on his face, which he
  is in the process of removing, under his arm a
  drawn sword. It is very gloomy. He approaches a
  door that is then opened. The Queen comes out in
  her night clothes with a lighted candle. Carlos
  kneels before her):*
Elizabeth!
QUEEN *(with quiet melancholy, lingering in his face):*
          And so we meet again!
CARLOS: And so we meet again!
                    (silence)
QUEEN *(attempts to compose herself):*

                              Arise! We will

Not weaken one another, Carlos. Not
By feeble tears can we give honor to
Our noble dear departed. Tears may flow
For lesser suffering!—It was for *you*
He sacrificed himself! He purchased your
Life with his precious own. And has this blood
Flowed for a phantom thing?—O Carlos, I
Have pledged myself security for you.
Because I promised him, he took his leave
From here most gladly. Will you make me out
A liar?
CARLOS *(with enthusiasm):*
        I will build a monument
For him, the like of which no king has had—
And over where his ashes rest will bloom
A paradise!
QUEEN: I hoped to find you thus!
That was the noble meaning of his death.
He chose me as the one to execute

His final wishes. Let me warn you. I
Will hold to the fulfillment of this oath.
—And still another legacy was put
By him, when doomed, into my hand—I gave
My word to him—and—why should I keep silent?
He gave his Carlos up to me—I will
Defy appearances—no longer tremble
Before mankind, will be brave as a friend
For once. My heart shall speak. He called our love
A virtue. I believe him, and my heart—
CARLOS: You must not finish this, my Queen—I have
    Been living in a long, oppressive dream.
    I was in love—but now I am awake.
    Forget what's past! Here are your letters back.
    You must destroy the ones I wrote. You need
    Fear no more fits of passion from me. That
    Is past. A purifying fire has purged
    My being. Now my passion dwells in graves
    Where dead men lie. No mortal appetite
    Can ever share this breast.
                (after a silence, grasping her hand)
                          I come to take
    My leave—O Mother, finally I see
    There is a greater good, more to be wished
    For, than possessing you—Just one short night
    Gave wings unto the sluggish current of
    My years, and turned me quickly to a man.
    I have no labor to perform in life
    Except the memory of him. Now past
    Are all my harvests—
       (He approaches the Queen, who has covered her face.)
                    Mother, have you nought
    To say to me?
QUEEN: Pay no attention to
    My tears—I cannot help them, Carlos, but
    You must believe me, I do marvel at you.
CARLOS: You were the only one who knew about
    Our compact, and for this association
    You will remain the thing most dear to me

In this whole world. I cannot give you friendship,
As yesterday I could not give my love
To any other woman—Still, if I
Ascend this throne through Providence, I will
Revere the widow of the King.
  (*The King, accompanied by the Grand Inquisitor and
  his grandees, appears in the background, unnoticed.*)
                                        Now I
Leave Spain, to see my father nevermore—
Not in this life again to see him. I
No longer value him. The voice of Nature
Has totally departed from my breast.
Be wife again to him, but he has lost
A son. You must return to do your duty,
While I must hasten to deliver my
Afflicted people from a tyrant's hand.
Madrid will see me as its King or never.
And now to say our last farewell!
                    (*He kisses her.*)
QUEEN: O Carlos!
  What are you doing to me?—I cannot
  Aspire to scale these heights of manly greatness,
  But I can comprehend and marvel at you.
CARLOS: Am I not strong, Elizabeth? I hold
  You here within my arms and do not waver.
  Just yesterday impending death's worst terrors
  Could not have dragged me from this very spot.
                    (*He releases her.*)
  But that is past. Now I can well defy
  All mortal fate. I held you in my arms
  And did not waver.—Hush! Did you hear that?
                    (*A clock strikes.*)
QUEEN: I hear nought but the frightful bell that tolls
  To mark our separation.
CARLOS: Good night, Mother.
  You will receive a letter from me, sent
  From Ghent, that will make public what has happened
  In secret here. I go now to pursue
  An open action aimed against the King.

My wish is that there shall be nothing more
Between us that is secret. *You* need not
Avoid the world's attention—Let this be
My last deceit.

> *(He is about to take his mask. The King steps*
> *between them.)*

KING: It is your last!

> *(The Queen falls in a faint.)*

CARLOS *(rushes to her and takes her in his arms):*

                    O Heaven,
O earth! Then is she dead?

KING *(coldly and quietly to the Grand Inquisitor):*

                    So, Cardinal,
Now I have done my part. See you do yours!

> *(He exits.)*
> *(Curtain.)*

Translated by A. Leslie
and Jeanne R. Willson

LETTERS ON
DON CARLOS

Letters on *Don Carlos*

First Letter

You tell me, dear friend, that the prevailing criticisms of *Don Carlos* have given you little satisfaction and that you think the greatest number of these have missed the real point of view of the author. It even seems to you that it may still be possible to save certain hazardous passages that the critics pronounced untenable; on the other hand, many misgivings that have been stirred up, you find in the continuity of the piece, if not fully answered, still foreseen and taken into account. In the case of most objections you found that the sagacity of the critics was far less to be admired than the complacency with which the most natural thought that transgressions, which at once catch the eye of the silliest person, might also have been evident to the author, who is seldom the least informed among his readers, and that they thus are dealing less with the subject itself than with the *reasons* that decided him on it. These reasons can, of course, be insufficient, can rest on a biased method of looking at things: but it should be the affair of the critic to show this insufficiency, this bias, if, indeed, he intends to acquire merit in the eyes of those upon whom he urges himself as judge or offers himself as adviser.

But, dear friend, how does it concern the author in the end whether his critic has a function or not? How much or how little discernment he has demonstrated? Let him decide that for himself. It is bad for the author and his work, if he allows its effect to be determined by the *gift of prophecy* and *fairness* of his critics, if he allows the impression it makes to be dependent on conditions that unite only in very few heads. This is one of the most defective situations in which an art work can find itself in, when it is left to the caprice of the spectator what interpretation he will make of it and when it requires patching up to shift him to the right point of view. If you wished to suggest to me·that my work finds itself in this situation, then you have said something very bad about it and you cause me to examine it again more carefully from this aspect. So it is of particular importance, it seems to me, to investigate whether everything that assists in the understanding of the play is contained within it and whether it was stated in such clear terms that it was easy for the reader to understand. So, dear friend, allow me to converse with you for a while concerning this matter. The play has become less familiar to me. I find myself now as if in a middle state between the artist and the spectator whereby it will perhaps be possible for me to combine the intimate acquaintance with the subject of the former with the impartiality of the latter.

It may have happened, after all—and I find it necessary to say this beforehand—it may have happened that I aroused other expectations in the early acts than I fulfilled in the later ones. S. Réal's novella, perhaps also my own remarks about it in the first issue of *Thalia,* may have directed the reader to a point of view from which it can no longer be regarded now. That is to say, during the time that I composed it, which because of many interruptions was a rather long time, much changed within me. It was inevitable that this work, too, would participate in the various fortunes that befell my way of thinking and of feeling during this time. Those things that in the beginning had fascinated me particularly in this plot had afterwards an effect that was much weaker and in the end had scarcely any at all. New ideas that meanwhile rose within me crowded out the earlier ones; Carlos himself had fallen in my favor, perhaps for no other reason than that I had advanced too far ahead of him in years, and for the opposite reason Marquis Posa had taken his place. So it happened then that I brought a completely different heart to the fourth and fifth acts. But the first three acts were in the hands of the public, the design of the whole could no longer be changed—thus I either had to suppress the piece entirely (and certainly a very small number of my readers would have thanked me for that), or I had to adapt the second half to the first as well as I could. If this was not done throughout in the most happy way, then it serves me as some comfort that a more capable hand than mine would not have succeeded much better. The main fault was that I had been occupied with the piece too long; but a dramatic work can and should be but the blossom of a single summer. The plan, too, was plotted too broadly for the limits and the rules of a dramatic work. This plan, for example, required that Marquis Posa win Philipp's unlimited trust; but to bring about this extraordinary effect the economy of the piece allowed me only a single scene.

These explanations will perhaps vindicate me with my friends but not to the world of art. But meanwhile may they only be inclined to bring to an end the many declamations with which the assault was made against me from that direction by the critics.

Second Letter

The character of the Marquis Posa is almost universally considered to be too idealistic; to what extent this point of contention has a basis will best be shown when we have traced the characteristic mode of action of this man back to its real substance. Here I am concerned, as you see, with two opposing factions. So those who would like to have him banished entirely from the ranks of normal beings must be shown to what extent he is related in essence to his fellow man, to what extent his convictions as well as his actions result from very human instincts and are founded in the chain of external circumstances; I need only make those who give him the appellation of divine aware of a few weak spots in him that are very human. The opinions that the Marquis expresses, the philosophy that guides him, the favorite sentiments that inspire him, as much as they do rise above everyday life, when regarded as mere ideas, cannot really be what exiles him with justification from the ranks of normal creatures. For what is there that cannot be endowed with life in the human mind, and what offspring of the brain that cannot develop into a passion in a glowing heart? Nor can it be his actions that, as seldom as this may indeed happen, have found their like in history itself; for the sacrifice of the Marquis for his friend has little or nothing to give it an advantage over the hero's death of a Curtius, a Regulus, or others. Then what is false and what is impossible would have to be either in the conflict of this way of thinking with the times or in its impotence and lack of vitality necessary to really ignite such actions. Thus I cannot understand the objections that are made against the naturalness of this character other than that in the century of Philipp II no person could have thought as Marquis Posa thought—that thoughts of this kind do not, as happens here, pass so easily into the will and into the deed—and that an idealistic enthusiasm is not usually put into effect with such consequences, not accompanied by such energy in action.

The objections made to this character, from the point of view of the times in which I have him appear, seem to me to speak much more *for* him than against him. Following the example of all great persons he has his origin between darkness and light, a distinguished, isolated appearance. The point in time in which he develops is one of fermentation of thought, of the battle of bias with reason, anarchy of opinion, the dawn of truth—from time immemorial the moment of birth of extraordinary men. The ideas of freedom and the nobility of man that a fortunate coincidence, perhaps a favorable education, cast into this finely tuned, impressionable soul astound it with their novelty and act upon it with all the strength of the unusual and the unexpected; the secrecy itself, with which they were probably communicated, would necessarily heighten the strength of their impression. They have not yet become commonplace from long, abrasive use that today makes their impression so dull; neither the babble of the schools nor the wit of men of the world has worn down their great imprint. Surrounded by these ideas his soul feels as if it were in a new and beautiful region that works upon it with all its dazzling light and transports it into the most delightful dream. The opposing wretched state of slavery and superstition causes it to be more and more fixedly attracted toward this favored world; the most beautiful dreams of freedom are truly dreamed in prison. Tell me yourself, my friend—where could the most daring idea of a republic of man, of universal tolerance and freedom of conscience be born into this world better and where more naturally than in close proximity to Philipp II and his Inquisition?

All of the Marquis' principles and favorite sentiments revolve around *republican* virtue. Even his sacrifice for his friend demonstrates this, for the capacity for sacrifice is the essence of all republican virtue.

The point in time in which he made his appearance was exactly that in which the talk of human rights and freedom of conscience was stronger than ever. The recent Reformation had first spread these ideas, and the unrest in Flanders kept them in circulation. His external independence, even his position as a Knight of Malta, give him the happy leisure to brood upon and bring to maturity his venturesome enthusiasm.

So in that age, and in that state in which the Marquis makes his appearance, and in the exterior things that surround him no reason can be found for him not to follow this philosophy, not to resign himself with fanatical devotion to it.

If history is rich in examples where all earthly things can be neglected for *opinions,* if the strength is given to the most unfathomable delusions to captivate the minds of men to such a degree that they are made capable of any sacrifice, it would be strange to deny this strength to the *truth.* In an age, finally, that is as rich as that one in examples of men risking their possessions and their lives for doctrines that have so little that is inspiring about them, it seems to me a character should not appear remarkable who dares to do something similar for the most sublime of all ideas; one would have to assume, then, that truth was less able to stir the human heart than delusions. Besides this, the Marquis is announced as a hero. In his early youth he has already given proof with his sword of a courage that he will later manifest for a more serious concern. Inspiring truths and a philosophy to elevate the soul, it seems to me, would necessarily lead to something quite different in a hero's soul than in the brain of a scholar or in the wasted heart of a weak man of the world.

There are two actions of the Marquis particularly, as you tell me, to which offense has been taken: his conduct toward the King in the tenth scene of the third act and his sacrifice for his friend. But it could be that the frankness with which he expresses his opinions to the King can be credited less to the account of his courage than to his accurate knowledge of the King's character, and, with the danger removed, the main objection to this scene is thereby also lifted. About that another time, when I will entertain

you on the subject of Philipp II; at present my concern was only
with Posa's sacrifice for the Prince, about which I want to communicate some thoughts to you in my next letter.

Third Letter

Recently you claimed to have found the evidence in *Don Carlos*
that the compelling *emotion of friendship* could be a subject for
tragedy that is just as moving as the compelling *emotion of love,*
and my answer that I had laid by a picture of such a friendship
for myself for the future seemed strange to you. So have you, too,
as most of my readers, assumed it is settled that it was the extreme
devotion of friendship that I have aimed at in the relationship between Carlos and Marquis Posa? And have you accordingly regarded both of these characters and perhaps the whole drama from
this point of view until now? But, dear friend, what if you really
have exaggerated the importance that I give this *friendship?* If it
was plainly evident from the entire context that this was *not* the
objective and absolutely could not be? What if the character of
the Marquis, as it proceeds from the sum of his actions, could not
be reconciled with such a friendship at all, and even if the best
evidence for the opposite could be drawn from his finest actions
that are credited to the account of friendship?

The first announcement of the relationship between these two
may have been misleading; but this was in appearance only, and
the slightest attention to the contrasting conduct of the two would
have served to dispel the error. By starting from their childhood
friendship the author does not detract from his higher intention,
on the contrary, this could not be spun out of any better thread.
The relationship in which the two enter here was reminiscent of
their earlier academic years. Harmony of sentiment, the same inclination toward the noble and beautiful, the same enthusiasm for
truth, freedom, and virtue had bound them to one another at that
time. A character like Posa's, which afterward unfolds as it happens in this piece, would of necessity have begun early to practice
this spirited power of emotion on a fruitful subject; a benevolence
that was subsequently to extend over the whole of humanity would
have to proceed from a more intimate bond. This creative and
ardent spirit had to have a subject soon on which to work; could

a finer one be offered him than a sensitive and warmly perceptive prince, susceptible to his effusions, voluntarily hastening to meet him? But even in these earlier times the severity of this character is evident in some features; even here Posa is the colder, the more belated friend, and his heart, already then too all-embracing to beat for one single living thing, had to be won by a great sacrifice.

> So I began to pester you with every
> Variety of tender brother-love.
> Your proud heart gave me cold return for this.
> . . . .
> You could disdain, despise the love I proferred
> But never drive me off. You could dismiss
> The prince three times, but three times he returned
> As supplicant, imploring you to love him . . .
> . . . .
> . . .   My royal blood
> Flowed basely under unrelenting blows.
> So vital was my obstinate desire
> To be beloved by Roderick.

Here a few indications are already given as to how little the devotion of the Marquis to the Prince is based on *personal* concord. Early he thought of him as the *sovereign's son,* early this idea forced itself between his heart and the supplications of his friend. Carlos opens his arms to him; the young cosmopolite kneels down before him. Feelings about freedom and the nobility of man were ripe in his soul earlier than friendship with Carlos; only later was this branch grafted onto the stronger stem. Even in the moment when his pride is overcome by the great sacrifice of his friend, he does not lose sight of the sovereign's son. "I will repay you," he says, "when *you* are the *king.*" Is it possible that in such a young heart, with this active and ever present feeling of the inequality of their rank, a *friendship* could grow, the essential condition of which is, after all, *equality?* So even at that time it was less love than gratitude, less friendship than compassion that won the *Marquis* for the Prince. The feelings, presentiments, dreams, resolves that forced their way, obscure and confused, into this boy's soul had to be passed on to be viewed by another soul, and Carlos was the only one who could share in these presentiments, these dreams, and who reciprocated them. A mind like Posa's needed to strive to make use of his superiority at an early age, and the loving Carlos adapted himself so submissively, so docilely to him. Posa saw himself in this fair mirror and was pleased with his image. Thus began this academic friendship.

But now they are parted from each other, and everything changes. Carlos arrives at the court of his father, and Posa flings himself into the world. The former, spoiled by his early attachment to the most noble and most ardent of youths, finds nothing in the whole circle of a despot's court to gratify his heart. Everything around him is empty and barren. Alone amidst the tumult of so many courtiers, depressed by the present, he takes comfort in sweet recollections of the past. Thus for him these early impressions remain warm and full of life; and his heart, fashioned for benevolence and lacking any worthy object, pines away in dreams that are never gratified. So he gradually becomes lost in a condition of *idle fancies, inactive contemplation.* In the perpetual battle with this situation his strengths erode, the unfriendly encounters with a father so unlike him spread a dismal melancholy over his nature—a worm gnawing at every blossom of his mind, the death of inspiration. Constricted, without energy, without employment. lost in his own daydreams, exhausted by grievous, unavailing conflict, driven by fear from one terrible extreme to the other, nc longer possessing the strength to rise again—in such a state h(finds his *first love.* In this condition he no longer has any strengtl to withstand it; all those former ideas that alone could have kep it in balance have become more unaccustomed to his soul; it con trols him with a tyrant's strength; thus he sinks into a painfu' blissful state of *suffering.* Now all of his forces are concentrate on a single object. A never-silenced desire holds his soul chaineu within. —How can it escape into the universe? Incapable of satisfying this desire, still less capable of overcoming it through inner strength, he wastes away perceptibly, half living, half dying; no distraction from the burning pain in his breast, no sympathetic heart revealing itself to him, to whom he might pour all this forth.

> . . . I have no one here,
> And there is no one in this whole, wide world
> As far as land lies 'neath my father's sway,

As far as ships may sail beneath his flag,
There is no spot, not even one, whereon
I can relieve my grief with tears . . .

Helplessness and his heart's need lead him back now to just that point where his heart's abundance had let him begin. More fervently does he feel the need for sympathy because he is *alone* and *unhappy*. Thus his returning friend finds him.

Meanwhile, things have gone very differently for him. Cast into the wide universe, with open mind, with all the strength of youth, all the urgency of genius, all the warmth of heart, he sees mankind acting on a large scale as on a small one; he finds the opportunity to test the ideals he has brought with him on the active forces of the whole breed. Everything that he hears, that he sees, he devours with lively enthusiasm; everything perceived in *reference* to those ideals, he reflects on and assimilates. Mankind shows itself to him in diverse varieties; he gets to know it in diverse regions, systems of government, degrees of education, and degrees of prosperity. Thus there gradually grows within him a combined and exalted concept of *man on the whole,* over against which every limited, smaller condition vanishes. Now he emerges from himself, in the great universe his soul expands into the distance. —Curious people who cast themselves into his pathway divert his attention, share in his regard and love. —In the place of an individual the whole race walks with him; a transitory, youthful emotional state expands into an all-embracing, unlimited philanthropy. From an idle enthusiast an effective man of action has come into existence. Those former dreams and presentiments that still lay dim and undeveloped in his soul have been refined to clear concepts; idle schemes are set into operation; a universal, vague impulse to act has changed into practical employment. The spirit of the people is studied by him, their strengths, their resources are weighed, their systems of government examined; in association with kindred minds his ideas gain versatility and shape; tried men of the world, like William of Orange, Coligny, and others, take from them the romantic and gradually tone them down to the pragmatic and useful.

Enriched with a thousand new, productive concepts, full of aspiring forces, creative drives, bold and comprehensive plans with a busy head, a glowing heart, permeated by the great, inspiring

ideas of universal human force and human nobility and more ardently inflamed for the happiness of this great totality that was
represented to him in so many individuals,* in this way he now
comes back from the great harvest, burning with the desire to find
a stage upon which he might realize these ideals, might bring those
assembled treasures into use. The state of affairs in Flanders pre-
sents itself to him. He finds everything there ready for a revolution.
Familiar with the spirit, the strengths, and the resources of the
people, which he calculates against the might of its oppressor, he
looks upon the undertaking as already finished. His ideal of republican freedom can find no more favorable moment and no more
receptive soil.

> . . . Such rich and blooming provinces!
> A vigorous, a noble people—and
> A good one—to be *father of this people,*
> That must, I thought, be godlike! . . .

The more miserable he finds these people, the nearer this desire
presses on his heart, the more he hastens to fulfill it. At this point,
and only *at this point,* does he actively remember his friend, whom
he left in Alcala with glowing sentiments on the happiness of man.
Now he imagines him to be the savior of the oppressed nation as

* In his subsequent conversation with the King these favorite ideas are brought to
light. "A single stroke done by your pen," he says to him, "and newly created is the
earth. Give us the right to think with freedom."

> . . . And generous,
> As strong, let happiness flow from your horn
> Of plenty—let men's souls mature within
> This universe of yours . . .
> . . . re-establish then
> The lost nobility of humankind.
> The common man may be again what he
> Has been, the purpose of the Crown—no duty
> Confines him but his brother's sacred rights.
> Then let the farmer glorify his plow,
> And grant the King, who cannot farm, his crown.
> The artist in his workshop, let him dream
> He is the sculptor of a better world.
> The thinker's flights need have no border now
> Except for finite Nature's limitations.

the instrument of his noble plans. Full of inexpressible love because he thinks of him as one with the favorite concern of his
heart, he hastens to Madrid to find those seeds of humanity and
heroic virtue, which he once sowed upon his soul, now as full
grown and to embrace in him the liberator of the Netherlands, the
future creator of his *imagined nation.*

More impassioned than ever, the latter rushes to meet him with
feverish intensity:

> Oh, let me clasp you to my heart and feel
> Your heart as it beats powerfully against me.
> Oh, now is everything made good . . .
> > . . . I hang
> Upon my Roderick's neck.

The reception is the most ardent: But how does Posa answer him?
He who left his friend behind in the full bloom of youth and finds
him again now resembling a wandering corpse, does he dwell on
this sad change? Does he seek long and anxiously for its source?
Does he descend to his friend's little concerns? Dismayed and stern
he returns this unwelcome reception:

> It was not thus that I had hoped to see
> Don Philipp's son . . .
> . . .   . . . for that
> Is not the lion-hearted youth to whom
> An oppressed people of heroic stock
> Send me—I stand here not as Roderick,
> Not as the playmate of the boy prince—
> A representative of all mankind
> Embraces you—the provinces of Flanders
> Do weep in truth upon your shoulder now.

Involuntarily his governing idea escapes him immediately in the
first moments of this reunion, so long in coming, where as a rule
there are so many more important trivial things to say, and Carlos
must summon all the pathetic aspects of his situation, must evoke

the most distant scenes of childhood in order to dislodge his friend's favorite idea, to awaken his sympathy, and to draw his attention to his own sad situation. Posa sees himself terribly deluded by the hopes with which he had hastened to his friend. He had expected a heroic character who longed for action, for which he would now offer an arena. He counted on that store of noble love for his fellow man, on the oath that he had made him on the Host broken in two in those rapturous days, and discovers his passion for his father's wife.—

> What you see here no longer is that Carlos,
> Who in Alcala took his leave from you.
> No more that Carlos who, emboldened, dared
> Anticipate the plan of our creator
> And in the days to come as total sovereign
> To plant a paradise in Spain—a whim
> So childish, yet it was most beautiful!
> But now those dreams are gone.

A hopeless passion that consumes all his strength, that puts his life itself in danger. How would a caring friend of the Prince, who was but *friend* alone and *nothing more,* have acted in this situation? And how did Posa, the man of the world, act? Posa, the Prince's friend and confidant, would have trembled much too much for the safety of his Carlos for him to have dared to offer him a hand in a dangerous meeting with his Queen. It would have been the duty of a friend to think of a way to suppress this passion and by no means to satisfy it. Posa, the defender of Flanders, acts quite differently. Nothing is more important to him than to end as quickly as possible this hopeless situation, in which the effective strengths of his friend are sinking, even though it may require a little risk. As long as his friend languishes in unappeased desire, he cannot be sensitive to another's affliction; as long as his powers are overwhelmed by melancholy, he cannot rise to a heroic resolve. Flanders can hope for nothing from this unhappy Carlos, but perhaps it can from a happy one. So he hastens to satisfy his most burning desire, he himself leads him to the feet of the Queen;

and, moreover, he does not stop at this alone. He no longer finds in the Prince's disposition the motives that had formerly raised him to heroic resolutions. What else can he do but kindle this extinguished hero's spirit at an untried flame and use the only passion that is present in the Prince's soul? He must join to this the new ideas that he wants to make prevail in it now. One look at the heart of the Queen convinces him that he may expect everything from her cooperation. It is only the first enthusiastic involvement that he intends to borrow from this passion. When she has helped to give his friend this beneficial boost, then he will not need her anymore, and he can be certain that her own action will cause her downfall. So the obstacle itself, which was put in the way of his great interest, this unhappy love itself, is now transformed into a tool to bring about that more momentous goal, and Flanders' fate must speak through the mouth of love to the heart of his friend.

> . . . I recognized within
> These hopeless flames the golden rays of hope.
> I meant to lead him into excellence,
> The proud and regal harvest, which can only
> Be slowly gathered by the generations,
> A sudden spring of wonder-working love
> Should speed upon its way. His virtue should
> Be ripened for me by this sunny glance.

Now from the hands of the Queen, Carlos receives the letters that Posa had brought for him from Flanders. The Queen calls back his faded spirit.

Even more visible is this subordination of the friendship to more important interests shown at the meeting in the monastery. The Prince's plan, presented to the King, has been disappointed; this, and a discovery which he believes he has made that will be advantageous to his passion, plunge him back more fiercely into the latter, and Posa thinks he sees pure sensuality mingled in this passion. Nothing could be less compatible with his more lofty plan. All the hopes that he has for his Netherlands, based on Carlos' love for the Queen, would crash down, if this love fell from its

heights. The indignation that he feels about it exposes his sentiments:

> How I must change my thoughts. Yes, once it was—
> It was so different. Then you were so rich,
> So warm, so rich! The circle of the world
> Could find a place within your bosom. All
> Of that is gone, devoured by *one* emotion,
> The victim of one small and selfish interest.
> Your heart has ceased to beat. There are no tears
> Left over for the wretched fortune of
> The province, not one small tear is left.
> O Carlos, you are desperately poor,
> Since you love no one but yourself.

Afraid of a similar relapse, he believes he must venture to use
strong measures. As long as Carlos remains near the Queen, he is
lost for the affair of Flanders. His presence in the Netherlands can
give a completely different turn to things there; so he does not
hesitate for a minute to get him there in the most forceful way.

> He will have to go
> Against the wishes of the King; he shall
> Proceed to Brussels secretly, and there
> With open arms the Flemish will await
> Him. At his signal all the Netherlands
> Will rise. The beneficial action gets
> Its strength from royal blood . . .

Would Carlos' *friend* have brought himself to play so presumptu-
ously with the good name, yes, even with the life, of his friend?
But Posa, to whom the deliverance of an oppressed people was a
far more pressing demand than the little affairs of a friend, Posa,
citizen of the world, could not help but act thus and no differently. All the steps that are undertaken by him in the course of the
play reveal a *venturesome daring* that only a heroic purpose can
inspire; friendship is often disheartened and always concerned.
Where up to now is there in the character of the Marquis even a

trace of this scrupulous attention to an isolated individual, of this all-exclusive preference in which alone the specific character of an intense friendship consists? Where for him is the interest in the Prince not subordinate to the higher interest in mankind? Firmly and tenaciously the Marquis goes his great cosmopolitan way, and everything that goes on around him is important to him only through the relation to this higher object in which it stands.

Fourth Letter

This confession might deprive him of a large part of his admirers, but he will console himself with the small share of new admirers that it wins for him, and a character like his, after all, could never hope for general approval. Lofty, effective benevolence toward the whole in no way excludes a loving interest in the joys and sorrows of an individual. That he loves mankind more than he loves Carlos does no damage to his friendship. Even if fate had not called him to a throne, he would ever have distinguished him from all others by a special, tender solicitude; he would have held him in his heart of hearts as Hamlet his Horatio. There is an opinion that benevolence becomes that much weaker and more tepid the more its objects accumulate; but this condition cannot apply to the Marquis. The object of his love appears to him in the fullest light of enthusiasm; glorious and radiant this image stands before his soul like the shape of a beloved. Since it is Carlos who is to realize this ideal of human happiness, he transfers it in this way to him, in this way he ultimately unites both inseparably in *one* feeling. In Carlos alone he now contemplates his ardently loved humanity; his friend is the focal point in which all his ideas of that composite whole assemble. But it produces an effect on him only in *one* object that he embraces with all the enthusiasm and all the strength of his soul:

> My heart, in that
> I dedicated it to only one,
> Included the whole world! In Carlos' soul
> Through me a paradise for millions was
> Created.

Here, then, is a love for *one* being without disregard for the universal—caring attention to a friendship without the unreasonableness, the exclusiveness of this intense devotion. Here universal, all-embracing philanthropy is compressed into a single flash of fire.

And should just that have damaged the involvement that it ennobled? This picture of friendship should lose in compassion and grace what it gained in scope? Carlos' friend should for that reason have less claim to our tears and our admiration because he combines his most ample expanse with the most limited expression of benevolent emotion and mitigates the divinity of universal love by its most human application?

With the ninth scene of the third act a whole new latitude is opened for this character.

Fifth Letter

Passion for the Queen has finally brought the Prince to the brink of destruction. Evidence of his guilt is in the hand of his father, and his reckless ardor has exposed him most perilously to the watchful suspicion of his enemies; he is in evident danger of becoming a victim of his insane love, his father's jealousy, a priest's hate, the vindictiveness of an insulted enemy and of a disdained lady-love. His situation from without requires the most urgent remedy, but it is even more required by the internal state of his mind, which threatens to bring to nought all the Marquis' expectations and plans. The Prince must be rescued from that danger, he must be snatched from that state of mind, if those plans for the liberation of Flanders are to be fulfilled; and it is the Marquis, from whom we expect both, who [on p. 187] himself holds out hope for this.

But on just that path, along which danger to the Prince is coming, a spiritual condition has also been produced in the King that causes him to feel for the first time the need for communication. The pangs of jealousy have taken him from the unnatural constraint of his rank back to the original state of humanity, have allowed him to feel the emptiness and artificiality of his despot's power and allowed desires to rise within him that neither power nor majesty can satisfy.

'Tis *King!* And only *King*
And *King* again! Is there no better answer
Than empty, hollow echoes? Here I beat
Upon this rock and ask for water, water
To ease my feverish thirst—and in return
He gives me gold.

A course of events exactly like the prevailing one, it seems to
me, or none, could have produced such a condition in a monarch
like Philipp II; and just such a condition had to be produced in
him in order to prepare for the following action and to make it
possible to bring the Marquis into close contact with him. Father
and son have been brought on very different paths to that point
where the author must have them; on very different paths they are
both drawn to the Marquis Posa, in whom alone their concerns,
previously disconnected, now press hard upon each other. By means
of Carlos' passion for the Queen and its inevitable effect on the
King, the whole course of the Marquis' life was determined; therefore it was also necessary that the whole piece open with this. In
comparison with that, the Marquis himself was necessarily placed
in shadow and had to content himself with a secondary involvement until he could take control of the whole action, because he
could receive from that alone all the ingredients for his future activity. Thus the attention of the spectator could absolutely not be
diverted from it ahead of time, and it was therefore necessary that
up to this point it occupy the attention as the main action, whereas
the concern that later was to become the predominant one was
indicated only by a suggestion from afar. But as soon as the edifice
is standing, the scaffold is removed. The story of Carlos' love, as
only a preliminary action, falls back to make way for that for
which it had alone done its work.

By that is meant those concealed motives of the Marquis that
are none else but the deliverance of Flanders and the future fate
of the nation; motives that had only been hinted at under the cover
of friendship now become evident and begin to take possession of
the entire attention. Carlos, as has become sufficiently clear from
what has gone before, was viewed by him only as the *single indispensable tool* for that one ardently and resolutely pursued goal
and as such was embraced with the same enthusiasm as the goal.

From this more universal motive there had to issue anxious interest in the weal and woe of his friend, even tender solicitude for the implement of his love, such as could have been produced only by the strongest *personal* sympathy. Carlos' friendship vouchsafes him the most complete enjoyment of his ideal. It is the focus of all his wishes and actions. He still knows no other or shorter way to achieve his high ideal of freedom and the prosperity of mankind than the one opened to him in Carlos. It never even occurred to him to look for this in another way; least of all did it ever occur to him to make this way directly *through the King*. Accordingly, when he is led to Philipp [on p. 206], he shows the greatest indifference.

> He wants to see me? Me? —To him I am
> A nothing, truly nought! —Here in this room!
> How pointless, how nonsensical! —What can
> It matter to him, if I am or not?
> You'll see, it leads to nothing.

But not for long does he abandon himself to this idle, this childish, astonishment. To a mind accustomed, as this one is, to perceive in each circumstance its usefulness, even to shape coincidence to his purpose with a creative hand, to conceive of each event in relation to his special ruling goal, the great use that can be made of this present moment does not remain long hidden. Even the smallest element of time is for him a sacredly entrusted treasure with which a profit must be made. It is still not a clear, coherent plan that he conceives; only a dim idea and scarcely even that, it is only a fleetingly rising notion that perhaps something might by chance be done here. He must appear before that one who holds the fate of so many millions in his hand. One must use the moment, he says to himself, that comes but once. And if it were but a spark of truth cast into the soul of this man, who has never yet heard the truth! Who knows how significantly Providence can manipulate this moment with him? —He does not imagine anything more by it than to make the best use he knows of a chance circumstance. In this frame of mind he awaits the King.

Sixth Letter

I will reserve for another occasion a more detailed explanation for you, if you have the desire to hear me, about the tone which Posa uses with the King from the very beginning, as in general about his whole behavior in this scene and the manner in which this is received by the King. Now I will be satisfied to dwell only on those things that are most intimately connected with the character of the Marquis. From a rational point of view, according to the Marquis' conception of the King, all he could hope to elicit from him was astonishment, combined with humiliation, that his great idea of himself and his trifling opinion of human beings might well allow for an exception, thence the natural inevitable embarrassment of a small mind before a great mind. This result could be salutary, even if it served only to shake the prejudices of this man for a moment, if it allowed him to feel that there were forces beyond his described circle, of which he had never allowed himself to dream. This single note could long reverberate in his life, and this impression could not help but remain with him longer, the more it was without precedent.

But Posa had really formed his opinion of the King too shallowly, too superficially, or even if he had been acquainted with him, he was nevertheless too little advised about his *current frame of mind* to *use* it in his calculations. This frame of mind was exceedingly favorable for him and provided a reception for his hasty words that he could not have expected on any principles of probability. This unexpected discovery gives him a more animated spirit, and the piece itself an entirely new turn. Made bold by a success that exceeded all his hope and set on fire by some traces of *humanity* that surprise him in the King, he goes astray for a moment to the extravagant idea of linking his ruling ideal of Flanders' fortune etc. directly to the person of the King, to bring it to fulfillment directly through him. This presumption puts him into a passion that opens the very fundament of his soul, brings all the offspring of his fantasy, all the results of his quiet thought to light, and clearly indicates how very much these ideals control him. Now, in this state of passion, all the inner workings become visible that have hitherto caused his actions, now he conducts himself like any fanatic who is overwhelmed by his ruling idea. He knows no more limits, in the ardor of his enthusiasm he *ennobles the King,* who listens to him with amazement, and forgets himself so far as to place hopes in him that he could blush at in the next quiet moment. He thinks no more of Carlos. What a long, roundabout way, only to wait for him! The King offers him far nearer and quicker satisfaction. Why postpone the prosperity of mankind till his successor?

Would Carlos' bosom friend forget himself so far, would any other passion but his ruling one have carried the Marquis *so* far? Are the concerns of friendship so changeable that it can be transferred with such little difficulty to another object? But everything is explained as soon as one *subordinates* friendship to that ruling passion. Then it is natural that the latter claims its rights at the first opportunity and does not long hesitate to exchange its resources and its implements.

The ardor and the ingenuousness with which Posa expounded to the King his special feelings, which were heretofore secrets between Carlos and himself, and the delusion that the King could understand them, yes, even fulfill them, was an evident act of disloyalty that he perpetrated against his friend Carlos. Posa, citizen of the world, was permitted to act in this way, and it can be forgiven him alone; in his bosom friend Carlos it would be just as condemnable as it would be inconceivable.

Certainly this delusion should last no longer than a few moments. The first surprise, the great emotion, one easily forgives; but if he continued to believe in this, even when calm, then he would in fairness fall in our eyes to the level of a dreamer. That it really had an effect on him is evident from several places where he jokes about it or earnestly purges himself of it. "Or say," he says to the Queen, "I have in mind to put my choice upon the throne?"

> QUEEN: No! No. Marquis.
> I will not, even as a joke, accuse
> You of this immature conceit. You are
> No dreamer who would undertake to do
> What cannot be completed.

MARQUIS: That, I think,
    Was just the question.

Carlos himself has looked deep enough into the soul of his friend
to find such a decision established in the way he acts, and what
he himself says about him on this occasion could by itself suffice
to put the point of view of the author beyond all doubt. "You,"
he tells him [p. 270], still under the delusion that the Marquis has
sacrificed him,

>   You will now achieve
> What I should have and could not. You will give
> To Spaniards as a gift the golden days
> That they had hoped in vain to get from me.
> For me 'tis over now forever! You
> Had recognized that. Oh, this frightful love
> Has carried off the early blossoms of
> My spirit irretrievably. For all
> Your noble hopes I am as good as dead.
> But Providence or chance has led you to
> The King. My secret is all it requires,
> And he is yours—and you can be his angel.
> For me there is no rescue—but perhaps
> For Spain!

And in another place he says to Count Lerma, in order to excuse
the presumed faithlessness of his friend:

>   He loved
> Me once, he loved me very much. I was
> As dear as his own soul. Oh that I know—
> A thousand proofs of that were given me.
> But should the millions, should his fatherland
> Not be still dearer to him than just *one?*
> His heart was far too great for just one friend,
> And my own happiness too small for him.
> He sacrificed me to his virtue.

Seventh Letter

Posa felt it was very good, however much his friend Carlos was forsaken by it, that he had made the King a confidant of his special feelings and had made an attempt on his heart. Precisely because he felt that these special feelings were the *real* bond of their friendship, he also knew no better than to think that he had broken this bond in the very moment when he profaned it with the King. Carlos did not know, but Posa knew very well that this philosophy and these plans for the future were the holy *Palladium of their friendship* and the important claim by which Carlos possessed his heart; precisely because he knew this and assumed in his heart that it also could not be unknown to Carlos—how could he dare to acknowledge to him that he had fraudulently used this Palladium? To confess to him what had gone on between him and the King could not help but mean just as much to his way of thinking as to proclaim to him that there had been a time when he meant nothing to him. But if Carlos' future calling to the throne, if the sovereign's son had no part in this friendship, if it was something independent and *completely* personal, then it could have been offended by those confidences to the King, but not betrayed, not torn apart; so this chance circumstance could have done no harm to the substance of their friendship. It was a delicacy, it was compassion that caused Posa, citizen of the world, to conceal from the *future* monarch the expectations that he had based on the *present* one; but Posa, Carlos' friend, could in no other way have offended more severely than by this reserve itself.

To be sure, the reasons that Posa gives himself, as well as later to his friend, about this reserve, the single source of all the subsequent confusion, are of a completely different sort. Act 4, Scene 6:

> The King has placed belief in this one vessel
> To which he charges his most holy secret,
> And this belief requires his gratitude.
> Why be loquacious when my silence will
> Not bring you harm? Perhaps will spare you? Why
> Point out the storm clouds hanging overhead
> To one who sleeps?

And in the third scene of Act 5:

>   . . . Then I,
> Infected by misled affection and
> Deceived by proud illusion that I could
> Conclude this daring venture without you,
> Conceal my risky secret from my friend.

But it will be evident to anyone who has but little insight into the heart of man that the Marquis seeks only to deceive himself with these reasons just quoted (that in themselves are far too weak to motivate such an important step)—because he does not dare to admit to himself the real reason. A far more correct disclosure about the current state of his mind is given in another place, from which it becomes clearly evident that there must have been moments in which he took counsel with himself as to whether he should not actually sacrifice his friend. "It would have been my chance," he says to the Queen,

>   to cause a whole
> New dawn to break above the Spanish Empire.
> The King bestowed his heart upon me. He
> Addressed me as his son—I bear his seal,
> And all his Albas are no more.
> . . . .
> I will give up the King . . .
> . . . In this unyielding land
> No rose will bloom for me again.—Those were
> But clowning gestures of a childish mind,
> Disclaimed with flaming cheeks by the grown man.
> Should I eradicate a hopeful spring
> That nears, in order to pretend there is
> A lukewarm glow of sunshine in the north?
> To ease a tired, old tyrant's final lashes
> I'd risk the greater freedom of the age?
> Such wretched glory I disdain. The fate
> Of Europe ripens with my noble friend.
> To him I handed Spain. But woe! Oh woe
> To me and him, if I should rue this act!

If I have chosen what was worse? If I
Have misread Providence's signals that
Meant to put *me*, not *him*, upon this throne.

So he did, after all, *choose*, and in order to choose, he must
then have thought of the opposite as a possibility. From all of
these quoted instances one recognizes plainly that the interest of
friendship is inferior to a higher interest, and that its direction
is determined for it by the higher interest. No one in the whole
play has judged this relationship between the two friends more
correctly than Philipp himself, from whom it was also first to be
expected. In the mouth of this keen observer of human nature I
put down my apologia and my own judgment of the hero of the
piece, and so, too, with his words may this inquiry be closed.

He made this sacrifice for whom?
For that mere boy, my son? Oh, not at all.
I will not credit that. A Posa does
Not die for a mere boy. The meager flame
Of friendship will not fill a Posa's heart.
It beat for all mankind. *His taste was for
The world with all its coming generations.*

Eighth Letter

But, you will say, why this whole inquiry? No matter if it was the
involuntary promptings of the heart, harmony of character, mu-
tual personal need for each other, or additional external circumstances and free choice, whatever created the bond of friendship
between these two—the consequences remain the same, and in the
course of the play itself nothing is altered by it. Why then this
effort to go far into the past to snatch the reader away from an
erroneous idea that is perhaps more pleasant for him than the
truth? What would the attraction of most moral phenomena be, if
each time one was forced to illuminate the innermost depths of
the human heart and, as it were, see it *becoming?* Enough for us
that everything Marquis Posa loves is brought together in the
Prince, is *represented* through him, or at least can be maintained

through him alone; that he combines this coincidental, limited interest, which he only lends to his friend, in the end inseparably with the nature of the same, and that everything he feels for him expresses itself in a personal inclination. Then we enjoy the pure beauty of this portrait of friendship as a simple, moral element, unconcerned as to no matter how many parts the philosopher may cut it up into.

But what if the settlement of this variation were important for the whole play? —That is to say, if the last objective of Posa's efforts is moved out *beyond* the Prince, then the latter, as a tool used for a higher purpose, is only so important to him if he satisfies another urge through his friendship than this friendship *alone,* then a narrower limit cannot very well be set for the play itself— thus the final purpose of the play must at least coincide with the Marquis' purpose. The grand destiny of a whole state, the prosperity of the human race down through many generations, in which all the endeavors of the Marquis, as we have seen, terminate, cannot very well be *episodes in a plot that has as its purpose the ending of a love story.* So if we have misunderstood one another about Posa's friendship, then I am afraid we have done so, too, about the final purpose of the whole tragedy. Let me show it to you from this new standpoint; perhaps many incongruities at which you have previously taken offense will disappear from this new aspect.

And what then would the so-called unity of the play be, if it should not be *love* and could never be *friendship?* The first three acts treat of the former, the two others of the latter, but the whole is concerned with neither one of the two. Friendship sacrifices itself and love is sacrificed; but it is neither the former nor the latter to which this sacrifice is brought by the other. So there must be some third thing present that is different from friendship and love, for which both have worked, and to which both are sacrificed— and if the play has a unity, where else could it be but in this third thing?

Call to mind, dear friend, a certain discussion about a favorite topic of our decade—about the spread of more pure, gentle humanity, about the highest possible freedom of *individuals,* along with the highest blossoming of the state, in short about the most perfect condition of mankind in its nature and its strengths, which is declared to be attainable—a discussion that became spirited between us and charmed our imaginations into one of those very lovely fantasies that the heart delights to revel in. We came to a close at that time with the fanciful wish that in the next Julian cycle chance, which has certainly performed greater wonders, might find it agreeable to arouse again our chain of thought, our dreams and convictions, fertilized with just such high spirits and with just as good intent, in the first-born son of a future ruler of ——— or ——— in this or the other hemisphere. What was only the mechanism of a serious conversation should, it struck me, in the case of such a mechanism as the tragedy, be lifted up to the position of honor of seriousness and of truth. What is not possible in the imagination? What is not permitted to the poet? Our discussion was long forgotten, when in the interim I made the acquaintance of the Prince of Spain; and I soon observed that this gifted youth might well be the one with whom we could bring our plan to realization. No sooner said than done! I found everything done for me, moreover, as if by a ministering spirit; the sense of freedom in the battle with despotism, the chains of stupidity shattered, thousand-year-old prejudices convulsed, a nation that demands the return of its human rights, republican virtues put into practice, clearer concepts in circulation, minds in ferment, hearts lifted by an inspired concern—and now to complete an auspicious constellation, a finely prepared young human being on the throne, in solitary, undisputed bloom issuing from hardship and suffering. Unhappy—we settled the matter so—the sovereign's son, in whom we meant to bring our ideal to fulfillment, must be unhappy.

> Be you
> A man upon King Philipp's throne! You have
> Become aware of sorrow—

He should not be taken out of the bosom of sensuality and happiness; the fine arts should not yet have laid hand on his development, the contemporary world not yet have pressed its stamp upon him. But how should a royal prince of the sixteenth century—the son of Philipp II—a pupil of the monastic people, whose scarcely awakened reason is watched over by such strict and keen-eyed keepers, attain this liberal philosophy? But look, even that was provided for. Fate gave him a friend—a friend in the decisive years when the bloom of the mind unfolds, ideals are conceived, and moral perception is purified—a gifted, sensitive youth, over whose education itself (what prevents me from assuming this?) a favorable star has watched, extraordinary good fortune has interceded, and whom some obscure wise man or other of his century has molded for this work. Thus this serene, human philosophy, which the Prince will practice on the throne, is the offspring of friendship. It clothes itself in all the charm of youth, in the full grace of poetry; it is stored in his heart with light and warmth; it is the first bloom of his being; it is his *first love*. It is of extreme importance to the Marquis to preserve for it this youthful animation, to let it continue with him as an object of great emotion, because only great emotion can help him overcome the difficulties that will oppose its execution. "You must tell him," he charges the Queen:

> For these grand visions of his youth he shall
> Be treated with esteem when he is older.
> He shall not open up the heart of this
> Most tender blossom to the deadly bug
> Of celebrated better judgment—that
> He might not be misled, if dusty wisdom
> Should slander heavenly enthusiasm.
> I said it to him once before—

So between the two friends there arises an *enthusiastic plan to bring about the most auspicious state that is attainable to human society,* and the drama at hand deals with *this enthusiastic plan as it, namely, appears in conflict with a passionate love.* But we were speaking of installing a *prince* who could truly bring about the highest possible ideal of civil happiness for his age—not of first educating this prince for the purpose, for this had to have taken place long before and thus could not very well be made the object of such an artistic production; still less of letting him really put his hand to this work, for how much would this have exceeded the narrow limits of a tragedy?—We were speaking only of *presenting* this prince, of making the frame of mind that must be at the base of such an effect dominant in him, and of elevating its *subjective* possibility to a high degree of probability, unconcerned whether good luck and coincidence will bring it about.

Ninth Letter

I want to explain myself more closely about the preceding.

The youth, namely, from whom we are to expect this extraordinary action, had to have first overcome desires that could be dangerous to such an undertaking; like that Roman, he had to hold his hand over a flame to convince us that he was man enough to triumph over pain; he had to go through a terrible trial by fire and in this fire prove true. Only then, when we have seen him contend successfully with an *internal* enemy, can we promise him the victory over the external obstacles that will hurl themselves against him on the reformer's course; only then, when we have seen him, in the years of sensuality, in spite of the passionate blood of youth defy temptation, can we be quite sure that it will no longer be dangerous to the grown man. And what passion could supply this effect in greater measure than the mightiest of all, *love?*

All of those passions that are to be feared for this great design I have saved him for, this single one excepted, have been cleared away out of his heart or have never dwelt within it. At a corrupt, immoral court he has retained the purity of original innocence; not his *love,* not even the exertion of his principles, but his moral instinct alone has protected him from this defilement.

> For passion's arrow splintered on this breast
> And long before Elizabeth here reigned.

In relation to the Princess of Eboli, who so often forgets herself toward him out of passion and design, he shows an innocence that comes near to *simplicity;* how many of those who read this scene would understand the Princess far quicker. My intention was to put such purity into his nature that no seduction can harm him. The kiss that he gives the Princess was, as he says himself, the first kiss of his life, and this was still a very virtuous kiss! But he should be seen also to be above a *more subtle* seduction; for that reason the whole episode of the Princess of Eboli, whose amorous arts prove unavailing against his *better love*. He should only have to deal with this love alone, and virtue will possess him entirely, if he succeeds in vanquishing this love, too; and this is what the play is about then. You will understand now, too, why the Prince is portrayed just *this way* and no differently; why I have permitted the noble beauty of this character to be troubled by so much vehemence, so much inconstant ardor, like clear water by its turbulent flow. A tender, benevolent heart, enthusiasm for the grand and beautiful, delicacy, courage, resoluteness, magnanimous generosity, these he should possess, fair and bright glimpses of spirit he should show, but wise he should not be. The great man to come should slumber within him, but his fiery blood should not yet allow him actually to be that man. Everything that makes an excellent sovereign, everything that can justify the expectation of his friend and the hopes of a world that awaits him, everything that must unite to realize the ideal set for him of a future state should be found together in this character, but it should not be developed, not yet separated from passion, not yet refined to pure gold. First of all, the important thing was to bring him closer to this perfection that he still lacks here; a more perfect character given to the Prince would have spared me the whole play. Likewise you will understand now why it was necessary to give the character of Philipp and his like-minded cohorts such a large range—an inexcusable error of these characters was to be nothing more than the machinery to develop and resolve a love story—and why, on the whole, such a wide field of action was left to *spiritual, political,* and *domestic* despotism. But since my real theme was to show the future *creator of the prosperity of man emerging* from the play, it was very much in place to present the *creator of their misfortune* beside him, and by means of an integral, horrifying painting of despotism to elevate its attractive opposite so much the more. We see the despot on his dismal throne, see him in want in the midst of his treasures, we learn from his mouth that he is *alone* amidst all his millions, that the furies of suspicion assail his sleep, that his vassals proffer him molten gold instead of a refreshing drink; we follow him into his lovely room, see there the ruler of half the world plead for *a human being,* and then—when fate has granted him this wish—like a madman himself destroy the gift that he was no longer worthy of. We see him ignorantly serve the lowest passions of his slaves, are eyewitnesses as they twist the rope on which they lead, like a child, the one who imagines himself to be the exclusive author of his deeds. We see him before whom they tremble on distant continents give a humiliating account before a domineering priest and avenge an insignificant transgression with a disgraceful punishment. We see him struggle against a nature and humanity that he cannot quite subdue, too proud to recognize their power, too feeble to evade them; escaped from all their gratifications, pursued by their weaknesses and fears, having removed himself from his species in order, as a thing between creature and creator, to arouse our sympathy. We disdain the greatness, but we mourn over his misunderstanding because we can gather even from this distortion itself traces of humanity that make him one of us, since he is miserable only because of the remaining traces of his humanity. But the more this horrible picture repels us, the stronger we are attracted by the representation of gentle humanitarianism that appears radiant before our eyes in Carlos, in his friend, and in the Queen.

And now, dear friend, survey the play once more from this new position. What you considered to be a surfeit will now perhaps be less so; in the *unity* of the play, about which we have now come to an understanding, all the individual components of it can be analyzed. I could go on still further with the thread I have begun, but let it be enough for me to have indicated to you by a few suggestions where the best information is contained in the play itself. It is possible that, in order to discover the principal idea of the play, more quiet reflection is required than is consistent with the hastiness with which one is accustomed to skim over writings of this type; but the goal that the artist has worked toward must certainly prove to be fulfilled at the end of the artistic work. What the tragedy is concluded with must be what it was concerned with, and now listen how Carlos parts from us and from his Queen:

> I have
> Been living in a long, oppressive dream.
> I was *in love*—but now I am awake.
> Forget what's past! Now finally I see
> There is a greater good, more to be wished
> For, than possessing you—Here are your letters.

You must destroy the ones I wrote. You need
Fear no more fits of passion from me. That
Is past. A purifying fire has purged
My being. I will build a monument
For him, the like of which no king has had—
And over where his ashes rest will bloom
A paradise!
QUEEN: I hoped to find you thus!
That was the noble meaning of his death.

Tenth Letter

I am neither an Illuminati nor a Mason, but if both fraternal orders have a moral purpose in common, and if this purpose is the
most important one for the society of men, then it must be at least
very closely related to the one that Marquis Posa proposed. What
the former seek to accomplish through a secret alliance of many
active members scattered throughout the world, the latter wants
to put into effect more perfectly and within a shorter length of
time by means of a single subject; namely, by means of a prince
who has the expectation of ascending the greatest throne in the
world and is given the ability to undertake such action through
this elevated vantage point. In this single subject the Marquis causes
the sequence of ideas and the method of perception to prevail,
from which that beneficent result must proceed as a necessary conclusion. To many people this subject might seem too abstract and
too serious for dramatic treatment, and if they are expecting nothing more than the picture of a passionate love, then I certainly
disappointed their expectations; but it seemed to me not totally
unworthy of an attempt "to draw truths, which to each person
who has good intentions toward his kind must be the *most holy*
and which till now were the property of scholarship alone, over
to the sphere of the arts, to inspire them with light and warmth,
and, planted in the human heart as actively operative motives, to
show them in a powerful battle with passion." If the spirit of tragedy was sniffing around at me for this infringement of boundaries,
then for that very reason some not entirely unimportant ideas that
are set down here are not lost on *the sincere finder,* whom it will

perhaps pleasantly surprise to see observations, which he remembers from his Montesquieu, employed and confirmed in a tragedy.

Eleventh Letter

Before I take my leave forever from our friend Posa, a few words more about his puzzling conduct toward the Prince and about his death.

Many people have reproached him that he, who fosters such a high concept of freedom and is incessantly talking about it, should nevertheless assume a despotic option over his friend, that he should guide him *blindly*, like someone underage, and precisely for that reason lead him to the brink of destruction. How, you say, can it be excused that Marquis Posa, instead of disclosing to the Prince straight out the relationship in which he now stands with the King, instead of discussing with him in a sensible way the necessary precautions and, by making him a confidant in his plan, at once prevent all hasty deeds to which lack of knowledge, mistrust, fear, and unconsidered passion could otherwise carry the Prince—and later actually did carry him—that he, instead of adopting such an innocent, natural way, prefers to take the most extreme risk, prefers to anticipate results that so easily might be averted, and then when they really happen attempts to improve them by a method that can turn out just as unfortunate as it is brutal and unnatural, namely, by the imprisonment of the Prince? He knew the tractable heart of his friend. The poet allowed him not long before to test the power with which he controlled it. Two words would have spared him this untoward device. Why does he take refuge in *intrigue* when by a *direct* action he would have reached his goal a great deal quicker and a great deal more certainly?

Because this outrageous and defective behavior of the Maltese brings about all the following situations and particularly his sacrifice, it is assumed a little hastily that the poet allowed himself to be carried away by this insignificant gain to do violence to the inner truth of this character and to mismanage the natural course of the action. Since this was certainly the most convenient and shortest way to reconcile oneself with the strange conduct of the

Maltese, one looked for no more *precise* explanation in the entire continuity of this character; for that would be too much to ask of a critic, to suspend his opinion just because the writer fares poorly from it. But I believed I had acquired some right to this fairness because more than once in the piece the more glorious position of truth has been sought after.

Doubtless! The character of the Marquis Posa would have gained in beauty and purity, if he had acted more straightforwardly throughout and had always remained above the ignoble expedient of intrigue. I acknowledge, too, this character lay close to my heart, but what I hold as the truth lay closer to me. I hold this to be truth, "that *love* for a *real object* and love for an ideal cannot help but be as unlike in their effects as they are different from one another in their nature—that the most unselfish, purest, and noblest person very often, because of enthusiastic devotion to *his idea* of virtue and happiness to be gained, is very often displayed dealing just as arbitrarily with individuals as even the most selfish despot, because the object of both their endeavors lies *within* them, not *outside* of them, and because the former, who shapes his actions after an inner mental picture, is at variance with the freedom of others almost as much as the latter, whose ultimate goal is *his own self.*" True greatness of mind often leads no less to the violation of the freedom of others than does selfishness and the lust for power, because it acts for the sake of the action, not for the sake of the individual subject. Even while it operates with constant regard to the whole, the smaller interest of the individual is only too easily lost in this broad aspect. Virtue acts grandly for the sake of law, enthusiasm for the sake of its ideal; love for the sake of its object. From the first type let us choose lawmakers, judges, kings; from the second, *heroes;* but only from the third, our friend. The first we *honor,* the second we *admire,* the third we *love.* Carlos found reason to rue it that he paid no heed to this distinction and made a great man his bosom friend.

> What is the Queen to *you?* Did *you* love her?
> And should your austere virtue answer to
> The unimportant worries of my love?
> . . . Oh, there is nothing to condemn,
> Not anything except my own delusion

That kept me till this day from comprehending
You are—as *great* as you are *tender*.

Noiselessly, without help, to work in quiet greatness is the Marquis' vision. Silently, as Providence cared for one who sleeps, he intends to resolve his friend's fate, he intends to rescue him, like a god—and precisely in this way he destroys him. That he looks aloft at his ideal of virtue too much and looks down too little at his friend became the ruin of them both. Carlos comes to grief because his friend is not content to save him in a common way.

And here, it seems to me, I meet with one of those not unremarkable pieces of practical wisdom from the moral world that cannot be completely foreign to anyone who has taken the time only to some extent to look around himself or to pay attention to the course of his own feelings. It is this: that the moral motives, which are derived from an *ideal of excellence that may be attained,* are not native to the human heart, and exactly because they must first be introduced therein through art, do not always have a salutary effect but very often, through a quite human transition, are exposed to harmful misuse. In his moral activity man should be guided by practical rules, not by artificial creations of theoretical reasoning. The very fact that every moral ideal or artistic structure of this sort is never any more than an idea, which, like all other ideas, shares in the limited point of view of the individual to whom it belongs, and thus in its application cannot also be fit for the general public in which man is accustomed to use it, this very fact, I am saying, would have to make it an extremely dangerous instrument in his hands; but it becomes even far more dangerous in the association that it assumes all too quickly with certain strong emotions that are to be found to a greater or lesser degree in the hearts of all men; lust for power, I mean, self-conceit, and pride that instantly seize upon it and mix inseparably with it. Give me the name, dear friend—just to choose one of innumerable examples—give me the name of the founder of an order or even of the order itself that—with the purest designs and most noble impulses—has always kept itself free of arbitrary acts in the application of *acts of violence* against the freedom of those outside of it, of the essence of *secrecy* and *lust for power*? That while pursuing a moral objective, no matter how free of any impure admixture—insofar as they consider this objective to be something independent and intend to attain it with all integrity, as it has presented itself to their reason—they have not been carried away unnoticed to violate some extraneous freedom, to neglect the attention to the rights of others that were otherwise most sacred to them, and not seldom to practice the most arbitrary despotism without changing their objective itself, without having sustained damage to their motives. I explain this phenomenon as the need of limited reason to *shorten* its path, simplify its business, and change personalities who distract and confuse it into generalities. From the common inclination of our minds toward love of power or from the endeavor to push away everything that hinders the play of our strength. For this reason I chose a totally benevolent character, completely above every selfish desire; I gave him the highest respect for the rights of others, I even gave him as a goal the creation of the universal *enjoyment of freedom,* and I believe I do not find myself in contradiction with practical experience when I allow him, on the way to that goal itself, to stray into despotism. It was part of my plan that he should be caught in this trap that is set for all who find themselves on the same path with him. How much would it have cost me, then, to bring him through this safe and sound and to give the reader, who has grown fond of him, the unmixed pleasure of all the other fine points of his character, if I had not considered it to be an incomparably greater gain to stand by human nature and to confirm an experience, which can never be pondered enough, by his example. I am of this opinion, that in moral matters one cannot without danger stray from natural, practical feelings in order to elevate oneself to general abstractions, that man entrusts himself with the greater certainty to the inspiration of his heart or to ever-present and individual feelings of right and wrong than to the dangerous guidance of universal rational ideas that he has artificially created for himself—for nothing leads to the *good* that is not *innate.*

Twelfth Letter

It only remains to say a few words about his sacrifice.

There has been criticism, of course, that he plunged headlong into a violent death he could have avoided. Everything, they say, was certainly not yet lost. Why could he not have fled just as well as his friend? Was he more rigorously watched than the other? Did not his friendship for Carlos itself make it his duty to save himself for his friend? And could he not be far more useful to him with his life than was probable with his death, even if everything had happened according to his plan? Could he not—by all means! What all would the quiet spectator not have done, and how much wiser and cleverer he would have managed with his life! What a shame that the Marquis enjoyed neither this happy composure nor the leisure time that was necessary for such a reasonable calculation. But, they will say, the unnatural and even ingenious means to which he takes recourse in order to die could not possibly present itself to him spontaneously and without prior thought; why could he not use the reflection and the time that these required just as well to devise a sensible plan of rescue, or better, just to grasp the one that lay so close to him, the one that is immediately evident to even the most nearsighted reader? If he does not want to die in order to be dead, or (as one of my reviewers put it) if he does not *want to die to be a martyr,* then it can scarcely be comprehended how the farfetched means to destruction can have presented itself to him before the far more normal means for rescue. There is much illusion in this criticism, and it is all the more worth the effort to discuss it.

This is the explanation:

First, this proposal is based on the false premise, refuted sufficiently by what has already been said, that the Marquis dies *only* for his friend, which cannot really occur after it has been demonstrated that *he has not lived for him* and that in the case of this friendship the circumstances are quite different. Thus he cannot really die to save the Prince; moreover, other and less violent expedients than death would likely have become evident to him, too— "he dies in order to do and to give everything he can for his ideal— deposited in the Prince's soul—and to do and give whatever a man can for something that is the most dear to him; in order to show to him, in the most emphatic way that he has in his power, how much he believes in the truth and beauty of this design and how important the fulfillment of it is to him"; he dies for the reason many great men have died for a truth they wanted the multitude to follow and take to heart; in order by his example to prove how very much it was worth it, that man should suffer all for it. When the lawgiver of Sparta saw his work finished and the Oracle of Delphi had made the statement that the Republic would flourish and endure as long as it honored Lycurgus' laws, he called the people of Sparta together and exacted a vow from them to let the new constitution remain unchallenged at least until he returned from a trip that he was just about to take. When this had been promised with a solemn oath, Lycurgus left the territory of Sparta, ceased from that moment on to take food, and the Republic awaited his return in vain. Before his death he gave explicit orders in addition that his ashes even be scattered on the ocean, so that not one atom of his being should return to Sparta and release his fellow citizens from their oath, if only by a pretense of justification. Could Lycurgus have seriously believed he could bind the Lacedaemonian people with this sophistry and secure his state constitution by such a mechanism? Is it even conceivable that such a wise man should have given up his life, that was so important for his country, for such a romantic notion? But it is very conceivable and worthy of him, it seems to me, that he gave it up in order, through the greatness and singularity of this death, to engrave an indelible impression of himself in the hearts of his Spartans and to diffuse a higher reverence over his work by making its author an object of compassion and admiration.

Second, it is not a matter here, as can easily be seen, of how *necessary,* how *natural,* and how *useful* this information was *in fact,* but rather how it *appeared* to the one who had to make use of it and how *easily* or with how much *difficulty* he came upon it. Thus it is far less the condition of things that must come into consideration here than it is the frame of mind of the one on whom these things have an effect. If the ideas that lead the Marquis to this heroic decision are *familiar* to him, and if they present themselves to him freely and vividly, then the decision is neither farfetched nor unnatural; if these ideas are, indeed, those that are pressing upon him and prevailing, and if those, on the other hand, that could lead him to a milder remedy, lie in the shadow, then the decision that he makes is *necessary;* if those feelings that would resist this decision in any other person have little power over him, then the execution of the same cannot cost him so very much. And it is this that we must now investigate.

First: Under what circumstances does he proceed to this decision? —In the most miserable state in which ever a man has found himself, where dread, doubt, annoyance at himself, grief, and desperation all at the same time assail his soul. *Dread:* he sees his friend on the point of disclosing a secret on which his life depends to the one person whom he knows to be his most fearful enemy. *Doubt:* he does not know if this secret has been divulged or not. If the Princess knows it, then he must deal with her as an accessory; if she does not know it yet, then one single word can make him a traitor, the murderer of his friend. *Annoyance at himself:* he alone, by his unfortunate reserve, has carried the Prince along to this rashness. *Grief and despair:* he sees his friend lost, he sees in his friend all those hopes lost that he had established in him.

> So deserted by the one, you throw
> Yourself into the arms of the Princess—
> Unhappy man! into a devil's arms;
> For *she* it was who had betrayed you. I
> Espy you going there. An awful thought
> Flies through my mind. I follow you. Too late.
> You lie there at her feet. And o'er your lips
> Already has passed your confession. Now
> For you there is no rescue—
> . . . It turns to night before my mind!
> There's nothing—nothing—no way out—no help—
> Not in the whole extent of Nature!

Then, at this moment when so many different emotions are raging in his soul, he must devise a means of rescue for his friend on the spur of the moment. What will it be? He has lost the proper use of his powers of judgment and along with them the thread of those things that only quiet reason is capable of following. He is no longer the master of his train of thought—he is thus controlled by those ideas that have attained the most illumination and the greatest familiarity with him.

And what is the nature of these? Who does not detect in the entire continuity of his life, as he lives it here in the play before our eyes, that his whole imagination is filled and pervaded with pictures of romantic greatness, that Plutarch's heroes live in his soul, and that consequently between alternatives the *heroic* one must first and above all present itself to him? Did not his previous scene with the King show us what and how much this man was capable of daring for that which he imagines to be true, beautiful, and excellent? —What is in turn more natural than that the annoyance with himself, which he feels in this moment, causes him to look first among those means of rescue that will cost him something; that he believes he owes it to justice to a certain extent to effect the rescue of his friend at *his own* expense, because it was his imprudence that plunged his friend into the danger? Take into consideration that he hastens urgently to pull himself out of this passive situation and to procure for himself again the independent control of his conduct and dominion over his emotions. But an intelligence like this one, you will grant me, looks for help *within* himself, not *outside* of himself; and if a man who is only *smart* would have let his first move be to examine from all sides the situation in which he finds himself, until he finally got the better of it, so it is, on the other hand, completely in character for the heroic visionary to shorten this process for himself, to place himself again in a position of esteem through some extraordinary *deed,* through an immediate enhancement of his condition. Thus the decision of the Marquis would be to a certain extent explainable as just a heroic palliative, by means of which he seeks to save himself from a momentary feeling of *hollowness* and *despondency,* the most dreadful state for such a mind. Add to that also that since his boyhood, from the very day when Carlos offered himself voluntarily to receive a painful punishment for him, the desire to reimburse him for this magnanimous deed troubled his soul, tormented him like an unpaid debt, and thus must reinforce no less the importance of the preceding reasons at this moment. That this memory really does occur to him is established in that passage where it involuntarily escapes him. Carlos urges him to flee before the consequences of his bold deed are fulfilled: "Was I so conscience-stricken," he answers him, "that time you bled for me—when still a boy?" The Queen, overcome by her grief, even accuses him of having long since carried this resolve around with him—

> You threw yourself into this deed that you
> Call noble. You cannot deny it now.
> I know you. You have thirsted for this chance.

Finally, I certainly do not mean to absolve the Marquis of all fanaticism. Fanaticism and enthusiasm border so closely on one another, their line of distinction is so fine, that in a state of intense excitement it can all too easily be transgressed. And the Marquis has only a few moments for this choice! The same attitude of mind in which he determines on the deed is the one also in which he takes the irrevocable step toward its execution. It will not be so good for him to look upon his decision again in another state of mind before he fulfills it—who knows if he might not have made it differently then! Such a different state of mind, for example, is the one in which he leaves the Queen. "Oh," he exclaims, "but life is beautiful!" But he makes this discovery too late. He wraps himself in the greatness of his deed, so that he may feel no regret about it.

Translated by Jeanne R. Wilson

ACKNOWLEDGMENTS

We gratefully acknowledge permission to reprint the following:

Friedrich von Schiller, *Intrigue and Love: A Bourgeois Tragedy,* translated by Charles E. Passage. Copyright © 1971 by Frederick Ungar Publishing Co., Inc. Reprinted by permission of the publisher.